American Indian Culture

American Indian Culture

Volume 2

Hides and Hidework—Syllabaries

Edited by

Carole A. Barrett
University of Mary

Harvey J. Markowitz
Washington and Lee University

SALEM PRESS, INC.
Pasadena, California   Hackensack, New Jersey

Most of the essays appearing within are drawn from *Ready Reference: American Indians* (1995), *Great Events from History: Revised North American Series* (1997), and *Racial and Ethnic Relations in America* (1999); essays have been updated and new essays have been added.

Library of Congress Cataloging-in-Publication Data
American Indian culture / edited by Carole A. Barrett, Harvey J. Markowitz.
    p. cm. — (Magill's choice)
    Includes bibliographical references and index.
    ISBN 1-58765-192-0 (set : alk. paper) — ISBN 1-58765-193-9 (vol. 1 : alk. paper) — ISBN 1-58765-194-7 (vol. 2 : alk. paper) — ISBN 1-58765-247-1 (vol. 3 : alk. paper)
    1. Indians of North America—Social life and customs. I. Barrett, Carole A. II. Markowitz, Harvey. III. Series.
    E98.S7A44 2004
    970.004'97—dc22

                                                              2004001362

First Printing

PRINTED IN THE UNITED STATES OF AMERICA

Contents

Alphabetical List of Contents. xxxiii

Hides and Hidework. 353
Hogan 355
Hohokam Culture 356
Horses. 362
Humor. 365
Hunting and Gathering 366
Husk Face Society 369

Igloo 370
Incest Taboo. 371
Indian Police and Judges 372
Irrigation 374

Joking Relations 375

Kachinas. 377
Kinnikinnick 379
Kinship and Social Organization 380
Kivas. 388
Knives 390
Kuksu Rituals and Society. 391

Lacrosse 395
Lances and Spears 396
Land Claims. 397
Language Families 402
Lean-To 412
Longhouse 414
Longhouse Religion 415

Contents

Manibozho 418
Maple Syrup and Sugar 420
Marriage and Divorce 422
Maru Cult 425
Masks 427
Mathematics 431
Mayan Civilization 432
Medicine and Modes of Curing: Post-contact 438
Medicine and Modes of Curing: Pre-contact 446
Medicine Bundles 454
Medicine Wheels 455
Menses and Menstruation 456
Metalwork 457
Midewiwin 459
Midwinter Ceremony 460
Military Societies 462
Missions and Missionaries 463
Mississippian Culture 468
Moccasins 473
Mogollon Culture 474
Money 479
Morning Star Ceremony 481
Mosaic and Inlay 482
Mother Earth 483
Mounds and Mound Builders 484
Music and Song 487

Names and Naming 496
Native American Church 498

Ohio Mound Builders 501
Okeepa 506
Olmec Civilization 507
Oral Literatures 512
Oratory 520
Ornaments 523

Contents

Paints and Painting. 524
Pan-Indianism 526
Parfleche. 531
Pemmican 532
Petroglyphs 533
Peyote and Peyote Religion 536
Pictographs 540
Pipestone Quarries 544
Pit House 545
Plank House 547
Pochteca 549
Political Organization and Leadership. 550
Potlatch 561
Pottery 563
Pow-wows and Celebrations 568
Praying Indians. 572
Projectile Points. 575
Puberty and Initiation Rites 576
Pueblo 580

Quetzalcóatl. 582
Quillwork 583

Ranching 585
Religion 586
Religious Specialists 595
Relocation 603
Repatriation. 608
Resource Use: Pre-contact 611
Resources 614
Rite of Consolation 617
Rites of Passage. 618

Sachem 622
Sacred, the. 623
Sacred Narratives. 630

Contents

Salmon. 633
Salt 635
Sand Painting 636
Scalps and Scalping 638
Sculpture 641
Secotan. 642
Secret Societies 644
Serpent Mounds 645
Shaker Church 647
Shaking Tent Ceremony 649
Shalako 651
Shells and Shellwork. 651
Shields 654
Sign Language 658
Silverworking. 659
Slavery. 662
Snake Dance 666
Social Control 667
Societies: Non-kin-based 670
Spirit Dancing 678
Sports Mascots 679
Squash. 683
Star Quilts 684
Stereotypes 686
Stomp Dance 691
Subsistence 692
Suicide. 702
Sun Dance. 703
Sweatlodges and Sweatbaths 709
Syllabaries. 711

Alphabetical List of Contents

Volume 1

Acorns. 1
Adobe 2
Adoption 3
Agriculture 5
Alcoholism 14
American Indian
   Studies 19
Anasazi Civilization 26
Appliqué and
   Ribbonwork 31
Architecture: Arctic. 35
Architecture: California 40
Architecture: Great Basin . . . 43
Architecture: Northeast 45
Architecture: Northwest
   Coast 49
Architecture: Plains. 53
Architecture: Plateau. 56
Architecture: Southeast 58
Architecture: Southwest 61
Architecture: Subarctic. 66
Art and Artists:
   Contemporary. 67
Arts and Crafts: Arctic 71
Arts and Crafts:
   California. 75
Arts and Crafts:
   Great Basin. 79
Arts and Crafts:
   Northeast. 83
Arts and Crafts:
   Northwest Coast 86

Arts and Crafts: Plains 90
Arts and Crafts:
   Plateau 94
Arts and Crafts:
   Southeast. 97
Arts and Crafts:
   Southwest. 100
Arts and Crafts:
   Subarctic 104
Astronomy. 106
Atlatl 108
Aztec Empire. 110

Ball Game and Courts. 115
Banner Stones 117
Baskets and Basketry 118
Beads and Beadwork 123
Beans 127
Berdache 128
Birchbark. 130
Black Drink 132
Black Hills 133
Bladder Festival 134
Blankets 136
Boarding and Residential
   Schools 138
Boats and Watercraft 143
Booger Dance 147
Bows, Arrows, and
   Quivers 148
Bragskins. 151
Buffalo 152

Buffalo Dance 155
Bundles, Sacred 156

Cacique. 160
Calumets and Pipe
    Bags 160
Captivity and Captivity
    Narratives 162
Chantways. 163
Chickee. 167
Children 168
Chilkat Blankets 173
Clans 174
Cliff Dwellings. 178
Clowns 180
Codices 182
Corn. 183
Corn Woman. 189
Cotton 190
Coup Sticks and
    Counting 191
Culture Areas 192

Dances and Dancing 202
Death and Mortuary
    Customs. 210
Deer Dance. 214
Demography. 215
Disease and Intergroup
    Contact 225
Dogs 230
Dream Catchers 231
Dress and Adornment 233
Drums 242

Earthlodge 243
Education: Post-contact. . . . 245
Education: Pre-contact 254

Effigy Mounds. 258
Elderly 260
Employment and
    Unemployment 263
Ethnophilosophy and
    Worldview 270

False Face Ceremony 279
Feast of the Dead 280
Feasts 281
Feathers and
    Featherwork 287
Fire and Firemaking. 289
Fish and Fishing. 291
Flutes 294
Food Preparation and
    Cooking. 295

Gambling. 298
Games and Contests 303
Gender Relations and
    Roles. 308
Ghost Dance 319
Gifts and Gift Giving 323
Gold and Goldworking. . . . 325
Gourd Dance. 327
Grass Dance 328
Grass House 329
Green Corn Dance. 330
Grooming 332
Guardian Spirits 336
Guns 337

Hako 339
Hamatsa 343
Hand Games. 344
Hand Tremblers 346
Headdresses 348

Volume 2

Hides and Hidework 353
Hogan 355
Hohokam Culture 356
Horses 362
Humor 365
Hunting and Gathering 366
Husk Face Society 369

Igloo 370
Incest Taboo 371
Indian Police and Judges . . . 372
Irrigation 374

Joking Relations 375

Kachinas 377
Kinnikinnick 379
Kinship and Social
    Organization 380
Kivas 388
Knives 390
Kuksu Rituals and
    Society 391

Lacrosse 395
Lances and Spears 396
Land Claims 397
Language Families 402
Lean-To 412
Longhouse 414
Longhouse Religion 415

Manibozho 418
Maple Syrup and Sugar . . . 420
Marriage and Divorce 422

Maru Cult 425
Masks 427
Mathematics 431
Mayan Civilization 432
Medicine and Modes of
    Curing: Post-contact 438
Medicine and Modes of
    Curing: Pre-contact 446
Medicine Bundles 454
Medicine Wheels 455
Menses and
    Menstruation 456
Metalwork 457
Midewiwin 459
Midwinter Ceremony 460
Military Societies 462
Missions and
    Missionaries 463
Mississippian Culture 468
Moccasins 473
Mogollon Culture 474
Money 479
Morning Star Ceremony . . . 481
Mosaic and Inlay 482
Mother Earth 483
Mounds and Mound
    Builders 484
Music and Song 487

Names and Naming 496
Native American Church . . . 498

Ohio Mound Builders 501
Okeepa 506
Olmec Civilization 507

Alphabetical List of Contents

Oral Literatures 512
Oratory 520
Ornaments 523

Paints and Painting 524
Pan-Indianism 526
Parfleche 531
Pemmican 532
Petroglyphs 533
Peyote and Peyote
    Religion 536
Pictographs 540
Pipestone Quarries 544
Pit House 545
Plank House 547
Pochteca 549
Political Organization
    and Leadership 550
Potlatch 561
Pottery 563
Pow-wows and
    Celebrations 568
Praying Indians 572
Projectile Points 575
Puberty and Initiation
    Rites 576
Pueblo 580

Quetzalcóatl 582
Quillwork 583

Ranching 585
Religion 586
Religious Specialists 595
Relocation 603
Repatriation 608
Resource Use:
    Pre-contact 611

Resources 614
Rite of Consolation 617
Rites of Passage 618

Sachem 622
Sacred, the 623
Sacred Narratives 630
Salmon 633
Salt 635
Sand Painting 636
Scalps and Scalping 638
Sculpture 641
Secotan 642
Secret Societies 644
Serpent Mounds 645
Shaker Church 647
Shaking Tent Ceremony . . . 649
Shalako 651
Shells and Shellwork 651
Shields 654
Sign Language 658
Silverworking 659
Slavery 662
Snake Dance 666
Social Control 667
Societies: Non-kin-based . . . 670
Spirit Dancing 678
Sports Mascots 679
Squash 683
Star Quilts 684
Stereotypes 686
Stomp Dance 691
Subsistence 692
Suicide 702
Sun Dance 703
Sweatlodges and
    Sweatbaths 709
Syllabaries 711

Volume 3

Symbolism in Art 713

Tanning. 715
Tattoos and Tattooing. 715
Technology. 717
Tipi 725
Tobacco. 727
Tobacco Society and
    Dance 728
Tomahawks 730
Tools 731
Torture 737
Totem Poles 739
Totems 741
Tourism. 743
Toys. 746
Trade 747
Transportation Modes 751
Tribal Colleges. 754
Tribal Councils. 759
Tribal Courts 761
Tricksters 763
Turquoise. 766
Twins 768

Urban Indians 769

Visions and Vision
    Quests. 774

Walam Olum. 777
Wampum. 778
War Bonnets 781
Warfare and Conflict 783
Wattle and Daub. 790

Weapons 791
Weaving 794
Weirs and Traps 799
Whales and Whaling 801
White Buffalo Society. 803
White Deerskin Dance 804
Wickiup. 805
Wigwam 806
Wild Rice. 808
Windigo 810
Wintercounts. 811
Witchcraft and Sorcery 812
Women 814
Women's Societies. 822

Zapotec Civilization. 824

Educational Institutions
    and Programs 829
Festivals and
    Pow-Wows 857
Glossary 874
Mediagraphy 888
Museums, Archives,
    and Libraries 938
Organizations, Agencies,
    and Societies 976
Tribes by Culture Area 985
Bibliography. 991
Web Resources 1019

Category Index. 1029
Culture Area Index 1037
Subject Index 1043

American Indian Culture

Hides and Hidework

Tribes affected: Pantribal

Significance: *Hide was used by virtually all native groups for a variety of utilitarian purposes.*

Hide, either tanned or untanned (rawhide), was used by nearly all Native American groups for clothing, hats, burden cases, pouches, shields, masks, snowshoes, moccasins, strapping, hafting of wood and stone tools, stone-boiling, slings, quivers, rattles, weapons, saddles, shelters, fishing floats, survival food, kayak and umiak coverings, and a variety of other utilitarian articles. Though land mammal hide was most commonly used, there were instances of bird, reptile, and even salmon skin being utilized for various purposes.

Hide tanning was laborious and sometimes labor intensive, particularly in the late summer or early fall when land mammal hides were prime. Consequently, a high division of labor existed for procuring and processing hides. Usually men were responsible for acquiring hides through hunting, trapping or snares, and, depending upon circumstances, skinning was accomplished by either gender. Once the animal's skin was removed (usually intact), women were responsible for processing the hide. In fact, a woman could gain considerable status through her proficiency with hides, particularly if the hide was to be decorated with porcupine quills, shells, feathers, or teeth.

A hide, if not to be used as rawhide, was processed in one of two ways: fur dressing, in which the hair was left on the hide, or complete hair removal. Fur dressing was a less complete method of tanning because the hide was not split, and limitations were imposed while tanning so as not to loosen the hair, which meant the hide frequently stiffened when wet. This type of tanning method was usually for clothing.

Tanning a hide required basically four major steps. Regardless of the method of tanning, the skin was first washed and pounded with a stone maul to remove blood, fat, and excess flesh. The pounding broke down and softened the grain of fibers, making the hide more adherent to the tanning chemicals. Next the hide was dehaired, a process which varied among Native American groups. One procedure was to bury the stretched hide in hardwood ashes several inches underground for several days. Another procedure for hair removal was to "sweat" the hide in controlled conditions of humidity or warmth. Some groups would soak the hide in urine to facilitate hair removal.

The next process was "beaming," which removed any remaining hair, subcutaneous fat, and blood. The hide was pegged with wooden stakes or horn to the ground, or stretched onto a nearly vertical frame, or placed sectionally over a smooth log. The beaming was done with either a large mammal rib, scapula, or tibiae to which was hafted a flat, dull, ovid stone. Scraping stones were frequently lunette-shaped to prevent piercing the hide, and often were not hafted, but handheld. Further washing of the hide completed this difficult process. Ideally, the hide was then soft and flexible, ready for tanning.

Among Native Americans there were essentially four methods of tanning, ones that required using either brains, urine, oil, or vegetables. Brain tanning, the most common method, required the brains of the animal to be kneaded into both sides of the pegged or loose hide. Any residue was later scraped away. The brains contained fat and an emulsifier. They were often mixed with animal liver, then kneaded with lichens to form small pads that were stored for future use. Sometimes this method of tanning was supplemented with washes from various deciduous tree barks, which actually was a combination of vegetable and brain tanning.

Urine tanning was common in the Arctic region; it required submersion and manipulation of the hide in human urine, sometimes stored in ice troughs. Both urine- and brain-tanned hides become stiff when dry after being wet, and to maintain suppleness, hides were smoked with punk wood in small tipi-like structures. Oil tanning, though restricted in use, was a method that required working the animal's fat and oil into the hide. In the Arctic and Subarctic, reindeer liver could supplement oil tanning. Vegetable tanning was accomplished with solutions from deciduous tree barks that contain tannin, such as oak, chestnut, and sumac trees. This procedure commonly required enclosing the hide in a bag containing the tanning solution until tanning was complete. Oils were sometimes used in addition to the tannic acids.

John Alan Ross

Source for Further Study
Dubin, Lois Sherr. *North American Indian Jewelry and Adornment: From Prehistory to the Present.* New York: Henry N. Abrams, 1999.

See also: Buffalo; Hunting and Gathering; Tanning.

Hogan

Tribe affected: Navajo
Significance: *Hogans are unique housing structures suited to the pastoral lifeways of the Navajo.*

The typical Navajo hogan is a large, comfortable, one-family dwelling place. The usual construction method starts with four support poles, which may represent the four sacred directions or the four sacred mountains that anchor the Navajo universe. The entryway, facing east, represents the union of sun and earth, as in Navajo creation myths. Around the foundation supports, a six-sided structure is built of logs, which are laid against lateral braces and then chinked with clay and rock. The roof curves in to form a low dome with a smoke hole in the center. The smoke hole and an entrance, covered with a blanket or sheepskin in winter, are the only openings.

The hogan is ideally suited to the high mesas of the Southwest with their dry winds and temperature extremes. From snowy winters to hot dry summers, the log and clay exterior of the hogan provides efficient insulation, while its rounded shape conserves heat in winter. The roomy hogan may also provide a temporary home

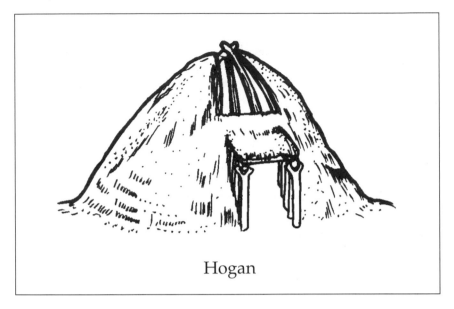

Hogan

to newborn lambs or pups, as well as a living space for their owners. Often, a brush shelter is built near the hogan. This allows for
outdoor cooking and dining during the summer. In places where
wood is scarce, hogans may be constructed of stone.

Helen Jaskoski

See also: Architecture: Southwest.

Hohokam Culture

Significance: *Adapting to the desert environment, these ancestors of the
modern Pimi and Papago established agricultural settlements and irrigation systems.*

One of four prehistoric cultures in the Southwest, the Hohokam
people, ancestors of the modern Pimi and Papago, lived in the
fertile valleys of the Salt and Gila Rivers in what is today southern Arizona. Artifacts show that this seemingly bleak region, the

Arizona-Sonora Desert, was home to the Hohokam for more than seventeen hundred years, but archaeologists are not certain where they originated. Were they descendants of the earlier Cochise people, who hunted and gathered in the same desert area, or did they migrate from Mexico? Much of their cultural history suggests a Mesoamerican influence; however, this could have been acquired through the extensive trade routes established by the Hohokam.

Development of Hohokam culture occurred in four phases: Pioneer, 300 B.C.E.-500 C.E.; Colonial, 500-900 C.E.; Sedentary, 900-1100 C.E.; and Classic, 1100-1400 C.E. The Hohokam culture was similar to the desert cultures of the Anasazi, Hakataya, and Mogollon, but a major difference was their complex irrigation system. Evidence from the Pioneer phase shows that the Hohokam lived in pit houses and began the cultivation of corn in their small villages. Floodplains along the rivers were rich with silt deposited from spring rains and snowmelt from nearby mountains. The earliest irrigation was probably achieved by directing the floodwaters.

About 300 B.C.E., during the Pioneer phase, the village of Skoaquick, or Snaketown, was founded on the north bank of the Gila River. The first canal was built there to divert river water to irrigate fields as far as three miles away. Early canals were shallow but very wide. Later, using technology from Mexico, the Hohokam built narrow, deep canals with many branches and lined them with clay to channel water more than thirty miles. Gates made of woven grass mats controlled the flow from large dams throughout the canal system. Archaeological evidence suggests that construction of the canals was done by men using digging sticks and stone hoes. Earth was carried away in baskets by women and was probably used in building their pyramid ceremonial platforms.

Continual maintenance was needed to keep the canals open after floods or thunderstorms, but this full-time technology provided a reliable subsistence for the Hohokam and supported a denser population. Instead of harvesting crops from the natural habitat, the Hohokam successfully brought agriculture into their villages to develop a stable farming society in which the men tended the fields instead of hunting.

As domesticated corn moved northward from Mexico, it evolved into a new type with a floury kernel more easily crushed when dry. The Hohokam harvested their domestic corn and prepared it by traditional desert-culture methods of sun-drying, parching in baskets with coals, and grinding dried kernels. Storage in large pits kept their surplus food secure for several years. The plentiful food supply allowed time for the creation of art, including shell carving, loom weaving, and pottery making. Images of Kokopelli, the humpbacked flute player, a fertility god believed to assure a good harvest, frequently decorated the pottery. Epic poems carried Hohokam cultural history through many generations.

The archaeological record shows that the Hohokam had no weapons; their bows, arrows, and spears were used for hunting deer, rabbits, and other small game to supplement their crops.

Area of the Hohokam Culture

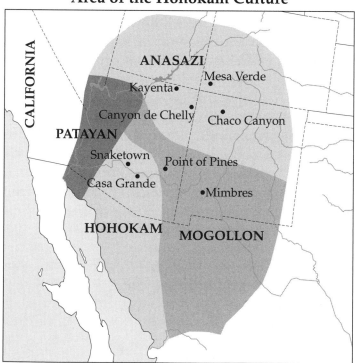

Deerskins and rabbit fur were used for ponchos, robes, and blankets. Cotton shirts and breechcloths were typical outfits for men, and apron-skirts of shredded fiber were worn by women. Both wore sandals of woven fiber and wickerwork. Other Hohokam artifacts include stone and clay pipes, cane cigarettes, noseplugs, wooden spoons, flutes, and prayer sticks. Stick and ring games, guessing games, gambling bones, and dice were also part of Hohokam culture.

Petroglyphs, pot shards, pyramids, and pit houses tell the story of Hohokam contact with Mexico. In addition to pottery and domestic crops, which by 600 C.E. included cotton, the Colonial phase shows the use of astronomy to calculate planting dates. Narrower, deeper canals were dug to control evaporation, ball courts were built for ceremonial use, and images of the feathered serpent were used in ceremonial art.

In the Sedentary phase, a smaller area of the desert was occupied by the Hohokam. Greater development occurred in the material culture, which showed more influence from Mexico: red-on-buff pottery, copper bells, turquoise mosaics, iron-pyrite mirrors, textiles, and bright-feathered macaws as pets in homes. During this period, Hohokam artists began the process of etching. The earliest people in the Western world to master the craft, they devised a method of covering the shells with pitch, carving the design, then dipping shells in the acidic juice of the saguaro cactus fruit. Along with salt, these shells were highly prized for exchange on the extensive trade route.

During the Classic phase, the Salados (a branch of the Anasazi people) moved into Hohokam territory, bringing a new architecture of multistory adobe houses. They introduced other varieties of corn, as well as beans and squash, and brought basketry, the newest art form. Always peaceful people, the Hohokam coexisted with the Salados, who assisted with the building of canals. By 1350 C.E., the complex network extended more than 150 miles. Of great importance to the Hohokam were the new songs and ceremonies brought by the Salado, for these kept the world in balance and assured a life of abundance and harmony.

As early as 300 B.C.E., Snaketown had been the year-round site of a village of about fifty families who relied on the production of domestic crops. It remained the center of Hohokam culture for fifteen hundred years. During the expansive period, more than one hundred pit houses covered the three-hundred-acre site. A highly developed social organization was needed to oversee the large population, produce abundant food, and maintain the network of canals. As their culture evolved from the Pioneer through the Classic phase, Hohokam social organization had shifted from small bands to tribes to chiefdoms to states.

In the early fifteenth century, the Hohokam abandoned Snaketown and other settlements, possibly because of a long period of drought. In the nineteenth century, Mormon farmers used part of the network of canals skillfully engineered almost two thousand years earlier. Continuing the legacy, a canal at Snaketown near present-day Phoenix was reconstructed in the twentieth century to divert water from the Salt River.

The ancient Hohokam spoke Uto-Aztecan, one of the seven Southwest language families, which also included Hopi, Pima, Yaqui-Mayo, and Huichol. In the Piman language, the term "Hohokam" translates as "the vanished ones." Myths and songs about the mysterious desert whirlwinds are found in Piman culture, inherited from their Hohokam ancestors. Perhaps the whirlwinds hold the secret of the vanished ones.

Gale M. Thompson

Sources for Further Study

Abbott, David R., ed. *Centuries of Decline During the Hohokam Classic Period at Pueblo Grande.* Tucson: University of Arizona Press, 2003. An examination of the collapse of Hohokam culture during the fourteenth century.

Ortiz, Alfonso, ed. *Southwest.* Vol. 9 in *Handbook of North American Indians,* edited by William C. Sturtevant. Washington, D.C.: Smithsonian Institution, 1979.

_____. *Southwest.* Vol. 10 in *Handbook of North American Indians,* edited by William C. Sturtevant. Washington, D.C.: Smithsonian Institution, 1983. These two volumes in the Smithsonian's multivolume history cover both the Pueblo (volume 9) and non-Pueblo (volume 10) peoples of the Southwest. Maps, photographs, illustrations, bibliographies, indexes.

Taylor, Colin, and William C. Sturtevant, eds. *The Native Americans: The Indigenous People of North America*. New York: Smithmark, 1991. Native American culture and lifestyle in nine culture areas, from the Arctic to the Southwest. Includes twenty-eight photographic spreads showing more than a thousand artifacts, dating from 1860 to 1920; 250 archival photographs, maps, and color plates, dating from 1850 to 1940; bibliography; catalog of artifacts; and index.

Thomas, David Hurst. *Exploring Ancient Native America: An Archeological Guide*. New York: Routledge, 1999. Overview of Native American cultures and the evolution of numerous Native American civilizations. References more than four hundred accessible sites in North America. Discusses new scientific data from burial mounds, petroglyphs, artifacts, and celestial observations. Photographs, drawings, maps, and index.

Underhill, Ruth M. *Red Man's America: A History of Indians in the United States*. Chicago: University of Chicago Press, 1953. Concise volume surveying origins, history, and definitive accounts of social customs, material culture, religion, and mythology. Written from the perspective of the first peoples of North America. Illustrations, maps, notes, extensive bibliography, and index.

See also: Agriculture; Architecture: Southwest; Anasazi Civilization; Corn; Irrigation; Mogollon Civilization; Pottery.

Horses

Tribes affected: Pantribal

Significance: *From the seventeenth century onward, the horse was an important aspect of many, if not most, North American Indian societies; it was most dominant in the lives of the Plains Indians.*

On his second voyage to the New World in 1493, Christopher Columbus imported the first horses to America. The settlement of Santo Domingo in Hispaniola became the horse-breeding center of the Caribbean islands. Subsequently, horse *rancherías*, both royal and private, were established in Cuba, Jamaica and other islands. When Hernán Cortés left Havana for the expedition to New Spain (Mexico) in 1519, he took with him sixteen horses, one of which foaled on board during the trip. After the fall of the Aztec empire, the Spaniards moved quickly to consolidate their gains. Antonio de Mendoza, the first viceroy of New Spain, faced the first serious challenge to Spanish rule since the conquest when natives rebelled in the northwestern province of Nueva Galicia, now the states of Jalisco and Nayarit. The rebellion, known as the Mixtón War of 1541-1542, caused the viceroy, for the first time, to send allied chieftains on horseback and use Spanish weapons to quell the uprising. It was with the Mixtón War that Native Americans started their long relationship with the horse.

Dispersion of Horses. From New Spain, horses moved northward when Francisco Vásquez de Coronado, in his expedition of 1540-1542, took fifteen hundred horses with him to New Mexico (only a few of these animals survived). The first important breeding and distribution center of horses in what is now the United States was established in 1598 by Juan de Oñate in the San Juan Pueblo settlement on the east bank of the Rio Grande River, about 30 miles north of present-day Santa Fe, New Mexico. From this location, the horse was farther dispersed in an ever-northward and northwestward direction, arriving in the following areas in approximately these years: Colorado, 1659; Wyoming/Idaho, 1690-1700;

Montana/Oregon/Washington, 1720-1730; Canada, 1730-1750; California, 1769-1775. In an eastern and northeastern direction, the horse was dispersed to the following areas: Texas/Oklahoma, 1600-1690; Nebraska/Kansas/South and North Dakota, 1720-1750.

Except for the Mixtón incident and reports that, in 1567, tribes were observed riding horses in the Sonora Valley of Mexico, there is nothing to suggest that Southwest natives were on horseback before the seventeenth century. When Native Americans acquired horses they did so by stealing them from the Spaniards. By early 1700, horses with Spanish brands had reached the northern Plains, transforming every aspect of life for the people in the region. Before the advent of the horse, people in the Plains area used dogs to help transport personal possessions on travois tied to the dog's back. The newly acquired horse became a "new superior dog" that was harnessed to a larger travois and was capable of transporting

The horse enabled the Plains Indians to use bigger travois to transport a larger volume of goods. *(Library of Congress)*

greater volumes of material. Dog names were given to horses, honoring their function; the Assiniboine had two names for horses: *Sho-a-thin-ga* and *Thongatch-shonga*, both signifying "great dog"; the Blackfoot had *Ponokamita*, "elk dog"; the Gros Ventre, *It-shouma-shunga*, "red dog." The Sioux word was *Shonk-a-Wakan*, "medicine dog"; and the Cree was *Mistamin*, "big dog."

Plains Horse Culture. Inevitably, horseback riding quickly followed the harnessed "big dogs," and with the acquisition of firearms, mounted hunting parties enjoyed easier access to the vast buffalo herds roaming the Plains. Greater meat supplies raised many tribes above subsistence levels, providing time to pursue warlike activities such as raids for the acquisition of horses owned by other tribes. Individual horse ownership became an integral part of social transactions, and standards of wealth were measured in number of horses owned. Spiritual and religious customs incorporated the horse as powerful medicine, and members of horse cults believed they received their powers from horses.

Horse breeding became commonplace among many tribes. The Flathead and Piegan acquired vast herds of horses (said to have numbered in the thousands), while the Nez Perce developed the outstanding, well-conformed, and spotted Appaloosa, which was known throughout the region as the hardiest and most reliable horse. The Blackfoot were the consummate horse keepers and trainers, and they practiced superior husbandry procedures. The Crow developed an honored horse "trading" tradition throughout the northern Plains and mountains. The Cheyenne attempted to steal horses without killing the members of the raided tribe, and the Comanche became the most dreaded and splendid horsemen of the Plains. The extermination of the buffalo, the sheer power of the western movement of European Americans, and the placement of the tribes on reservations ended the Native American horse culture.

Moises Roizen

See also: Buffalo; Dogs.

Humor

Tribes affected: Pantribal

Significance: *North American Indian humor, in various forms, pervades various native traditions and serves important social functions.*

Playfulness, practical jokes, and other forms of humor were—and are—widespread among North American Indians. Lightheartedness might be used as a way of dealing with traditional restraints on expressing emotions. In the controlled setting of a village or family unit, arguments deriving from inevitable tensions could be very disruptive of common order. Conveying one's point of view through humor rather than contention allowed for a socially acceptable release of emotions which might otherwise lead to socially harmful conflict.

Humor also served as a way of keeping interpersonal aggressions under control, conveying a desired message of rebuke without the likelihood of physical retribution. An example is the tradition of "joking relations," often cousins, who might use sarcasm to suggest corrections in undesirable behaviors. These cousins monitored each other's actions, making pointed comments about a young man's aptitude as a warrior, a young woman's resistance to getting married, or an inappropriate choice of potential mate. In this way humor served as a way of discouraging deviant behavior and encouraging group norms while keeping the rebuke at a safe distance from the harmony of the immediate family.

Similarly, a pejorative nickname based on undesirable physical attributes or lack of appropriate manly or womanly behavior might serve as an incentive to overcome limitations and conform to group norms. An unflattering name suggesting immaturity, unattractiveness, or unworthiness might follow someone through life or might later be replaced with a more desirable name. For example, the Shawnee Prophet was once known as Lalawethika (the Drum or Rattle) because of his boastfulness. After his spiritual awakening, however, he became known as Tenskwatawa—the Open Door.

Indian cultures frowned on sarcasm or ridicule directed from parents toward their children in the interest of preserving family unity and protecting budding egos. At the same time, children—in the tolerant upbringing common to many native people—were often allowed to use humor and practical jokes, even against family members. Humor allowed important messages about behavior to be communicated in nonthreatening ways and thereby served as an important reinforcement of the community.

Thomas P. Carroll

See also: Joking Relations; Names and Naming; Social Control.

Hunting and Gathering

Tribes affected: Prehistoric and pantribal
Significance: *Hunting and gathering societies could not amass surplus food supplies, but they generally met their needs adequately and had significant leisure time.*

"Hunting and gathering" refers to the economic activities of the simplest and historically earliest form of human society. Hunters and gatherers were migrant people possessing only rudimentary technology who traveled a fixed territory in pursuit of seasonal produce and game animals. Because they were usually ignorant of techniques of food preservation, hunters and gatherers did not collect surplus, thereby making them susceptible to occasional food shortages. Usually, however, tribes were so well adapted that even in the most marginal areas they easily supplied their continuing caloric needs by utilizing a wide range of food sources. Indeed, hunters and gatherers maintained the most leisurely lifestyle of any human societies, often devoting a scant two or three hours per day to subsistence activities.

Hunting and gathering tribes contained several small bands of less than fifty members, all related by kinship or marriage. Occasionally kinship was fictive. Within bands the nuclear family was

A late nineteenth century Paiute woman gathering seeds in southern Nevada. *(National Archives)*

the primary economic and social unit. Bands usually maintained a central camp, and food sharing was a principal feature of life. Occasionally bands met on ceremonial occasions or for the exchange, through marriage, of men or women.

Of all human societies, hunting and gathering bands were the most egalitarian. Although bands usually acknowledged a headman, his role was merely advisory, and his status was in recognition of unusual prowess in a vital skill such as hunting. Likewise, there was greater sexual equality than among other types of societies. Among the Ute of the Great Basin, for example, instruction of women in abortion techniques and enforced sexual abstinence for more than a year after childbirth freed women from overly burdensome maternal responsibilities. Trial marriages were common, and divorce could be accomplished simply by returning to the parental camp.

Division of labor was by sex, with men hunting and women gathering food. Warfare and political functions were male responsibilities, as were religious and ceremonial leadership; elaborate rituals often surrounded a hunt. Child rearing and domestic activities such as cooking, basketmaking, sewing, and tanning hides were female duties. Hunting was awarded the highest social significance, which resulted in male dominance. Yet fully two-thirds or more of caloric needs were met by women's gathering activities.

Lacking higher authorities, discipline was usually performed within families. Ostracism and gossip within the band were also effective deterrents of crime. Tensions were often diffused by elaborate and ritualized methods such as insult singing.

Because they were limited by their nomadic lifestyles, material possessions among hunters and gatherers were usually few. Oral traditions, including storytelling and historical renditions, however, were often elaborate. Unusual storytelling ability was valued, often conferring high status. Likewise, decorative arts could also be elaborate. The greatest pre-contact concentration of hunting and gathering tribes in North America was in the semi-arid Great Basin of Nevada, California, Oregon, Idaho, and Utah. By the mid-twentieth century, all American Indian hunting and gathering tribes had abandoned their traditional lifestyles.

Mary E. Virginia

Sources for Further Study

Lee, Richard B., and Richard Daly, eds. *The Cambridge Encyclopedia of Hunters and Gatherers.* New York: Cambridge University Press, 1999.

Panter-Brick, Catherine, Robert H. Layton, and Peter Rowley-Conwy, eds. *Hunter-gatherers: An Interdisciplinary Perspective.* New York: Cambridge University Press, 2001.

See also: Gender Relations and Roles; Subsistence.

Husk Face Society

Tribes affected: Iroquois tribes
Significance: *Also called the Bushy Heads, the Husk Faces are an Iroquoian medicine society ministering to specific illnesses and conducting certain ritual functions.*

Husk Faces wear masks braided or woven from cornhusks. Paraphernalia also includes wooden hoes, shovels, and paddles for spreading or combing ashes. Membership in the Husk Face Society includes both men and women and comes as the result of dreaming of, or visioning, agricultural spirits, which ranking members of the society recognize. Husk Faces function in the Midwinter Ceremony in a key role as clowns. The female members dress as men and the men as women. They also reverse dance roles in the Midwinter Ceremony, and before departing they usually prophesy an abundant corn harvest for the coming year. Husk Faces herald the arrival of False Face Society members during the autumnal Thanksgiving Ceremony. Public appearances at Green Corn and other ceremonies include functioning to dispel disease. During False Face ceremonies, the Husk Faces act as "doorkeepers." Husk Face masks include protruded mouth holes from which healers expel a curative blow on hot coals. Husk Face Society members seem to handle hot coals with ease.

Glenn J. Schiffman

Source for Further Study

Fenton, William N. *The False Faces of the Iroquois*. Norman: University of Oklahoma Press, 1987.

See also: Clowns; Masks; Midwinter Ceremony.

Igloo

Tribes affected: Primarily Inuit (Eskimo) groups in the Arctic culture area

Significance: *Igloos were the main dwelling structures of central Arctic tribes.*

Igloos, found mostly in the central Arctic, were hemispherical structures of varying size made of wind-compacted snow. Blocks were cut with bone or baleen knives. When placed one atop another in an inclined plane, each course of snow blocks decreased in circumference until the very top, which was completed with a capblock. Additional insulation was provided by shoveling loose snow atop the completed structure. A window for light was made of ice. It normally took two men three hours to build such a structure.

The domoid igloo was divided into a living/cooking area and raised sleeping platform. The entrance tunnel sump was always lowest, so that entering cold air was warmed and then exited through a small opening over the sleeping area. It was important

Igloo

that the insulation effect not be reduced by the interior becoming too warm and the ice melting. Igloo size varied from accommodation for an extended family to a large ceremonial structure. On occasion, individual igloos situated at productive resource areas, particularly ice-sealing sites, were joined by tunnels.

John Alan Ross

See also: Architecture: Arctic.

Incest Taboo

Tribes affected: Pantribal
Significance: *This proscription was and continues to be taken very seriously by American Indian cultures.*

The incest taboo is the near-universal prohibition against marrying close biological relatives. Incest was condemned in very grave terms by American Indian cultures, even to the extent of being associated with witchcraft and sorcery. The practice of incest was sometimes blamed for reduced success in hunting and other misfortunes which befell communities. The ban on incest involved not only marriage but also any sexual intercourse with forbidden classes of relatives. Such classes included, but were not limited to, biological parents and siblings.

Prohibited relatives also often included parallel cousins (that is, a man marrying his father's brother's daughter or his mother's sister's daughter). In some cultures the same denotation was applied to such cousins as was applied to siblings, as if to reinforce the prohibition on any marital or sexual relationship. One way of examining the likely acceptability of a match between relatives is thus by examining the terms used for the relationships between them.

No such widespread ban, however, existed on relationships between cross cousins (a man marrying his father's sister's daughter or his mother's brother's daughter). In some cultures these marriages were not only permitted but also encouraged, and an alternative partner was wed only when no acceptable cross cousin was available. In such communities, kinship terms for in-laws are often not present, since there is a biological relationship between both parties and their parents. A man was also usually allowed to marry his brother's widow.

Related to the prohibition of incest is the practice of exogamy. Exogamy refers to certain traditional restrictions on marriage that are not based on such close biological ties. One example is the requirement that one marry outside one's clan. Another, local exogamy, dictates bans on marriage within a geographical community, requiring suitors to take a spouse from another location. Exogamy within families may be patrilineal, restricting marriage and sexual bonds with a greater number of relatives of the father; matrilineal, restricting a greater number of relatives of the mother; or bilateral, restricting equal numbers of relatives of both parents.

Thomas P. Carroll

See also: Clans; Kinship and Social Organization; Marriage and Divorce.

Indian Police and Judges

Tribes affected: Pantribal
Significance: *In 1878, a native police force and judicial system were created to administer justice on reservations.*

In 1817, the United States Supreme Court ruled that federal courts had jurisdiction over all cases, criminal and civil, in "Indian country." The army served as the police force for Native Americans, and trials were held in federal courts. That policy remained in effect until 1878, when Secretary of the Interior Carl Schurz recommended to Congress the creation of the United States Indian Police. Schurz received warnings from army officers in the West that starving Indians on reservations were becoming desperate and that a rebellion could break out at any time. Since the army did not

Sioux Indian police at the Pine Ridge Agency in the late 1880's. *(National Archives)*

have enough troops available to react quickly to such an alarming possibility, it was suggested that Indians themselves be trained to handle such problems. Congress approved the creation of a native police force under the control of Office of Indian Affairs agents. Within three years, 162 officers and 653 privates, all Native Americans, were working at forty agencies in the West.

Congress gave the Indian police the authority to guard reservations against trespassers, find and return "truants" from the reservation, arrest people for drunkenness, and provide other police services. The officers and their men generally received high praise from Indians and white agents for their conduct. Indians respected their own police much more than they did white military personnel.

In 1883, the Department of the Interior authorized creation of Courts of Indian Offenses. The police were to serve as judges in these courts. Policemen serving as both judges and arresting officers created conflicts in many trials, so Congress approved hiring new Native American judges, even though it meant spending a little more money. Some whites in Congress and in white areas surrounding reservations, however, feared giving Native Americans full control of their criminal justice system. In 1885, the secretary of the interior acted to limit the types of crimes heard in the Indian courts. Indian judges could no longer hear cases concerning murder, manslaughter, rape, assault, arson, burglary, or larceny. These crimes were returned to the jurisdiction of United States marshals and federal district courts. Indian judges could try cases involving only petty criminal offenses. Despite these limits, the Indian police and courts proved a successful reform in treatment of Native Americans by allowing for more self-government on reservations.

Leslie V. Tischauser

Source for Further Study
Hagan, William T. *Indian Police and Judges: Experiments in Acculturation and Control*. Lincoln: University of Nebraska Press, 1980.

See also: Tribal Courts.

Irrigation

Tribes affected: Southwestern tribes
Significance: *Irrigation permitted some tribes of the Southwest, particularly in prehistoric times, to practice effective agriculture in arid lands.*

Irrigation, the bringing of water to agricultural fields, was practiced widely in pre-Columbian Mexico and Peru, but it was used relatively little by prehistoric North American Indians. Most of eastern North America had adequate rainfall for agriculture, and much of western North America was so dry that agriculture was impractical. As a result, irrigation in pre-Columbian North America was restricted to the Southwest. There, the earliest known irrigation was practiced by people of the Hohokam archaeological tradition, beginning around 100 C.E.

The earliest canals were modest in scope, unlined, and without sophisticated water control features. By 700, they had been expanded to a massive network, including one main canal at least 17 miles long; in addition, control features such as trash gates, head gates, and plunge pools had been added to the system. A few centuries later, the canals were lined to reduce loss from seepage. By 1400, however, Hohokam irrigation had diminished to small-scale ditches with far less engineering sophistication than the earlier systems, and this sort of irrigation was continued by the Pima. Other historic tribes using irrigation include the Pueblo peoples and the Colorado River tribes (Mojave and Yuma), who probably adopted their irrigation practices from the Spanish.

Russell J. Barber

See also: Agriculture; Hohokam Culture; Technology.

Joking Relations

Tribes affected: Widespread but not pantribal
Significance: *Joking relations refer to the humorous and informal relations between certain relatives in many Indian tribes.*

A feature of many North American kinship systems is joking relations. Joking relations are almost always paired with, and given definition by, a corresponding set of avoidance relations. In avoidance relations, kin are to act in a reserved, formal fashion with each other; in some cases, kin in avoidance relations are actually to avoid each other physically. In joking relations, by contrast, certain kin engage in free and easy bantering and talk with each other. The kin with whom one may joke are typically a person's grandparents and cross cousins. (A cross cousin is a relative related to a person through that person's father's sister or mother's brother.) Avoidance relations are typically with one's parents, siblings of the opposite sex, and parallel cousins. (Parallel cousins are related through the father's brother or the mother's sister.) North American Indians typically also practiced a strong avoidance relationship between sons- and mothers-in-law; for example, among the Crow, if a man's mother-in-law entered an area, a son-in-law would excuse himself and leave.

Kin with whom a person has avoidance relations are people with whom a person may not have sexual intercourse; if sex between such individuals did occur, it would be judged incest, a crime North American Indians strongly proscribed. To avoid even the appearance of the possibility of incestuous relationships with some relatives, Indians did not joke about or even talk about any topic even remotely related to sex with those kin. Avoidance relations were formal, and behavior around avoidance kin was carefully controlled.

By comparison, joking relations were very informal and often bawdy. With these kin, people were relaxed; mock aggression and sexual allusion were common. Joking kin often tried to outdo one another in the obscenity of references to one another's sexual exploits or attributes. Children were taught from infancy to delight in considering some joking kin in sexual and conjugal terms, and sexual intercourse was permitted between cross cousins. A nonsexual relationship of mutual indulgence existed between grandparents and grandchildren. While a person's interactions with parents were formal, informality, personal warmth, and easygoing bantering marked interactions between grandparents and grandchildren.

In some cultures, such as the Hidatsa, joking relations served an additional function: creating conformity through teasing. A Hidatsa man would tease a joking relative who had achieved few war honors or would tease a member of the Black Mouth secret society, which served as a kind of police force among the Hidatsa, who was thought to be unjust. Once again, the informality of the situation made the circumstances humorous and acceptable, but an important social message was delivered at the same time. Generally, however, joking relations were primarily a source of recreation and entertainment for those involved.

David J. Minderhout

See also: Children; Humor; Incest Taboo; Kinship and Social Organization.

Kachinas

Tribes affected: Pueblo tribes
Significance: *The kachina cult, concerned with the growth of crops and the fertility of all life, is found among all the Puebloans in the Southwest.*

The term "kachina" has three distinct meanings: a spirit being, a dancer wearing a mask who impersonates one of the spirits in ceremonial dances, and a wooden figurine or doll made to resemble one of the spirits. These kachina dolls, the best examples of woodcarving found among the Puebloans, are made primarily by the Hopi and to a lesser extent by the Zuñi, although belief in the kachina spirits is common to all the groups.

Kachinas are spirits of the dead who act as intermediaries between humankind and the gods and who bring the clouds and the rain. Some Puebloans, the Hopi among them, believe that the kachinas live on mountaintops, while others, such as the Zuñi, believe that they live under the lakes. The Hopi kachinas leave their mountain home to live in the villages for six months each year, arriving in late February for an initiation ceremony called the Powamu and returning after the Niman Ceremony, or Home Dance, in July. While they are in the villages, the kachinas are represented in various dances and ceremonies by men wearing masks. There are two major categories of masks: those representing the greater, or most sacred, spirits, which are simple and unchanging, and those representing the lesser spirits, which have more spectacular, and changeable, features such as ears, noses, or beaks.

Masked figures very similar to modern kachina masks have been found in ancient kiva murals at Hopi and in the Rio Grande Valley, as well as in pictographs located throughout the Southwest. Additionally, a small wooden effigy with the face painted to resemble a mask, found at the prehistoric site of Double Butte Cave in Arizona, bears a similarity to Hopi "cradle dolls," the simple flat kachina dolls tied to a baby's cradle. All these suggest a prehistoric origin for the kachina cult.

Members of the Hopi tribe making kachina figures during the mid-1930's. *(Museum of New Mexico)*

It is not certain when the Puebloans began to carve modern versions of kachina dolls, although there are no examples dating earlier than about 1850, nor are there any references to them in the literature of the period. Kachina dolls are carved from cottonwood root and painted by the men of the pueblo to be given to their daughters or nieces in order to teach them the mask, costume, and body markings of each kachina spirit. Therefore, the doll must be accurate and detailed, especially the mask features. The dolls, although referring to religious spirits, are not religious objects themselves and are not worshiped as idols.

The commercialization of the kachina doll began sometime in the 1880's, when the traders who came into the Southwest began to sell the dolls to collectors. This resulted in a greater naturalism in the modeling of the figures as well as the addition of pieces of cloth, fur, and feathers to replace features earlier represented by carving and painting. "Action dolls"—those carved in more active positions—have also been developed to appeal to the collector.

LouAnn Faris Culley

Sources for Further Study

Day, Jonathan S. *Traditional Hopi Kachinas: A New Generation of Carvers.* Flagstaff, Ariz.: Northland, 2000.

Schaafsma, Polly, ed. *Kachinas in the Pueblo World.* Salt Lake City: University of Utah Press, 2000.

See also: Arts and Crafts: Southwest; Masks; Religion; Sculpture.

Kinnikinnick

Tribes affected: Pantribal
Significance: *This plant was used by Native Americans in many ways.*

Kinnikinnick, a member of the heather family, is a low, trailing, evergreen shrub that forms dense mats in well-drained sandy soils throughout much of North America. Wherever the plant was found, the leaves and berries were utilized by Native Americans in a variety of ways.

Some groups believed the plant was placed on earth primarily for use as a tobacco. Most commonly, the leaves were picked, dried, and smoked as a substitute for tobacco or used as a mixture with other plants, including wild tobacco, huckleberry leaves, "Indian marijuana," dwarf wild rose, and red osier dogwood. After the plant had flowered, the leaf was dried, toasted, and often greased. The smoke has a sweet smell, and it can make the uninitiated smoker dizzy. The Lillooet sometimes made temporary pipe stems from the dried roots.

The berries were eaten raw or after cooking, which made them more palatable, particularly when cooked slowly in bear, salmon, moose, deer, mountain goat, seal, or sturgeon grease. Kinnikinnick berries were used in meat and soups and, after the introduction of flour, were made into dumplings. The leaf was used commonly for making tea by boiling the dried leaves; the tea was drunk medicinally as a diuretic or tonic.

John Alan Ross

See also: Medicine and Modes of Curing: Pre-contact; Tobacco.

Kinship and Social Organization

Tribes affected: Pantribal

Significance: *Kinship relationships of various types have often formed the basis for political and social customs among native North Americans, including systems both much like and vastly different from those of Europeans.*

Like almost all cultures around the world, traditional American Indian cultures considered family relationships to be of paramount importance. Family relationships could be quite complex, as could the larger units of social organization. Therefore, a number of terms must be noted before American Indian social organization can be examined.

The largest societal group was the tribe, or nation. The precise number of tribes that have existed in North America is difficult to ascertain, since many were virtually exterminated by the European invaders, but they certainly numbered in the hundreds. Within some tribes were moieties, two subgroups within the tribe, often identified with particular animals. The next group was the clan, identified by close familial relationship. Finally there was the family group, extended or immediate. Among various Indian tribes, these groups were of varying importance.

The term "matrilineal" describes a society in which lineage, property, and various powers are passed down from mother to daughter. Patrilineal societies pass property and power from father to son. Patrilocal societies are those in which wives move into their husbands' households; in matrilocal societies, men move into their wives' households.

Finally, before further discussion of social organization, it should be noted that some traditions and customs have survived to the present day, whereas others have not. Almost all of those that have continued have been changed—some dramatically—by contact with the dominant European American culture. A prime example of such changes is the fact that most Indians today are at least nominally Christian, and all live within the American legal system. Polygamy used to be common among Indian tribes; today, at least legally, it is nonexistent. Tribal chiefs still exist, but they are ultimately under the control of the United States government. While there will be a brief discussion of modern conditions, all the following will be referred to in the past tense as an indication that times have changed since first contact between Europeans and Indians.

Lineage Patterns. Unlike European traditions, in which the male line is almost always considered predominant, there are a number of different traditions among Indians. Matrilineage was quite common. In many Indian cultures, the men spent most of their time outside, hunting and fishing or conducting warfare. The women were in charge of the household and often tended crops. In some cases, such as certain Inuit groups, the men customarily lived in "men's houses," while the regular households were composed entirely of women and children.

In the Southwest, patrilineal descent was more common. Power and property were passed from father to son or from brother to brother. Wives often moved into their husbands' households at marriage.

In a few cases there was bilateral lineage, and the naming and meaning of various relatives were complex indeed. Some tribes described fathers and fathers' brothers by the same term, while differentiating between mothers and mothers' sisters. Many variations took place. Unfortunately, since many of these customs had already been altered before they were seriously studied, the situations can be confusing.

Marriage within a clan was almost always forbidden. In some cases, the marriage had to be outside the moiety. In some cultures, notably the Subarctic tribes, marriage between cousins was encouraged, but incest was almost a universal taboo. While it is impossible to determine how ancient taboos originated, as they are usually assigned to the dictates of gods and spirits, these rules are remarkably logical in terms of modern genetics, which also discourages marriage between close relatives.

Patterns of Descent

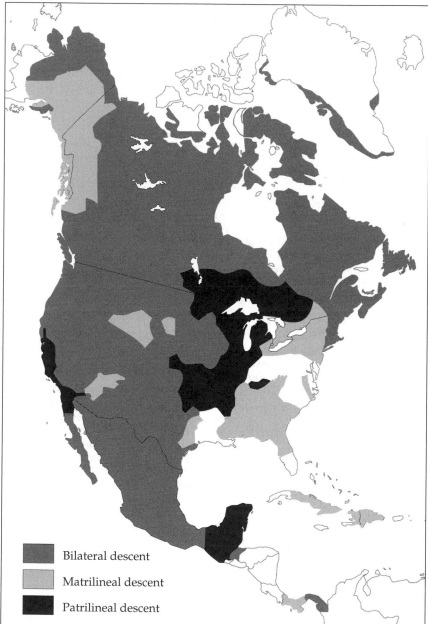

Bilateral descent

Matrilineal descent

Patrilineal descent

Source: After Driver, Harold E., and William C. Massey, *Comparative Studies of North American Indians*, 1957.

The one common custom among many Indian tribes that was totally abolished (at least legally) by U.S. law was polygamy. In many Indian cultures it was customary for a man, especially a man of power and influence, to have several wives. In some tribes, the number of wives a man married was an important sign of prestige.

Political Power. The common stereotype of the old chief sitting on his blanket and decreeing orders for the tribe was actually a very uncommon system of government among American Indians. There were some such chiefs, certainly; the Natchez of Alabama and Louisiana, for example, were ruled by a chief called the Great Sun, who was practically considered a god, was bowed to regardless of what he said, and was carried on a litter. Lesser men left his presence by walking backward. He was an absolute dictator.

Much more common, however, was a chief who was chosen by election, inherited his title but could be deposed by common opinion, or simply became chief because he proved himself in battle or had great wealth.

The Athapaskan peoples of the Subarctic, whose political system is probably the best understood because they were among the last Indians to be significantly influenced by white culture, elected their chief. This chief was far from dictatorial, and he was answerable to a village council. Chosen for his abilities, he was not necessarily an old man or significantly involved in religious ceremonies.

In many cases, religious leaders were also political leaders. The shamans among the Eskimos (Inuits) were probably the most powerful people in their tribes, but the political structure there was very loose, and occasionally great warriors achieved political power for a time. The Crow of the northwestern Plains had a chief with widespread power, but he became chief by agreement of the tribal members.

Gender Roles. Gender roles among American Indians, including the division of labor between men and women and the amounts of social and political power held by each, were first observed and studied by European men who applied their own strong cultural biases and perceptions to what they observed. As a consequence, gender roles in American Indian societies represent an area of study that has been subject to some debate and reinterpretation. As a general rule, men were hunters, warriors, and the official leaders, while women kept up the homes and often tended crops. Such division is not surprising for societies that were largely agrarian or were oriented toward hunting or fishing; preindustrial European societies functioned in much the same way.

Yet there were a number of exceptions. While men almost always were officially in charge, women sometimes held considerable power. Among the Hopi, for example, the individual households were the most important unit, and they were run by women. The household had a sacred bundle (fetish), which was owned by the oldest woman in the household and passed down from mother to daughter. The ceremonies involving these fetishes were held by the brother or son of this woman. The village chief was a man, and the chief generally was more a mediator than a ruler. This post was handed down from father to son. There was also a war chief, who had dictatorial powers in time of war but was chosen on the basis of his ability rather than lineage.

Social Organization. The degree of social organization within and among groups varied widely among tribes, from loosely knit groups of small families to huge nations with complex political structures.

Probably the most highly organized group of North American Indians were the Iroquois. This was a league of six nations, the Mohawk, Seneca, Oneida, Tuscarora, Cayuga, and Onondaga. While these groups spoke a common language family and had many customs in common, their uniting was mainly a result of their warfare with the Algonquians, the other major group in New York and southeastern Quebec. The union was strengthened when the French, the first European settlers in the area, sided with the Algonquians. In the French and Indian War, the Iroquois Confederacy sided with the English.

The prehistoric traditions of the Iroquois are hard to determine, because they had very early contact with Europeans, and this contact was usually violent. It is known, however, that Iroquois society was probably the closest to a genuinely matriarchal society in North America.

Among the Iroquois, the women owned the property, arranged the marriages, and ruled the extended families, who lived in large numbers in longhouses—log cabins that could hold a great number of people of several generations. The original rulers were called sachems, but they were more mediators in tribal disagreements than rulers or dictators. Early European reports suggested that the real power was held by the women.

At the opposite extreme were the tribes of the Subarctic and Arctic, including the Athapaskans, Eskimos (Inuits), and Aleuts. These people had an extremely loose political structure. Where there were chiefs at all, they were generally either elected or simply assumed to be in charge because they had proved themselves. These people were not particularly warlike; they were often nomadic, moving in search of game.

Generally, the family unit was the most important social structure. The family unit varied from a small, nuclear family consisting of a husband, one or more wives, and any number of children, to large, extended families spanning several generations. A group of families constituted a clan, with common historical ancestors, often supposedly descended from a spirit or even an animal. Beyond the clan was the moiety. Paramount in most cases was the tribe, although even here there were great differences. In the Northeast, the tribe tended to be highly powerful, with a complex political structure. In the Northwest, small clans tended to be most powerful. In the Southwest, larger clans prevailed, and disputes among clans were settled by councils of chiefs.

Contemporary Conditions. As stated previously, American Indian societies today—although some traditions continue and others are being rediscovered and reintroduced—reflect the disruption and cultural adaptation brought about by centuries of contact with European-derived culture. In addition to the wide variety of traditional lifeways of American Indians, which continue to provide differences among tribes, the structures of contemporary Indian societies are strongly affected by where Indians live today. Broadly speaking, three categories may be delineated: those who live in urban areas or large towns, those who live on reservations, and those who live in very remote areas (as in the Subarctic).

American Indians in cities and towns, although still facing certain biases and prejudices, have generally acculturated to the dominant white culture. Moreover, because there has been considerable intermarriage, it is not always obvious that an individual is of Indian descent. Reservation Indians, on the other hand, are more likely to have preserved the old rituals, and reservation villages often still have chiefs and shamans. (It might be noted, however, that income from tourism has sometimes also played a part in the maintenance or reestablishment of certain ceremonies or customs.)

There are still some Indians, mostly in very remote areas, who have been little affected by white culture. Probably the most widespread group still holding to ancient customs in many ways are the Athapaskans of Alaska, the Yukon, and the Northwest Territories. They live in log cabins in tiny villages, usually with no more than eighty or ninety residents. White residents, or even visitors, are rare apart from a few government officials and schoolteachers. English is the working language, but the native languages are used for traditional ceremonies. Typically, at a major event such as a birth, marriage, or death, two ceremonies will be held. One is in the ancient language (complete with dances and songs) and is usually barred to whites; the other is a Christian ceremony similar to one that might be held in any city or town in North America.

Marc Goldstein

Sources for Further Study

Bandi, Hans-George. *Eskimo Prehistory*. College: University of Alaska Press, 1979. An archaeological study of early Eskimos, including illustrations, diagrams, and maps, discussing their culture from arrival upon the American continent.

DeMallie, Raymond J., and Alfonso Ortiz, eds. *North American Indian Anthropology: Essays on Society and Culture.* Norman: University of Oklahoma Press, 1994. A collection of essays on kinship and social organization, law, art, ethnicity, politics, and religion.

Hamilton, Charles. *Cry of the Thunderbird: The American Indian's Own Story.* New ed. Norman: University of Oklahoma Press, 1972. A compilation of articles by American Indians about their culture, including memories of childhood, historical beginnings, and contemporary conditions.

Morgan, Lewis Henry. *Systems of Consanguinity and Affinity of the Human Family.* Introduction by Elisabeth Tooker. Lincoln: University of Nebraska Press, 1997. This book was originally published in 1871. Morgan studied the kinship systems of more than one hundred cultures—exploring the similarities and dissimilarities among the groups.

Osalt, Wendell H. *This Land Was Theirs: A Study of North American Indians.* 7th ed. Mountain View, Calif.: Mayfield, 2001. Description of representative tribes in various regions; includes photographs and maps showing tribal areas.

Spencer, Robert F., Jesse D. Jennings, et al. *The Native Americans.* 2d ed. New York: Harper & Row, 1977. An encyclopedic discussion of American Indian culture, from prehistory to contemporary times.

Viola, Herman J. *After Columbus: The Smithsonian Chronicles of the American Indians.* Washington, D.C.: Smithsonian Institution Press, 1990. A history of North American Indian cultures, with a particular emphasis on the changes in those cultures as a result of European influence.

See also: Clans; Gender Relations and Roles; Marriage and Divorce; Political Organization and Leadership; Social Control; Societies: Non-kin-based; Women.

Kivas

Tribes affected: Pueblo people (prehistoric to modern)

Significance: *The kiva is a circular, semi-subterranean structure used for ceremonial purposes; each tribal clan or society, usually exclusively male, has its own kiva, where members meet to commune with the spirits and with one another.*

The kiva first appeared in the Southwest among the prehistoric Mogollon, Hohokam, and Anasazi cultures. The Mogollon were the first to begin building permanent houses; it is likely that they conceived and developed their architecture themselves, without outside influence. By circa 100 c.e., the Mogollon circular pit house consisted of a hole several feet deep that was lined with poles and brush to create low sidewalls; a single center post supported a conical roof. A short, sloping ramp on one side served as an entryway, and a hole in the center of the roof provided a vent for the fire pit. As the Mogollon constructed their pit house villages, they always built one extra structure, usually deeper and larger, which served as the kiva—their ceremonial center.

The Hohokam were also pit house builders, but their structures differed from those of the Mogollon both in design and in construction techniques. Starting with a large rectangular hole 20 to 30 feet in length, the Hohokam then built an entire "wattle-and-daub" structure within the pit. This method, consisting of small posts interlaced with brush and packed with mud and clay, offered better protection from the elements. The roof now had a double pitch, but entry was still gained through a sloping ramp on one side. Like the Mogollon, they designated one large pit house as a ceremonial kiva.

About 500 c.e., the Modified Basket Maker Anasazi developed a circular pit house, about 5 feet deep and up to 25 feet in diameter. The walls of the pit were plastered with clay, and entrance was by ladder through the smoke hole. In the packed earthen floor, a small hole near the central fire pit represented *sipapu*, the opening through which humankind emerged onto the face of the earth, according to Puebloan legends of creation. Originally, the Anasazi pit house served as both home and ceremonial center; low stone walls were eventually used to divide the pit house into two separate spaces, one for daily living and one for ceremonial functions.

The Pueblo Anasazi refined the earlier pit house into a more formal ceremonial structure which was deeper in the ground; it had stone-lined walls and floor, a stone bench around the inside, and stone pilasters to support the roof. When the Anasazi built their stone pueblos consisting of long, slightly curved rows of contiguous rooms, they placed their kivas in the center.

From ancient times to the present, the kiva has served as the center of Puebloan ceremonial life. Every pueblo has several kivas, one for each of the clans or societies that play roles in influencing the spirits on behalf of all the people. Clan membership and access to the kivas are reserved for men only. Thus, the kiva also serves as

Early twentieth century corn dancers entering a kiva in San Ildefonso Pueblo. *(Edward S. Curtis/Museum of New Mexico)*

a clubhouse for the men, giving them a place to work and socialize that is exclusively their own—an important function in a matrilineal society.

LouAnn Faris Culley

See also: Architecture: Southwest; Mogollon Civilization; Pit House; Pueblo; Religion; Sacred, the.

Knives

Tribes affected: Pantribal
Significance: *Knives have been in use throughout prehistoric and historic times.*

Knives, which may be defined simply as tools for cutting, doubtless were carried across the Bering Strait land bridge when the ancestors of American Indians entered the Americas tens of thousands of years ago. These early knives would have resembled those in common use throughout the prehistoric period: stone knives flaked on both faces to form a sharp edge. Some knives, mostly for special purposes, were made from other materials or by other techniques in the prehistoric era. These included the cold-hammered copper knives used as grave offerings by Indians around the Great Lakes from 2500 to 500 B.C.E. and the bone snow knives used by Inuits for cutting blocks for igloo construction. Another Inuit knife, the ulu, or "woman's knife," was half-moon-shaped and made from ground slate. With the advent of Europeans, metals became more available for knives, arriving sometimes as trade knives and sometimes as other iron items that were remade into knives by Indian craftspeople. One special type of knife was the crooked knife, used by the Iroquois especially for carving false face masks. The crooked knife was made of trade iron but was based on an earlier native design made of bone.

Russell J. Barber

Sources for Further Study

Taylor, Colin F. *Native American Weapons*. Norman: University of Oklahoma Press, 2001.

Tully, Lawrence N., and Steven N. Tully. *Field Guide to Flint Arrowheads and Knives of the North American Indian: Identification and Values*. Paducah, Ky.: Collector Books, 1998.

Yeager, C. G. *Arrowheads and Stone Artifacts: A Practical Guide for the Amateur Archaeologist*. 2d ed. Boulder, Colo.: Pruett, 2000.

See also: Lances and Spears; Projectile Points; Tools; Weapons.

Kuksu Rituals and Society

Tribes affected: Costano, Maidu, Miwok, Patwin (Southern Wintu), Pomo, Northern Yokuts

Significance: *The Kuksu ritual and the emergence of the Kuksu society represent a shift from traditional religious beliefs that resulted from contact with European Americans.*

The "Kuksu complex," as it is sometimes called by anthropologists, refers to an integrated set of rituals or ceremonies originally practiced by the river Patwin of the central Sacramento Valley of California. In its traditional context, Kuksu ritual provided for the initiation of young males into adulthood. Through time, however, as a result of contact with Spanish, Mexican, and Anglo populations and influence from the Native American Ghost Dance, the Kuksu cycle became the domain of a secret society dedicated to revitalizing native culture. As this became more and more the case, the influence of the Kuksu society spread to include a significant number of tribal groups in central-northern California.

The Kuksu Rituals. The Kuksu rituals, as they were traditionally practiced, took place in semi-subterranean houses and involved dancers who impersonated important mythical spirits and deities. For example, the lead dancer typically played the part of

Moki, a spirit of great significance in the scheme of Patwin cosmology. Other spirit characters were Tuya ("Big-Headed Dancer") and Chelito—who helped coordinate the movements of Tuya.

Of all the Kuksu ceremonies, Hesi was the most important. This ceremony began the ritual cycle which ran from fall to spring. The Hesi ritual took four days to complete and, as is typical of many Native American ceremonies, was conducted in a highly formal and prescriptive manner. Each dancer had to know the precise set of choreographed movements associated with each of the spirit characters. If a dancer made a mistake, he ran the risk of insulting the spirit and, thus, creating the possibility of bringing bad luck to the village.

Most of the Kuksu rituals involved elaborate use of performance paraphernalia. Masks, veiled headdresses, feathered cloaks, and drums (otherwise rare in California) were all used to enhance the performances of the dancers. Most of these materials actually allowed the dancers to impersonate various spirits, especially those associated with creation myths, and to enhance the status of the dancers as mystics. In the Hesi ritual, for example, young initiates were subjected to a dance that involved the symbolic killing of the initiates. The dancers pretended, through clever manipulation of knives and other sharp objects, to slit the throats of the initiates. After this was done the dancers, most of whom were actual shamans, acted out the revival of their subjects.

Cultural Functions. As mentioned above, the Kuksu ceremonies originally functioned primarily as a means of initiating adolescent males into the status of adults. Anthropologists and historians have also pointed to a number of more subtle functions. For example, most of the religious themes employed in these ceremonies relied to a significant degree on references to mythical characters. This suggests that a major function of these ceremonies involved the reinforcement of mythic stories of cosmogony (origins) and cosmology (the nature of the cosmos). As such, these dances and ceremonies not only had the general effect of telling members of society how the world came into existence but also afforded a way to make these ideas concrete and visible through ritual action.

Anthropologists have also noted that the Kuksu complex defined status differences across both age and gender dimensions. For example, two levels of status based on age were always clearly defined through the structure and carrying out of Kuksu ceremonies: young male initiates and their elders. Furthermore, the ceremonies essentially acted out much of the content of stories and myths, and these stories often carried themes indicating fundamental differences between the roles of males and females. Women, for example, were not allowed to attend Kuksu ceremonies; thus, by way of their exclusion, women were defined as fundamentally different from men. Moreover, many of the stories acted out in the dances pointed to specific tasks associated with men. This had the effect of reinforcing a division of labor into male and female activities.

Another emphasis found throughout the Kuksu cycle centered on the status and role of traditional healers. Among the Pomo, for example, the term "Kuksu" was used to refer to a specific type of healer. This individual was usually responsible for organizing and carrying out those ceremonies connected with the Kuksu cycle. This suggests, at least to some anthropologists, that shamans were extending their roles beyond part-time healing into a different function—that of community organizers. Moreover, some shamans were able to obtain greater overall status by way of elevating their participation in Kuksu rituals.

The Kuksu Society and Cult. As more and more people of European descent began to settle in central-northern California, inevitable problems associated with close and immediate contact with Native American groups arose. During the 1870's, 1880's, and 1890's, the Ghost Dance of the Great Basin and elsewhere in North America extended its influence into California. Kuksu practitioners began to incorporate elements of the Ghost Dance into their rituals. Prior to this time, the Kuksu had been organized into a secret society; with the introduction of Ghost Dance elements, the Kuksu society began to stimulate the formation of a reactionary organization whose primary goal was to invoke dead ancestors who would presumably expel whites from North America. Social scientists have referred to these types of associations as "revitalization" movements, for the underlying purpose of such movements was to revitalize a culture through purging all foreign and hostile elements. By 1900, many of the groups that had been involved with a more traditional approach to Kuksu themes had converted to a Ghost Dance version. This continued into the 1920's, when Kuksu eventually died out.

Michael Findlay

Sources for Further Study

Frickeberg, Walter, et al. *Pre-Columbian American Religions*. New York: Holt, Rinehart and Winston, 1968.

Heizer, Robert F., and M. A. Whipple. *The California Indians: A Source Book*. 2d ed. Berkeley: University of California Press, 1971.

Hultkrantz, Ake. *The Religions of the American Indians*. Berkeley: University of California Press, 1979.

Kroeber, Alfred L. *The Patwin and Their Neighbors*. Berkeley: University of California Press, 1932.

Loeb, Edwin Meyer. *The Eastern Kuksu Cult*. Berkeley: University of California Press, 1933.

_____. *The Western Kuksu Cult*. Berkeley: University of California Press, 1932.

See also: Dances and Dancing; Drums; Ghost Dance; Puberty and Initiation Rites; Religion.

Lacrosse

Tribes affected: Pantribal except for the Southwest

Significance: *The most widespread and popular game among Indians in North America, lacrosse often had ceremonial significance; European settlers learned the game, and it became popular in North America and parts of Europe.*

The actual origins of the game are unknown, but based on its widespread popularity and similarity of rules throughout North America, it is believed to be more than a thousand years old. It was played on fields of varying sizes of up to 2 miles long and 200 yards wide. Teams attempted to score by throwing a hard wooden or sand-filled buckskin ball through a goal. Players carried sticks of 3 to 5 feet in length with a woven leather pouch on the end used to carry, throw, and catch the ball. This feature is emphasized in the French name "lacrosse," meaning "the stick." The game was often part of ceremonial events including healing ceremonies and a regular part of celebrations. While it was usually a man's game, in some areas women also played. Contests were also a means of friendly tribal rivalry and were often the focus for wagering.

European settlers in Canada and the United States learned and adopted the game. Today it remains popular among Indian peoples, most notably the Iroquois. It is also firmly established as a college sport and is growing in popularity at the high school level.

Charles Louis Kammer III

Sources for Further Study

Fisher, Donald M. *Lacrosse: A History of the Game.* Baltimore: Johns Hopkins University Press, 2002.

Hoyt-Goldsmith, Diane. *Lacrosse: The National Game of the Iroquois.* New York: Holiday House, 1998.

Oxendine, Joseph B. *American Indian Sports Heritage.* Lincoln: University of Nebraska Press, 1995.

See also: Games and Contests.

Lances and Spears

Tribes affected: Pantribal
Significance: *Lances and spears were widely used since ancient times as weapons of battle and hunting; they were also used as symbols in religious ceremonies.*

The lance and spear were widely distributed hunting and war weapons, but they were used most extensively by the Inuit and Plains tribes. The Inuit used them primarily for hunting. The Plains tribes made most extensive use of them in warfare, probably because they were especially well suited to being thrown from horseback.

The lance originated in ancient times as an effective distance weapon, reducing the risk of injury and producing surer results than could be obtained from using close-quarter weapons such as knives. The distance and force with which the lance could be propelled were significantly increased by means of a throwing stick. The spear or lance consisted of a projectile point, similar to an arrowhead, affixed to a long shaft of wood. The specific materials used and the lance's form depended on environmental demands and available materials.

Besides being used as weapons for hunting or combat, lances and spears acquired religious and ceremonial significance. Among

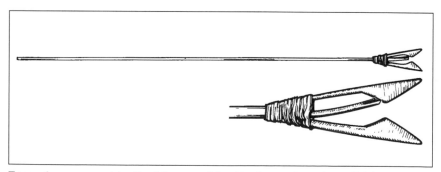

Type of spear used by the Micmac of the Northeast for salmon fishing; the two barbs around the point hold the speared fish in place.

some tribes they were housed in elaborately decorated sheaths that signified the society, office, or status of the owner.

Laurence Miller

Source for Further Study

Taylor, Colin F. *Native American Weapons*. Norman: University of Oklahoma Press, 2001.

See also: Atlatl; Bows, Arrows, and Quivers; Knives; Projectile Points; Tools; Weapons.

Land Claims

Tribes affected: Pantribal

Significance: *American Indians are using a variety of means to repossess land that was taken from them by conquest, treaty, or court decision.*

Land claims are a key component in conflicts between American Indians and federal, state, and local governments throughout North America. The claims stem from the repeated seizure of Indian lands by non-Indians since the beginning of European contact.

History. American Indians have seen their land taken from them by military conquest, by treaty, by depopulation, and by court action. For example, in the United States, in the 1810 case of *Fletcher v. Peck*, U.S. Supreme Court justice John Marshall ruled that American Indian lands were "effectively vacant" and could be taken from Indians without their consent. Subsequent U.S. court cases in the early nineteenth century ruled that the federal government had precedent rights over American Indians by the fact of discovery; Indian nations were seen as "domestic to and dependent upon" the U.S. government, which could make decisions on their behalf.

Even the reservation land guaranteed to American Indians in

An advertisement from 1879 selling land the U.S. government bought from the Chickasaw, Choctaw, Creek, and Seminole tribes. The land was originally intended for settlement by other Indians and former slaves. *(Library of Congress)*

the more than three hundred treaties signed between Indians and the U.S. government between 1790 and 1870 was open to non-Indian exploitation. The General Allotment Act of 1887 ended the traditional Indian land tenure system of communal ownership by assigning plots of land as private property to individual Indians on reservations; family heads were assigned 160 acres, for example. Because there were far fewer Indians than land parcels in 1887, the General Allotment Act gave the federal government the right to lease "surplus" reservation land to non-Indians or to incorporate it into national parks or forests. In this way, American Indians lost effective control of two-thirds of the acreage assigned to them by treaty. Individual Indians were also given the right to dispose of their reservation allotment, and many individuals found themselves coerced by poverty or pressure from non-Indians to lease their holdings to non-Indians. On some reservations, such as the Crow Reservation in Montana, non-Indians control nearly half of reservation land.

Modern Issues. Many American Indians see land claims as basic to their efforts to improve their economic status and to gain an increased sense of self-worth and autonomy. American Indians have used a variety of means—including peaceful demonstrations, violent confrontations, and legal actions against governments or individuals in courts—to gain access to land taken from them.

In the United States, Indians have often turned to the federal court system to enforce the terms of treaties or to set aside the effects of the General Allotment Act. The courts have been reluctant, however, to return land leased or owned by non-Indians; in some cases, Indians have instead been awarded restitution or access to former treaty lands for hunting, trapping, or fishing.

For example, in 1983, a federal court in Wisconsin gave Indians the right to hunt and fish by traditional methods both on and off their reservations in that state. This led to occasional violent confrontations between Indians and non-Indian sport fishermen when Indians asserted their treaty rights to set their own season and size limit for fishing. Similarly, in 1986, a federal court in Minnesota awarded each individual of the White Earth Chippewa (Ojibwa) compensation for land lost to the General Allotment Act based on the value of the land at the time it was lost plus 5 percent compound interest; an additional six million dollars was granted the tribe for economic development of the reservation. Individuals who did not agree with the court's decision were granted the right to sue for outright return of land within a given time period, but of thirty-nine Chippewa who elected this procedure, none prevailed.

Similar land claim conflicts have occurred in Canada and Mexico. While the Canadian government has asserted the rights of Indians and Inuits to self-government on native lands since 1989, the actual implementation of those rights has been controversial. For example, in 1991, the Canadian government created a new 770,000-square-mile Arctic territory called Nunavut and assigned 136,000 square miles to the Inuit. In return, however, the Inuit were required to renounce their claims to all ancestral lands, especially those areas rich in oil, gas, and minerals. Many Inuit found that to

Effect of Allotment on Land Ownership, 1890-1970

| Year | Indian-Owned | | Government- Owned | Total |
	Trust Allotted	Tribal		
1890	—	104,314,000	—	104,314,000
1900	6,737,000	77,865,000	—	84,602,000
1910	31,094,000	41,052,000	—	72,146,000
1920	37,159,000	35,502,000	—	72,661,000
1930	—	32,097,000	—	32,097,000
1940	17,574,000	36,047,000	1,786,000	55,407,000
1949	16,534,000	38,608,000	863,000	56,005,000
1960	12,235,000	41,226,000	4,618,000	58,079,000
1970	10,698,000	39,642,000	5,068,000	55,408,000

Note: Figures represent acres, rounded off to thousands, under Bureau of Indian Affairs jurisdiction. Dash (—) indicates unavailable data.

Source: U.S. Department of Commerce, Bureau of the Census, *Historical Statistics of the United States, Colonial Times to 1970, Part 1*. Washington, D.C.: U.S. Government Printing Office, 1975.

be too steep a price to pay for land that they effectively possessed anyway. In other cases as well, the Canadian government insisted that Indians give up all traditional land claims as part of any agreement on land use and self-government.

In Mexico, Maya Indians in 1992 peacefully marched 1,000 kilometers across Mexico to protest the loss of traditional lands as well as to publicize other grievances; in return, the Mexican government pledged to resolve local land disputes in the state of Chiapas and to finance hundreds of small community development projects. The failure of the Mexican government to fulfill its pledges led to a January, 1994, uprising in Chiapas in which Indians battled with government troops; nearly one hundred persons were reported to have been killed, and a former governor of Chiapas was kidnapped.

Means of Land Acquisition. Between passage of the General Allotment Act of 1887 and this 1934 legislation, the U.S. government took more than 90 million acres of Indian land. Today in the United States, the more than five hundred federally recognized Indian tribes hold only about 2 percent of U.S. land, or approximately 50 million acres. Most of this area is broken into widely scattered and small parcels, often in arid, rocky, and rural or remote areas. The largest reservation is that of the Navajo, which holds an area in the Southwest as big as the state of West Virginia. However, this size is an exception; most reservations are only small pockets of land, and some tribes have no land of their own.

Tribes can acquire land in trust by purchase from federal surplus lands or by an act of Congress. It is also possible for the the Department of Interior to take land into trust for American Indian tribes, a power conferred in 1934 through the Indian Reorganization Act, which was designed in part to compensate Native Americans for previous unjust takings of their land. In 1983, the Indian Land Consolidation Act authorized any tribe, subject to approval of the Department of Interior, to exchange or sell tribal lands to eliminate undivided fractional interests in Indian trust or restricted lands or to consolidate its tribal holdings. Several amendments to this key piece of legislation have occurred since.

Today much of the litigation and other activity surrounding land claims is directed toward acquisition of lands that historically were occupied by the tribes. Since 1934, the Department of Interior has taken into trust for American Indians approximately 9 million acres, but that is only 10 percent of the lands lost. In all sections of the North American continent Indians see land claims as central to their disputes with non-Indians. Legal proceedings and court cases to secure land continue across North America—involving tribes as disparate as the Chippewa, Sioux, Yakima, and Iroquois—and Congress continues to consider bills on land-into-trust issues.

David J. Minderhout, updated by Christina J. Moose

Sources for Further Study

Anaya, S. James. "Native Land Claims in the United States: The Unatoned-for Spirit of Place." *Cultural Survival Quarterly* 17, no. 4 (1994): 52-55.

Benedek, Emily. *The Wind Won't Know Me: A History of the Navajo-Hopi Land Dispute.* New York: Knopf, 1992.

Brugge, David M. *The Navajo-Hopi Land Dispute: An American Tragedy.* Albuquerque: University of New Mexico, 1994.

Carrillo, Jo, ed. *Readings in American Indian Law: Recalling the Rhythm of Survival.* Philadelphia: Temple University Press, 1998.

Churchill, Ward. "The Earth Is Our Mother: Struggles for American Indian Land and Liberation in the Contemporary United States." In *The State of Native America: Genocide, Colonization, and Resistance.* Boston: South End Press, 1992.

Elias, Peter D. "Anthropology and Aboriginal Claims Research." In *Anthropology, Public Policy, and Native Peoples in Canada.* Edited by Noel Dyck and James B. Waldram. Montreal: McGill-Queen's University Press, 1993.

Goldschmidt, Walter R., and Theodore H. Haas. *Haa Aani, Our Land: Tlingit and Haida Land Rights and Use.* Edited with an introduction by Thomas F. Thornton. Seattle: University of Washington Press, 1999.

Menzies, Charles R. "Stories from Home: First Nations, Land Claims, and Euro-Canadians." *American Ethnologist* 21, no. 4 (1994): 776-791.

See also: Black Hills; Resources.

Language Families

Tribes affected: Pantribal

Significance: *A language family's existence indicates that its member languages have descended from a common, ancient source; that fact helps scholars reconstruct the origins and kinship of tribes.*

Anthropologists believe that humans first reached North America via a land bridge that intermittently connected Alaska and Siberia between twenty thousand and five thousand years ago. They came in a series of migrations, some separated by thousands of years, and (the theory holds) each migrating group spoke a single language. As a group slowly spread through North America and perhaps into Central and South America, it fragmented into subgroups that settled different areas along the way. Many subgroups lost contact with one another. The original language the group spoke changed, because all languages evolve, and it changed at different rates and in different manners among the subgroups as each developed a distinct culture.

Soon subgroups spoke mutually unintelligible versions of the ancestral tongue; in other words, each had its own language. So disparate had the descendant languages become that when Europeans arrived on the American continents in the late fifteenth and early sixteenth centuries, they encountered what seemed to them a bewildering variety of languages radically unlike their own.

Typology and Genetic Classifications. Yet despite the apparent diversity, underlying relationships exist among the languages. There are basically two ways to describe a linguistic relationship. The first, called typology, classifies languages based on structural similarities. Soon after American linguistics began, scholars noted that most Indian languages are polysynthetic (or incorporative), a type that combines major grammatical features into single words. In this sense, New World languages seemed distinct from all other languages then known. Typology, however, does not necessarily prove historical kinship. For example, according to typological criteria, English is more like Japanese than it is like German, to which English has a known historical connection.

The second method, genetic classification, hunts for these historical connections. Historical and comparative linguists analyze languages to discover features that can only have been inherited from the same source. When they find similar pronunciations, words and affixes, and grammatical features among two or more languages that cannot be explained by coincidence or by borrowing, these languages must share a family relationship—a genealogy— just as organisms descended from the same parent share physical traits. Linguists often use the metaphor of a tree to characterize the relationships: An ancestral language (also called a "proto" language) splits into branches, each branch into sub-branches, and sub-branches into separate languages. The term "family" refers collectively to the descendants of the ancestral language, which lends its name to the family. A grouping of multiple families is called a superfamily or phylum.

Even if the parent language no longer exists, its living offspring reveal much of its nature. By using modern evidence to reconstruct an ancient tongue's sounds, words, and grammar, linguists offer potential evidence of humankind's prehistoric character, evidence parallel to the ruins and middens studied by archaeologists and the skeletal remains studied by paleontologists. Since the early nineteenth century, reapplying linguistic methods developed during the study of the Indo-European languages, scholars have had notable success; many American Indian languages do indeed belong in families. Yet a number of topics—how many families, which languages belong in each, and what the families say about the original settlement of the Americas—have remained controversial from their beginnings.

History of Classifications. In *A Guide to the World's Languages* (1987), Merritt Ruhlen lists 627 Indian and Eskimo languages in the Americas, many of which are extinct and known only from short word lists that European explorers compiled. Although their methods were often crude, these explorers were the first contributors to American linguistics. The first formal studies of individual North American languages appeared in the mid-seventeenth century: John Eliot's Natick grammar in 1666 and Roger Williams' Narragansett phrase book in 1643. As European colonists moved westward and more Indian languages became known, affinities among them led to speculations about their relationships. Thomas Jefferson, for example, wrote in 1789 that a common parentage might become apparent from a study of Indian vocabularies and suggested New World languages may have a kinship to Asian languages, an idea that scholars began exploring seriously in the late twentieth century.

Attempts to define the genetic relationship of American Indian languages began in the mid-nineteenth century. The first comprehensive study came from Albert Gallatin in 1836 (revised and expanded in 1848). Gallatin, a secretary of war, distributed a questionnaire to Indian language experts nationwide, soliciting information on six hundred words and some grammatical features. Gallatin made his classification by systematically comparing the responses. He grouped all North American languages, except those of California, into thirty-two families.

Gallatin's classification remained the standard until 1891, when separate studies by Daniel Brinton and John Wesley Powell appeared. Brinton, who included all the languages in both North and South America about which he could get information, perceived a fundamental unity behind them, although he separated them into about eighty families for each continent in *The American Race*. Powell, as director of the Bureau of American Ethnology and a founder of the American Anthropological Association, had access to much more information than Brinton did; he also had a staff of linguists to help him. His article in the bureau's seventh annual report, however, treated only those languages north of Mexico. Based on comparisons of vocabulary, Powell and his staff distinguished fifty-eight language families and isolates (languages which do not show kinship to other languages). The report served as the basis for subsequent investigations in North American linguistics well into the twentieth century, while Brinton's book did much the same for the languages of South America.

American linguistics has been divided by a dispute over methods, a dispute that gradually arose between Columbia University anthropologist Franz Boas and several former students, principally Edward Sapir. Boas collected and analyzed information on a remarkable number of Indian languages, and early in his career he suggested that structural similarities among some languages bespoke a common origin. Later he changed his mind about the validity of genetic groupings and criticized the findings of his students. Those students, collecting and assessing languages on their own, especially in California, worked to classify them in ever larger families. In an influential 1929 *Encyclopædia Britannica* article, Sapir tentatively proposed six families for all of North America and parts of Mexico and Central America because of similarities in vocabulary and grammar: Eskimo-Aleut, Algonquian-Mosan, Na-Dene, Penutian, Aztec-Tanoan, and Hokan-Siouan. Specialists in individual families denounced Sapir's broad classifications, some claiming that the resemblances he cited were purely fanciful and others faulting him for not distinguishing adequately between coincidental similarities, borrowings, and true cognates when he compared vocabulary items. The controversy persisted through the rest of the century; traditionalist linguists, in the spirit of Boas, resisted large-scale classifications and argued with reductionists, who followed Sapir in proposing families. The two sides were somewhat facetiously known as "splitters" and "lumpers."

Traditionalist Classification. In their introduction to *The Languages of Native America* (1979), Lyle Campbell and Marianne Mithun, rejecting the simple vocabulary comparisons of reductionists, listed three criteria for genetic classifications that would satisfy the traditionalists. First, only purely linguistic evidence is admissible; the findings of cultural anthropologists or archaeologists, for example, are irrelevant. Second, only resemblances between languages that include both sound and meaning are to be considered. If two or more languages have only a similar sound structure (such as the same number and type of consonants) or only employ the same method for constructing words (such as the use of suffixes to turn verbs into nouns), the kinship, Campbell and Mithun argue, should be viewed with skepticism. Basically, in this view, linguists should look for as many cognates as possible. Cognates (from Latin, meaning "born together") are words in different languages that have similar sounds and meanings because they derive from the same word in an ancestral language. For example, English *yoke*, Latin *iugum*, and German *Joch* are cognates deriving from the hypothetical Indo-European form *jugo*.

Third, comparisons of sounds, words, and grammatical features must not be conducted piecemeal; they must be accompanied by a hypothesis systematically explaining how changes took place. That is, linguists must discover laws of change from a parent language to its offspring languages. Only then will the relation between the offspring languages be proved. Additionally, they warn that not enough attention has been paid to "areal diffusion," or the borrowing of words and (less often) grammatical features between groups living close to one another. Such borrowings prove only physical proximity, not common origins and kinship.

Applying these criteria and cautions, Campbell and Mithun list 62 language families and isolates for North America. Their classifications are pointedly conservative and uncontroversial, intended to summarize contemporary research and serve as a starting point for further work. They recognize that many of the languages they list as isolates and some of the major branches will eventually be proved to belong together, but they refuse to allow lumping based on comparisons of vocabulary alone. Still, they follow Sapir in some cases, notably the universally accepted Eskimo-Aleut and Na-Dene families; however, they completely reject four of his six groupings.

Campbell and Mithun insist that the watchword for linguistics should be "demonstration," not "lumping," in order to give American Indian linguistics a scientific rigor. Yet their call for rigor and their criteria have placed traditionalists in something of a dilemma. Their 62 families for North America and the 117 families posited for South America by the traditionalist Cestmir Loukotka in 1968 amount to considerable linguistic diversity, far more than exists in Europe or Africa—both of which were settled long before the Americas. In general, anthropologists have found that cultural diversity increases with time. That a more recently settled region such as the Americas should show greater linguistic diversity than an older cultural area such as Africa flouts this principle. Furthermore, paleoanthropological evidence fails to support such great diversity, a fact which has made some linguists unhappy with the traditionalist approach.

Reductionist Classification. In 1987 Stanford University's Joseph H. Greenberg published *Language in the Americas*, among the most controversial books about historical linguistics published in the twentieth century. In it he sweeps aside the traditionalists' cautions, which he argues are largely specious. He claims that it is not necessary to reconstruct sound laws in order to show linguistic relationships. If two or more languages contain a sufficient number of cognates, then it is reasonable to assume that those languages descend from a common protolanguage. To ignore cognates because no sound laws exist to explain their varying forms, Greenberg argues, eliminates much valuable evidence.

Greenberg and Ruhlen, his former student, applied their system of "multilateral analysis" to hundreds of languages. For this method, they compiled lists of words for universal concepts and natural phenomena, such as pronouns, terms for family members, names for body parts, and names for water, because such words are seldom borrowed. Then they compared the words for a particular concept all at once, not language by language as traditionalists would have it. Together they discerned the etymologies (historical roots of modern words) of about five hundred words and found 107 grammatical features existing in more than one language. From this evidence, Greenberg concluded that all the languages in the Americas belong to one of three phyla: Eskimo-Aleut, Na-Dene, and Amerind.

Eskimo-Aleut includes ten languages and is spoken by about eighty-five thousand people living on the Aleutian Islands and in a belt of land that extends from western Alaska across the top of Canada to the coasts of Greenland. The Eskimo branches fall into two sub-branches, western (or Yupik) and eastern (or Inuit), which meet at Alaska's Norton Sound. Because it has relatively little diversity, Eskimo-Aleut is thought to be the youngest of the three phyla.

Na-Dene contains three independent languages, Haida, Tlingit, and Eyak, which together have perhaps two thousand speakers, and a large branch, Athapaskan, which has thirty-two languages, most notably Chipewyan, Beaver, Apache, and Navajo. Navajo, with about 149,000 speakers, is the largest single Indian language in North America and the only one with a growing number of speakers. The Na-Dene phylum spreads from central Alaska as far as Hudson Bay in the east and south well into British Columbia. There are also small linguistic islands of Athapaskan in coastal Washington, Oregon, and Northern California and a large island that covers a substantial portion of New Mexico and Arizona.

There has been little controversy about Eskimo-Aleut and Na-Dene, but Amerind, by far the largest group with 583 languages, was immediately denounced by traditionalists, who not only rejected the phylum but many of the branches and sub-branches in it because Greenberg does not distinguish typological similarities from genetic similarities. The large number of etymologies, however, has impressed some scholars. Most telling is the appearance of *n* in first-person pronouns and *m* in second-person pronouns in all Amerind subgroups, while *i-* is a common third-person marker; such widespread features for basic language concepts, Greenberg contends, can only point to a common ancestral language.

Greenberg and Ruhlen divide the Amerind phylum into six major stocks, two of which apply to North America. Northern Amerind contains Almosan-Keresiouan (sixty-nine languages), which in its sub-branches has such famous languages as Blackfoot, Cheyenne, Arapaho, Cree, Ojibwa, Shawnee, Massachusett, Tillamook, Crow, Dakota, Pawnee, Mohawk, and Cherokee; Penutian (sixty-eight languages), with Chinook, Nez Perce, Natchez, Choctaw, Alabama, and Yucatec; and Hokan (twenty-eight languages), with Pomo, Mojave, Yuma, and Washoe. Central Amerind includes Tanoan (forty-nine languages), with Kiowa and Taos; Uto-Aztecan (twenty-five languages), with Hopi, Paiute, Shoshone, Comanche, and Nahuatl (the Aztec language); and Oto-Manguean (seventeen languages). The remaining four major stocks, Chibchan-Paezan (forty-three languages), Andean (eighteen languages), Equatorial-Tucanoan (192 languages), and Ge-Pano-Carib (117 languages), occupy South America and the Caribbean islands. Quechau, an Andean language in Colombia, Ecuador, Peru, and Bolivia, has the largest number of speakers, about eight million.

Greenberg remarks that his broad approach to classification is a beginning, not an end in itself. Detailed reconstructions of languages and sound laws, the scrutiny which traditionalists demand, are still needed to work out the details in his proposal. Although he admits that some features of his groupings may need revising after such examinations, he remains confident that the overall plan is correct. He further proposes that the three American phyla show connections to Old World language groups. Eskimo-Aleut may belong in Eurasiatic, a postulated immense superfamily whose members include English, Turkic, and Japanese; Amerind may also be related to Eurasiatic, but much more distantly. Since *Language in the Americas* appeared, some Russian and American scholars have placed Na-Dene and Caucasian (languages of central Russia) in Dene-Caucasian, with possible affiliation to Sino-Tibetan, a family that includes the Chinese languages. Ultimately, Greenberg suggests, all modern languages may descend from a single stock, which he calls Proto-Sapiens and others have called Proto-World and Proto-Human.

Nonlinguistic Evidence. Despite the debate among linguists, Greenberg's Eskimo-Aleut, Na-Dene, and Amerind categories have found some support from other scientific disciplines. The findings all appear to substantiate the theory that American Indians and Eskimos crossed from Asia in at least three migrations that correspond to the three language phyla. The first, the ancestors of Amerind speakers, came no more recently than twelve thousand years ago and may correspond, in anthropological terms, to the Clovis, or Paleo-Indian, culture. The Na-Dene migration began to arrive sometime between seven and ten thousand years ago and probably became the Paleo-Arctic culture. The Eskimo-Aleuts came last, about four to five thousand years ago, and may have been the Thule culture, although that identification is uncertain. The periods are so vague because the archaeological and linguistic evidence is difficult to date precisely.

Geneticists also have found that American Indians belong in three distinct groups. A team led by L. L. Cavalli-Sforza studied variations in Rh factor, a blood antigen, by population; Cavalli-Sforza claims that Greenberg's language phyla accord with his genetic groups. Studies of variations in mitochondrial deoxyribonucleic acid (DNA) by Douglas C. Wallace also appear to support Greenberg. Finally, analyses of human teeth, immunoglobulin G, and blood serums in modern Indian populations have produced corroborating findings.

A majority of linguists reject, or at least are skeptical of, the multilateral analysis Greenberg and Ruhlen used to reach their conclusions. At the same time, most assume that large-scale relationships do exist among the more than six hundred known Indian languages, which language-by-language comparison and deduction of sound laws will eventually confirm. Thus, scientists largely agree that the Americas were populated by a small number of groups who traveled from Asia and whose languages slowly differentiated as the groups spread throughout the New World.

Roger Smith

Sources for Further Study

Bright, William, et al., eds. *Linguistics in North America*. Vol. 10 in *Current Trends in Linguistics*, edited by Thomas A. Sebeok. The Hague: Mouton, 1973. Essays devoted to the history of American linguistics, protolanguages, and the mutual influence of languages within regions present summary information on genetic and typological classifications.

Campbell, Lyle. *American Indian Languages: The Historical Linguistics of Native America*. New York: Oxford University Press, 1997. An analysis of the history of Native American languages.

Campbell, Lyle, and Marianne Mithun, eds. *The Languages of Native America: Historical and Comparative Assessment*. Austin: University of Texas Press, 1979. The editors propose sixty-two language families and isolates, based on rigorous and systematic classification methods, and contributors summarize research on seventeen of the families.

Greenberg, Joseph H. *Language in the Americas*. Stanford, Calif.: Stanford University Press, 1987. This controversial book classifies all languages in North and South America into three phyla based on correspondences in vocabulary and grammar.

Greenberg, Joseph H., and Merritt Ruhlen. "Linguistic Origins of Native Americans." *Scientific American* 267 (November, 1992): 94-99. Summarizes the authors' classification of American languages into three phyla, discusses their relation to Old World language families, and outlines corroborating evidence from genetics and anthropology.

Mithun, Marianne. *The Languages of Native North America*. New York: Cambridge University Press, 1999. An exhaustive and scholarly study of native North American languages.

Ruhlen, Merritt. *Classification*. Vol. 1 in *A Guide to the World's Languages*. Stanford, Calif.: Stanford University Press, 1987. An illuminating chapter on classification methods helps make sense of the long-standing controversy over American Indian languages; another chapter presents major classification proposals for them and repeats Greenberg's conclusions.

See also: Culture Areas; Sign Language.

Lean-To

Tribes affected: Pantribal
Significance: *Lean-tos were most useful as quickly constructed, temporary shelters.*

Lean-tos were used as temporary structures throughout North America, mostly for shelter, windbreaks, or privacy when people were in transit or at resource exploitation sites. A lean-to was basically an inclined rectangular or V-shaped side roof that was freestanding using several vertical supporting upright poles. It might also be supported against a tree or large boulder. The main attribute of this simple but effective structure was its ease of construction; natives utilized natural materials available on the site such as tules, cattails, strips of bark, plaited willow, seaweed, leaves, grass, or even clothing or blankets. The size of the structure was depen-

Lean-to

dent upon materials at hand, number of occupants, and time required to construct the shelter.

A basic lean-to could accommodate four to five persons; in the Great Basin, these structures were relatively large and were used for several weeks or even months by an extended family. Lean-tos were strategically situated so the prevailing wind was at a right angle to the opening, to draft away any smoke or embers from a cooking or warming fire. With more complex lean-tos, the bearing poles were carefully tied and stored in or against a tree for future use.

John Alan Ross

See also: Architecture: Plateau; Architecture: Subarctic.

Longhouse

Tribes affected: Primarily Iroquois, Northwest Coast tribes
Significance: *The longhouse is a distinctive architectural structure used by various tribes for housing in traditional times and used as the setting for religious ceremonies today.*

The longhouse is an architectural form that occurs widely throughout the world, including native North America, Africa, Micronesia, and Scandinavia. The longhouse is, as the name implies, relatively long and narrow, often reaching 50 to 70 feet in length and 12 to 15 feet in width. Longhouses usually have several fires for cooking and heating arrayed along their central axis, each maintained by a nuclear family. The nuclear families within a longhouse usually are closely related and form a matrilineal extended family. In North America, longhouses have been traditional for the Iroquois and various the Northwest Coast tribes. Among the Iroquois, the longhouse is a symbol of traditional values and, when it was the primary form of housing, was the site of various tradi-

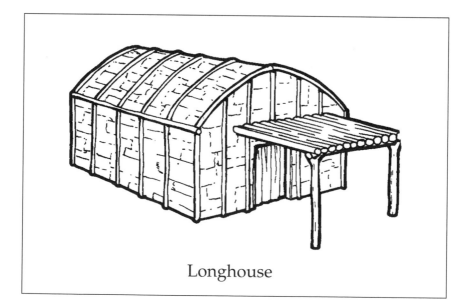

Longhouse

tional religious ceremonies. Though today Iroquois live mostly in single-family housing, the religious association of the longhouse has been continued. The religion of Handsome Lake, commonly called the "Longhouse religion," holds its ceremonies in a longhouse dedicated to that purpose. Most Northwest Coast tribes use longhouses solely for potlatches and other ceremonies.

Russell J. Barber

See also: Architecture: Northeast; Architecture: Northwest Coast; Longhouse Religion.

Longhouse Religion

Tribes affected: Seneca, other Iroquois tribes
Significance: *The Longhouse religion, influential among the Iroquois, particularly the Senecas, stressed the importance of the family and the harmful effects of such "sins" as promiscuity, wife beating, and alcoholism.*

The Longhouse religion, or the *Gaiwiio*, "the good word," is the modern religious tradition that traces its roots to the Seneca prophet Handsome Lake, who delivered his prophecies in 1810. His first vision occurred in 1799. Handsome Lake was born at the Seneca village Canawaugus, near Avon, New York. He was a recognized Seneca chief, as was his half-brother, Cornplanter. Cornplanter was the better known of the two among non-Indians, having traveled widely on behalf of Seneca and general Native American issues.

In June, 1799, Handsome Lake was seriously ill and fell unconscious. He reported having a vision while in this state. In this vision he saw three men holding berry bushes; they offered berries to Handsome Lake. The berries had a healing effect, and as he recovered, he began to talk with the three men. It was understood that there was one man missing, a fourth, whom Handsome Lake later identified with the Great Spirit, who would come again at a later time. During his conversations with the three men, Handsome

Lake heard them condemn alcoholism, pronounce a death sentence on a witch, and condemn witchcraft generally. Handsome Lake himself was told not to drink anymore. Furthermore, Handsome Lake was given to understand that his sins were not unforgivable and that he was to teach his people the proper way to live.

Handsome Lake had many such visions after this initial one, and over sixteen years of activity, a "Code" of teachings was gathered and became a part of Seneca oral tradition. The Code sounds very similar to apocalyptic biblical visions, such as those found in the books of Daniel and Revelation, in that it describes visions of heaven and hell and involves a conversation between a mortal and a being who describes what the person is seeing, emphasizing the importance of the message. Among the more significant of the visions of Handsome Lake are his reports of punishments in hell for specific sins, such as stinginess, alcoholism, witchcraft, sexual promiscuity, wife beating, gambling, and quarrelsome family relations. Each of these sins was associated with a particularly graphic punishment in hell.

As the Code reads in Arthur C. Parker's 1913 edition (based on oral tradition as it existed in 1910), it is a series of admonitions and bits of advice on preserving personal piety and family life and rejecting alcohol, gambling, and other threats to social existence. The Code is worded in a concerned and compassionate tone, as advice from the Great Spirit.

It is clear that the enumerated sins are signs of social breakdown and trouble among the Senecas themselves in times of contact with European American culture. Indeed, the religion of Handsome Lake was to become a significant response to and survival mechanism for the Seneca people. By 1861, traditional religion among the Senecas had been almost entirely replaced by membership in either a Christian missionary church or the Longhouse religion based on the teachings of Handsome Lake. Many Senecas then, as now, saw little conflict in active membership in both movements.

Most of the information about the early development of the Handsome Lake religion, and the visions of Handsome Lake himself, come from two main sources. Arthur C. Parker, working with a descendant of Cornplanter, sponsored a project involving Edward Cornplanter and a Seneca Baptist Christian, who translated into English the oral tradition as recollected by Cornplanter himself in about 1910.

The other main source of information are the journals of Quaker workers who lived with the Senecas at the time of Handsome Lake's visions and were on hand to record many of those visions at the precise time of Handsome Lake's activity. In 1798, the Quakers sponsored the work of Henry Simmons, Jr., Joel Swayne, and Halliday Jackson. They were not so much missionaries as relief workers whose intention was to teach trades and skills such as agriculture and spinning and to teach reading and writing to any young Senecas who were interested in attending regular school sessions, held at first in Cornplanter's home. The journals of these Quaker workers represent eyewitness accounts. The journals have been edited and published by Anthony F. C. Wallace.

The modern practice of the Longhouse religion is largely a private affair, not open to non-Indian investigation. In response to modern questions, respondents generally reply with answers similar to the following: "I do not have the right to exploit this tradition, since it is not mine to give—I am only a follower." Modern practitioners frequently describe the Longhouse religion as "a way of living and feeling that is our way" or say that "the Earth is filled with gifts, and we should give thanks for what is received, according to the Code of Handsome Lake."

From written accounts, it is possible to summarize Longhouse religious practice as highly personal and often emotional; it involves strong encouragement to maintain a pure lifestyle according to the teachings of Handsome Lake and emphasizes such important matters as alcoholism and family unity. Furthermore, regular occasions are set aside for recounting the Code of Handsome Lake, which must be read before noon; this may take from three to five days. Modern estimates of Longhouse religious practice suggest that nearly half of the Seneca-Iroquois are active participants and that adherents stretch from modern New York into southern Canada, and into Oklahoma on Seneca reservations there. Non-Indian students interested in the Longhouse religion should exercise great care in investigating this tradition with Seneca members, keeping in mind the sad history of exploitation that is very much in the minds of most Native American practitioners of native religious traditions, such as the Longhouse religion, the Shaker Church, the use of peyote (as in the Native American Church), and other expressions of religious faith.

Daniel L. Smith-Christopher

Sources for Further Study

Handsome Lake. *The Code of Handsome Lake.* Bulletin 163. Edited by Arthur C. Parker. New York: New York State Museum, 1913.

Swatzler, David, and Henry C. Simmons. *A Friend Among the Senecas: The Quaker Mission to Cornplanter's People.* Mechanicsburg, Pa.: Stackpole Books, 2000.

Wallace, Anthony F. C. *Death and Rebirth of the Seneca.* New York: Alfred A. Knopf, 1973.

_____, ed. "Halliday Jackson's Journal to the Seneca Indians, 1798-1800." Part 1. *Pennsylvania History* 19, no. 2 (1952): 117-147.

_____, ed. "Halliday Jackson's Journal to the Seneca Indians, 1798-1800." Part 2. *Pennsylvania History* 19, no. 3 (1952): 325-349.

See also: Longhouse; Religion; Visions and Vision Quests.

Manibozho

Tribe affected: Ojibwa

Significance: *Manibozho—legendary wise man, prophet, and messenger from the Great Spirit—was also a trickster who was sometimes outdone by his own tricks.*

Tales of Manibozho are told throughout the Great Lakes region, where he is also known as Nanabozho, Nana, Wenebojo, and the Great Hare. Manibozho was a messenger from Gitche Manitou

(Great Spirit). His grandmother, Nokomis, was daughter of the Moon; his father was the West Wind. Shortly after Manibozho's magical birth near Gitchee Gumee (Lake Superior), he turned himself into a white rabbit. Manibozho changed his form at will—to a tree, a rock, or any animal.

Manibozho was said to have brought his people the gift of fire. He also invented kinnikinnick (smoking mixture), created the Midewiwin (Grand Medicine Society), and remade the earth after the great flood.

According to one story about Manibozho, one day while he was picking berries, a flock of geese landed on the nearby lake. Determined to catch as many as possible, he wove a rope of cedar bark strips. Swimming quietly under the floating birds, he strung them all together by tying their legs. His greedy task took so long he gasped loudly for air when he came up. The geese took flight, with the middle goose in the lead and the others forming a *V*, with Manibozho dangling at one end. He shouted for them to stop, but they flew on. Letting go, he landed in a swamp. Wild geese have been flying in a *V* ever since.

People listened respectfully when Manibozho sang of flying far and high, but later they sang, "High in the sky, geese are calling. Down from the sky, Nana is falling."

Once a great creator and magician, Manibozho was turned to stone by Gitche Manitou and now lies sleeping as an island in Gitchee Gumee. Tales of Manibozho still abound; they are told in the winter, when spirits of the forest are asleep.

Gale M. Thompson

See also: Kinnikinnick; Midewiwin; Oral Literatures; Tricksters.

Maple Syrup and Sugar

Tribes affected: Northeast tribes
Significance: *Maple syrup and possibly maple sugar were used by tribes of the Northeast as foodstuffs and occasionally as trade goods.*

Many indigenous tribal peoples in the Northeastern Woodlands relied on the saps and gums of certain trees for food and gum products. Among these trees were spruces, birches, and maples. The last often supplied the tribes with a sweet, syrupy substance they mixed with other foodstuffs and possibly boiled down to make sugar. Tribes from the Abenaki of northern New England and Quebec to the Chippewa (Ojibwa) of Minnesota and Ontario tapped the abundant maples for these products.

The techniques of gathering the sap varied only slightly. The Abenaki cut a slanting gash and inserted an elderberry twig spile with its pith hollowed out and collected the drips in birchbark containers. The Chippewa used a cedar spile. Later, with the introduction of metal technology by European Americans, the iron or tin spile came into use (the dating for this switch is unclear). Once they had gathered enough syrup, tribal peoples used the sweetener in various ways. The Iroquois mixed it with corn mush. The Chippewa stirred it into wild rice, vegetables, and fish dishes, blended it with water for a beverage, and stuffed sugar into duck bills for portable candy treats for their children. What they could not use immediately, the Chippewa stored in mococks, sewn birchbark packages that often held five pounds of sugar. Tribes in Michigan, such as the Ottawa, apparently distributed the syrup and sugar as a trade good.

There exists some dispute among historians about the sugar-making capacities of the indigenous people. One school of thought holds that tribal peoples did not begin to boil down the syrup until the arrival of reliable iron pots from the Europeans. They point to the absence of description in contemporary travelers' accounts. The other camp believes that sugar making definitely predated European contact, perhaps by centuries. The Abenaki, according to the second theory, employed birchbark pails and clay pots for the boiling.

Whatever the case, early European American settlers soon adapted the customs themselves eagerly. Many a colonist depended on maple syrup for a nip of sweetness, because it was more plentiful and cheaper than cane products on the frontier. Over the centuries, maple syrup and sugar production became a thriving industry in the Northeast and Canada to the point that states such as Vermont have become stereotypically identified with those products. Demonstrations and images of sap gathering and sugar making, however, rarely point to the indigenous origins of the practice.

Thomas L. Altherr

See also: Food Preparation and Cooking.

Two women cooking cane sugar at the Seminole Indian Agency in the early 1940's. *(National Archives)*

Marriage and Divorce

Tribes affected: Pantribal
Significance: *For the American Indian, the integrity of the family was paramount; divorce was possible, but it was not expected.*

Marriage customs differed from tribe to tribe. In the Northeast and Plains tribes there was usually not a ceremony to celebrate the wedding, but there were very strict arrangements made between the two uniting families before the couple came together. The groom usually contacted the girl discreetly but personally to see whether she would accept him. This encounter might be a formal courting situation, or it might only be a quick look at a public event. Marriage partners had often known each other all their lives; even if not in personal contact with each other, they knew the families involved.

Establishing the Marriage. Once the young man believed that there was a mutual attraction, he would contact the bride's family to arrange the terms of the union. Usually, it was the groom who would provide for the bride's family. The amount of goods brought to the girl's family was in accord with the status of the family and the girl. A virtuous, reserved, industrious girl who would bring honor to a man's home commanded respect. That respect was publicly demonstrated by bringing goods to her family. Among Plains tribes this could include a number of horses, weapons, cooking utensils, tanned hides, clothing decorated with quillwork or beadwork, tanned and painted robes, and food. If accepted, these items were distributed among the girl's relatives. Among most tribes, the bride's family reciprocated with a feast and gifts for the groom's relatives. During these events, many items were also given to the new couple so that when they began their lives together it would be in the manner to which they were accustomed. Among the Hopi and Zuñi of the Southwest the marriage was less public, with the man moving in with his bride's family. No marriages with members of one's own clan were permitted.

Divorce. It was not unusual for a young man to come to stay at the home of his potential in-laws for a week or more prior to the wedding ceremony. In this way, the couple could decide without any pressure whether they were compatible. Likewise, marriages could be easily terminated by the woman. She had only to put her husband's personal items—his clothing and weapons—outside the door of their abode and the divorce was complete. Divorce was not uncommon, but it was the exception rather than the norm. Most couples lived in harmony according to custom, but if there was disharmony it was thought best to separate. The house, household goods, and any children were to be cared for by the wife. The husband took his things and returned to the house of his mother or another female relative. It was not unheard of for men to remain single for years or not to marry at all. These men added another presence to the households of their female relatives, helpful in supplying food and teaching the children in the households. They often had obligations to their sisters' children. This was the case in most matrilineal tribes. Patrilineal tribes, such as the Ojibwa, differed somewhat because the right to use land was passed from father or uncle to son or nephew. In this case, a divorced woman took her household goods and children and returned to her family's area.

An Apache bride is pictured in her wedding attire. *(National Archives)*

Marriage was considered a lifetime commitment. Infidelity was frowned upon, although a man could take a second wife in the form of a captured woman of another tribe or, more often, a younger sister or cousin of his wife. If the man were able to provide for such a large family, he would choose a wife who was compatible with his first wife to maintain harmony in his home. Sometimes when the second or third wife was especially troublesome, the first wife, who retained primacy, would demand that the husband return her to her family. An unhappy home was rarely chosen over removing the person in question. In some tribes, wives were shared with guests for their pleasure. This did not imply any disrespect for the wife; it was done as a comforting gesture to a man risking his life in travel. Any children that were born belonged to the wife and were an accepted part of the household. Most women practiced birth control with native herbs, so unwanted children were rare.

Sexual Relations. Most tribes considered sexual behavior to be private; within the communal atmosphere of the home, it was practiced discreetly. Girls were warned not to succumb to boys' advances and were usually chaperoned by an older female relative when they became teenagers. Girls were expected to be virgins when they married in most (but not all) tribes, although if they had tried marriage and found it unsuitable, it was not held against them. Because mutual respect between a virtuous woman and a man who was a bountiful provider was the basis for an honorable home, all members of the extended family tried to provide an environment to support good behavior. Unmarried pregnancy was rare. The integrity of the family was foremost. Behavior within marriage was designed to bring esteem to the family and to create a harmonious home.

Elopements were another way of uniting. There was no exchange of goods and no honoring between families, so this alternative was less desired. Still, it was considered a socially acceptable way for a young couple to begin if neither had much social standing and neither could provide goods. Even among those who could, it was an acceptable, though not esteemed, way to come together. Occasionally, women who were not faithful were physically punished. Among some Plains tribes, women had their noses cut off in retribution for their behavior.

Nancy H. Omaha Boy

Sources for Further Study

Embree, Edwin R. *Indians of the Americas*. Boston: Houghton Mifflin, 1939. Reprint. New York: Collier Books, 1970.

Gourse, Leslie. *Native American Courtship and Marriage Traditions*. New York: Hippocrence Books, 2000.

Parsons, Elsie Clews, ed. *American Indian Life*. New York: Dover, 1992.

Plane, Ann Marie. *Colonial Intimacies: Indian Marriage in Early New England*. Ithaca, N.Y.: Cornell University Press, 2000.

Powers, Marla N. *Oglala Women: Myth, Ritual, and Reality*. Chicago: University of Chicago Press, 1986.

Reader's Digest. *America's Fascinating Indian Heritage*. Pleasantville, N.Y.: Author, 1978.

Spencer, Robert F., Jesse D. Jennings, et al. *The Native Americans*. 2d ed. New York: Harper & Row, 1977.

See also: Children; Clans; Gender Relations and Roles; Kinship and Social Organization; Women.

Maru Cult

Tribe affected: Pomo

Significance: *The Maru cult, a revitalization movement, has beliefs in common with the Ghost Dance movement.*

The Maru cult of the California Pomo (surrounding the Clear Lake area in Northern California) is a direct offshoot of the Ghost Dance, which began as a religious ceremony and ideology in the 1870's and resurfaced in the 1890's among Plains Indians. The Ghost

Dance involved various ideological aspects, among them a return to Indian ways and a rejection of settler culture. As such, the Ghost Dance, and the many religious movements it inspired, was seen as "revivalist," a religious response to social circumstances of breakdown and change brought about by contact between two alien cultures—and the power difference between them.

The inequality in settler/Indian relations may explain why many tribal members sought supernatural comfort and deliverance, believing that the simple ways of traditional warfare were not effective against the encroaching settler. The main influence of the Ghost Dance movements in California were the "Earthlodge" cults, which arrived in Pomo territory as early as 1872. In its Pomo manifestation, the cult was led by a "Maru," or "dreamer," who was the head functionary of religious ceremonies. Originally, the selecting of lodges for these ceremonies was inspired by the notion that large houses (dome-roofed constructions, of which some pictures are available) were to be a place of refuge from an anticipated destruction. The influence of Christian missionaries can be discerned in the Noah's Ark theme of these longhouse constructions.

A Maru who dreams becomes the individual leader of the ceremonies. He or she (for, since 1920, women have played an increasingly large role in the Maru ceremonies) who dreams and calls the ceremonies dictates the rules of the ceremony itself, and the dream is highly respected as a source of direction from supernatural promptings. The actual ceremony usually involves an opening flag-raising to "purify" the hall where the ceremonies are to take place. Prominent in most observations of the Maru cult are "Big-Head Dancers" (so named because of their large headdresses), typically four in number, and a number of drummers and singers. There are other dancers who must also observe a number of purity rules throughout the occupation of the ceremony itself. The ceremony may last many days and may vary in the style of dances and songs that are performed, all according to the dreams of the specific Maru.

Although less frequent today, Maru ceremonies are still observed, and it is not unusual for non-Pomo, or part-Pomo, peoples to be recognized as "dreamers" who may call for the ceremonies to begin. The occasion for the ceremonies varies, but is always dependent on the dream instructions of the Maru.

Daniel L. Smith-Christopher

Source for Further Study

Meighan, Clement W., and Francis Riddell. *The Maru Cult of the Pomo Indians: A California Ghost Dance Survival.* Los Angeles: Southwest Museum Papers, 1972.

See also: Dances and Dancing; Ghost Dance.

Masks

Tribes affected: Aleut, Bella Coola, Cherokee, Eskimo, Haida, Iroquois tribes, Kwakiutl, Lenni Lenape, Makah, Maya, Naskapi, Navajo, Nootka, Plains tribes, Pueblo tribes, Salish, Seneca, Tlingit, Tsimshian, others

Significance: *Masks have been used by many American Indian tribes since prehistoric times for ceremonial, social, and religious purposes, allowing access to and control of the spiritual world.*

The making and wearing of masks was an art form that served religious, social, and artistic purposes for American Indians. Putting on a "false face" could provide protection or disguise, be used as a vehicle for contact with supernatural powers, or enhance the role of storytelling.

Types of Masks. The simplest way of wearing a mask was to paint the face. This allowed the wearer to present a different persona easily by changing the color of the face and by emphasizing certain features. By painting the face, a transformation of personality took place, giving the wearer a different outlook and the ability to affect the impression and response of others.

In the prehistoric times, masks were used to control the spiritual world and for magical purposes. By putting on a false face it was believed that one could engage the power of the surrounding spirits, who, being good or evil, had an impact on one's life. Masks were considered holy and sacred objects in themselves as they had the power to transform the wearer into the representative spirit. Very often they were used in ritual dances to exorcise evil or invoke blessing. Masks made the powers visible, and the wearer could become one with the spiritual power. Some Indians believed that the spirits of deceased ancestors returned in a mask.

Ceremonial use included such occasions as initiations, war dances, and fertility rites. Storytelling and dramatization of symbolic legends made use of masks and provided entertainment. In the Southwest masks were used to invoke spirits to help in providing rain, and in the Northwest masks were related to the clan totem, the spirit protector of the clan.

A masked dancer from the Cowichan tribe. *(Library of Congress)*

Masks were made of wood, animal hides, and plant fibers in North America and of wood, metals, stone, and clay in Central and South America. Which material was used depended upon the region and its natural resources and the degree of development in the use of masks, which varied from tribe to tribe.

Regional Examples. The Northwest Coast area had perhaps the greatest development in the quality and use of masks. They were

used in curing ceremonies and midwinter performances of dramatized myths and legends in song and dance. The masks were made
by carvers (who were held in high esteem by the community) of
wood, generally cedar, and were colorfully and boldly painted,
with dark green being a favorite color. The Kwakiutl made highly
expressive, complex masks with moveable parts such as beaks.
Masks were often in the form of a human face, or the head of a bird,
animal, or spirit, all having supernatural power. Clan masks represented the clan totem. A shaman wearing a mask could be transformed into the animal or spirit represented by the mask. Sometimes masks were double-layered, representing the duality of the
inner human spiritual form and the outer animal form.

Eskimos (Inuits) used masks in acting out cosmic dramas. Their
masks displayed animal features representing a host of beings and
phenomena. Some masks were hinged; others were made of fur.
They also made large wooden masks to represent and honor the
dead; they were left unpainted and bore solemn expressions.

In the Southwest, Pueblo Indians made simple head coverings
of animal hides that were painted and decorated with feathers,
cloth, herbs, and carved wooden beaks. Rounded heads represented the male, and square heads represented the female; the respective shapes could also represent deities or lesser spirits.

Masks were sacred to the Pueblos, who did not allow exact photographic reproductions of them. The wearer had to be purified before wearing a mask, and masks were ceremonially sanctified with
sacred pollen or corn meal before being stored in the kiva. Most
Pueblo masks represented spirits, with a few representing animals. The kachina dancer portrayed the spirit of a deceased clan
member who lived in the underworld and was called upon for aid
in assuring rain and good crops.

In the Eastern Woodlands region, masks were used to drive
away evil spirits. Wooden masks were worn only by men, but
Husk Faces, made of bands of braided corn husks, were worn by
both men and women. The Iroquois made masks for False Face
Ceremonies to exorcise demons. These masks had distorted features, long hair, and deeply set eyes, and they were painted in red

and/or black. The Iroquois also made buffalo-head masks that were used in the Buffalo Dance. The Cherokee made masks for hunting, as aids to help them get close to game animals. Their masks boldly emphasized the distinctive features of animals, such as the eyes, ears, nose, or antlers. The Living Solid Face mask of the Lenni Lenape (Delaware) was considered a helpful spirit and guide as well as a living mask.

In Mesoamerica, mask making was a complex art form in which masks were used to record the history, religion, and aesthetics of the people. Made of a wide variety of materials, masks were symbolic expressions of beliefs and were worn at ritual dances.

Masks made by American Indians today are still used for ceremonial purposes. Among some tribes, masks are also made for commercial purposes.

Diane C. Van Noord

Sources for Further Study

Berlo, Janet Catherine. *Native North American Art*. New York: Oxford University Press, 1998.

Conn, Richard. *Native American Art in the Denver Art Museum*. Denver: Denver Art Museum, 1979.

Cordry, Donald. *Mexican Masks*. Austin: University of Texas Press, 1980.

Dubin, Lois Sherr. *North American Indian Jewelry and Adornment: From Prehistory to the Present*. New York: Henry N. Abrams, 1999.

Furst, Peter T., and Jill L. Furst. *North American Indian Art*. New York: Rizzoli International, 1982.

LaFarge, Oliver, et al. *Introduction to American Indian Art*. Glorieta, N.Mex.: Rio Grande Press, 1973.

Macgowan, Kenneth, and Herman Rosse. Reprint. 1923. *Masks and Demons*. New York: Kraus Reprint, 1972.

Wherry, Joseph H. *Indian Masks and Myths of the West*. New York: Thomas Y. Crowell, 1974.

See also: Dances and Dancing; False Face Ceremony; Husk Face Society; Kachinas; Paints and Painting; Religion; Totems.

Mathematics

Tribes affected: Pantribal

Significance: *The most highly developed mathematical systems in the pre-contact Americas were the Mayan and Aztec calendar systems, but number systems for counting were developed by most tribes.*

Mathematical skills developed by American Indian tribes included the development of number systems—words and symbols used for calendrical measurement and economic bookkeeping. In the former case, this allowed the passage of days, months, seasons, and years to be independently followed; in the latter case, it simply meant counting objects, people, animals, and so on. Hunting tribes, for example, had little use for extensive number systems, since small numbers were sufficient for enumeration in the counting of objects such as spears, knives, fish, and canoes.

Similar to the number systems of most ancient cultures throughout the world, many number systems of North America were based on the decimal system, meaning that their numbers were based on groupings of ten. (The origin of the decimal system, noted by Aristotle long ago, was a result of the fact that humans are born with ten fingers and ten toes.) Almost one-third of American Indian tribes that have been studied used the decimal system. In North America, this included the Algonquian, Iroquois, Salish, and Sioux. In parts of California, number systems were based on groupings of twenty, known as the vigesimal system. Other systems based on two, three, and five (the binary, ternary, and quinary systems, respectively) were also used. To derive numbers, most tribes used additive and multiplicative principles and, to a lesser extent, subtractive and divisive principles. Nine was considered one less than ten, and eleven was one greater than ten. Repeated addition (multiplication) was used for large numbers. The fingers and toes of five men could be used to count one hundred objects. To preserve a record of counted objects a pile of stones could be used, one stone for each object counted. Bundles of sticks were also used to count and keep track of days, one stick being removed from a bundle to represent the passage of a day. A tally of years was kept by scratching notches in sticks.

The complex Mayan and Aztec calendar systems used both the 365-day year and a 260-day cycle tied to the cultures' religious rituals. In the Mayan system, the more accurate of the two, there were 360 "named" days in the years and 5 unnamed days. The 360-day period of named days was called the *tun* and was composed of eighteen *uinals*, or months, of twenty days each. The 260-day and 365-day cycles overlapped; every fifty-two years the two cycles returned to the same relative positions; scholars refer to this fifty-two-year period as the Calendar Round. Every day—18.980 in all—in the round had a unique combination of day numbers and names and month numbers and names.

Nicholas C. Thomas

See also: Aztec Empire; Mayan Civilization.

Mayan Civilization

Significance: *These Mesoamericans contributed profound achievements in art, mathematics, astronomy, and architecture.*

Mayan history is divided into three periods: Preclassic (2000 B.C.E.-200 C.E.), Classic (200-900 C.E.), and Postclassic (900 C.E. to the Spanish conquest). The Maya lived in an area that included the present-day Mexican states of Chiapas, Tabasco, Campeche, Yucatan, and Quintana Roo, in addition to the countries of Belize, Guatemala, Honduras, and El Salvador. Scholars who study the Maya have divided the entire region into three subregions: the southern subregion of Guatemala highlands and the Pacific coast; the central subregion of northern Guatemala, its adjacent lowlands, and the Petén region; and the northern subregion of the Yucatan peninsula. The highland areas of southern Guatemala and Chiapas flourished during the late Preclassic period; lowland areas in the Petén region reached their height during the Classic pe-

Area of the Mayan Civilization

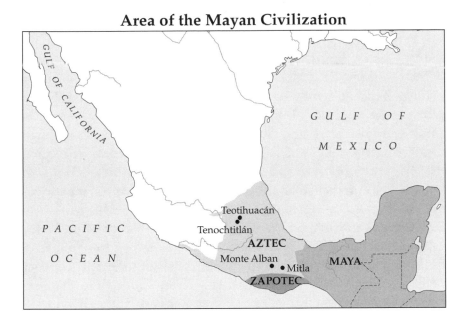

riod; and the area in the Yucatan Peninsula prospered in the late Classic and Postclassic periods.

The end of the Preclassic period and the beginning of the Classic period, when the Maya flourished, had formerly been defined by the appearance of vaulted stone architecture, monumental inscriptions, and polychrome pottery. However, subsequent finds have revealed that each of these traits appeared at different times during the Terminal Preclassic. Consequently the "official" end of the Preclassic period and beginning of the Classic period has been changed from 300 to 250 or 200 c.e. During the late Preclassic period, writing, mathematics, architecture, astronomy, and calendars were used, but these were all more fully developed in the Classic period.

A few city-states, such as El Mirador and Kaminaljuyu, developed in the Preclassic period, but it was the Classic period that witnessed the rise of the larger, more advanced city-states for which the Maya are known. One of the earliest and largest of the Classic-period centers was Tikal, located in the Petén region of Guatemala.

It covered a six-square-mile area, contained more than three thousand constructions, and had an estimated forty thousand inhabitants. One pyramid, 224 feet high, is the tallest pre-Columbian edifice in America. Copán, which was in Honduras, 250 miles southeast of Tikal, may have been a scientific center specializing in astronomy. Although the Maya did not have telescopes, jade tubes were used, which helped to concentrate their vision on selected celestial bodies. Their knowledge of astronomy was such that they not only had an accurate calendar of 365 days but also were able to predict solar and lunar eclipses, as well as the movement of Venus.

Palenque, in Chiapas, Mexico, had an aqueduct to direct water from a nearby stream to the center of the city and contained a building called the Palace, which was 228 feet long and 180 feet deep, with a four-story tower with an internal stairway. Perhaps its most famous feature is the tomb of the ruler Pacal, who died in 683 after ruling for sixty-eight years. The lid of the sarcophagus was a five-ton, twelve-foot slab of limestone carved with a bas-relief image of the ruler as he entered the jaws of death in the underworld. Palenque also is special for the fact that two women ruled before Pacal assumed the throne.

Bonampak, also located in Chiapas, is best known for its Temple of Frescoes. The frescoes depict many activities and scenes of daily life not represented elsewhere. Some of these representations have helped scholars to realize that the Maya were not the peaceful people they once were believed to be.

Other important centers in the Yucatan peninsula, such as Chichén Itzá, began in the Classic period but continued to flourish in the Postclassic period under the influence of the Toltecs, who invaded Mayan territory in the tenth century. Some of the aforementioned centers had previously experienced a foreign influence early in the Classic period. In the fifth century, Teotihuacán, which was located in the central basin of Mexico, began to spread its influence throughout southern Mesoamerica, including the Mayan cities of Kaminaljuyu, Copán, and Tikal. This influence ended in the eighth century, and there has been speculation that this was a factor in the demise of the Classic period at the end of the ninth century.

The Classic period was characterized by the construction of impressive structures, often one on top of the other. Either existing structures were demolished and the material was used in the new construction, or a new and larger structure enveloped the older one. Buildings were typically covered with stucco. If it was an important structure, the date would be recorded and the event would be celebrated with a religious ceremony that included bloodletting.

Some of the main features of Mayan architecture were large, flat-topped stone pyramids with steps that led to a temple decorated with tiled pediments known as "roof combs"; buildings covered with bas-reliefs; jutting corbeled arches or vaults; ballcourts; large public squares or plazas; and stelae, altars, and monoliths inscribed with names, dates, and important events. A major feature of the large ceremonial centers was the formal plaza lined by public buildings. Much of this was made possible by the Mayan practice of cementing the cut stones together. They had perfected the use of mortar, plaster, and stucco.

Society was highly stratified. At the top was an elite who ruled and enjoyed special privileges. It was the function of the common people to provide not only necessities but also luxuries for the elite. There were probably a number of strata between the royal family and the common farmers, based on birth or occupation, which may have been hereditary. Each city-state had its own ruling dynasty, which is believed to have been by patrilineal primogeniture accessible to others only through marriage. The inequality of treatment did not end with death; while the nobility were buried in tombs, the peasants were buried under the floor in their homes.

Religion was of central importance to Mayan culture. Myriad gods controlled everything and therefore had to be consulted and appeased constantly. Mayan religious concerns encouraged the development of astronomy and mathematics. Each day and number had its patron deity. When a child was born, a priest would predict its future with the aid of astrological charts and books. Each day and each moment was governed by a different god. Depending on the exact day and time of its birth, a child would owe a special devotion to the ascendant deity throughout its lifetime. Religious ceremonies were of the utmost importance. An important aspect of some religious ceremonies was the practice of shedding human blood. Bloodletting took the form of human sacrifices— either of enemies or possibly of devout martyrs—and nonfatal self-mutilation. The latter seems to have been a common practice, which entailed the piercing of the tongue, lips, earlobes, or penis. The blood was sometimes dripped onto paper strips that then were burned. In addition to giving nurture and praise to the gods, the Maya believed contact could be made with gods or deceased ancestors by the letting of blood.

The Classic period was marked by competition and conflict. There was an extensive system of short- and long-distance trade, not only among the Maya but with other indigenous peoples as well. Economic success brought growth and prosperity to the many city-states, but it also brought increased competition for territory and power. Warfare was a frequent outcome. Some of the conquered rivals provided sacrificial victims to satisfy the gods; others were beheaded, with the heads possibly used as trophies. During this period, Tikal was defeated by Caracol, which later was defeated by Dos Pilas. Thus fortunes changed for communities and individuals alike.

The end of the classic Mayan civilization was both swift and mysterious. Numerous theories attempt to explain the rather sudden and widespread demise of the prosperous lowland Mayan communities. Undoubtedly, there were both internal and external causes. The former may have included environmental degradation, overpopulation relative to the food supply, disease and malnutrition, a revolution of peasants against the elite, and decay of the artistic, political, and intellectual superstructure of society. Invasion and economic collapse due to changes in other parts of Mesoamerica are possible external causes. While the southern part of the Mayan civilization was undergoing collapse and depopulation, the centers in northern Yucatan continued to prosper and some southward immigration occurred to fill the vacuum. The succeeding Postclassic period, which witnessed the dominance of the Yucatan area, continued until the Spanish conquest in the mid-sixteenth century.

Philip E. Lampe

Sources for Further Study

The Cambridge History of the Native Peoples of the Americas. 3 vols. New York: Cambridge University Press, 1996-2000. The Aztec, Mayan, Olmec, and Zapotec civilizations are studied before and after contact with Europeans.

Carrasco, David. *Religions of Mesoamerica.* San Francisco: Harper & Row, 1990. Includes chapters on Mayan religion and closely related practices.

Hammond, Norman. *Ancient Maya Civilization.* New Brunswick, N.J.: Rutgers University Press, 1982. Good synthesis of available data, with scholars' theories and interpretations.

Henderson, John. *The World of the Ancient Maya.* Ithaca, N.Y.: Cornell University Press, 1981. Examines Mayan culture from the earliest settlements through the period of Spanish conquest.

Ivanoff, Pierre. *Maya Monuments of Civilization.* New York: Madison Square Press, 1973. Photographs and brief text on many important sites.

Landa, Diego de. *Yucatan Before and After the Conquest.* Translated by William Gates. New York: Dover, 1978. Historical explanation of manuscript by Landa, which is the source of much of the information available on Mayan history and culture.

See also: Astronomy; Ball Game and Courts; Codices; Culture Areas; Mathematics; Religion.

Medicine and Modes of Curing: Post-contact

Tribes affected: Pantribal
Significance: *Meeting the health care needs of contemporary American Indians, especially those living on reservations, is largely the responsibility of the Indian Health Service.*

By the middle of the nineteenth century, the American Indian population had been decimated by three centuries of contact with Europeans and European Americans. Among the primary factors in this vast depopulation was the devastation caused by infectious European diseases (such as smallpox), against which Indians did not have immunity. Moreover, by the mid- to late nineteenth century, nearly all the native population of the United States had been consigned to reservations. These reservations, found today in thirty-two states, are located primarily in Alaska, Arizona, Minnesota, Montana, New Mexico, South Dakota, Utah, Washington, and Wisconsin.

In various treaties with the federal government, Indians were historically guaranteed health care services. Until the late nineteenth century, such care was under the jurisdiction of the Department of War and was provided by military doctors stationed on or near reservations. Some health care was also provided by religious and social groups. It was not until 1921 that the federal government, in the Snyder Act, officially mandated that health services be provided to American Indians.

By the middle of the twentieth century, Indian health care had come under the jurisdiction of the Indian Health Service of the federal Public Health Service. Central issues such as the rural location of many American Indians, the widespread existence of Indian poverty, and the high incidence of certain health problems among Indians—especially accidental death, diabetes, depression, and many alcohol-related diseases—have complicated the problem of providing adequate health care to Indians.

Early Indian Health Care. In many cases, nineteenth century peace treaties between the federal government and the Indian tribes who agreed to live on reservations included some sort of health care provisions. Initially, the radically underfunded programs aimed at meeting these needs were of two types. First, health funds were combined with funds aimed at general education and were administered by either religious or philanthropic organizations that operated with widely varying degrees of success. Second, the Department of War used the most appropriate—or convenient—personnel at military posts close to the individual reservations to carry out Indian medical care and training in health-related areas such as sanitation. The quality of the health care Indians received varied greatly and depended on the attitudes of the personnel who were involved in it.

Development of the Indian Health Service. In the middle of the nineteenth century, the U.S. Department of the Interior was created. At this time civilians took over Indian health care entirely as this charge passed into the hands of the Bureau of Indian Affairs (BIA). While initially inefficient at providing health care, the BIA began to organize a medical care division in the middle of the 1870's. This division grew slowly; by the 1920's its main efforts were in the treatment of trachoma, tuberculosis, and the other contagious diseases that were endemic among reservation populations. Indians were given the right of American citizenship in 1924. Regrettably, however, the next thirty years saw relatively little overall improvement of their health, despite the efforts of the health care practitioners who worked among them.

In 1955 the Public Health Service took over Indian health care via the Division of Indian Health, which is now called the Indian Health Service. This change was mandated by Public Law 83-568 (the Transfer Act), which stated that "all the functions, responsibilities, authorities, and duties . . . relating to the maintenance and operation of . . . health facilities for Indians, and conservation of Indian health . . . shall be administered by the Surgeon General of the Public Health Service." Three factors enabled the Indian Health

Service to operate more efficiently than had previous agencies concerned with American Indian health.

First and foremost of these was the widespread use of antibiotics such as penicillin, which could cure many diseases very quickly and gave Indians more faith in the efficacy of white medicine. Second, federal legislation made it possible for physicians and other health professionals to serve in the Public Health Service Officer Corps instead of performing active military service. This brought a great many more qualified individuals into the Indian Health Service. Third, many of the Indians who had served in the U.S. armed forces during World War II had returned to their reservations. Now familiar with life and medical care off reservations, they became an essential cadre of advocates for the Indian Health Service; they also soon represented many members of its staff.

Another valuable aspect of the Indian Health Service is its efficient hierarchical organization and governance at all of its levels from the national office to its management areas to its service units (often a whole tribe). The hierarchy leads to swifter action and to better communication than was possible under other systems. One problem associated with the Indian Health Service is the lack of choice of individual physicians; reservation inhabitants must accept the care of a reservation's appointed doctors or must purchase their own health care.

Health Service Weaknesses and Solutions. Most weaknesses of the Indian Health Service arise from its relatively inadequate funding, the transience and undersupply of its biomedical staff, and the fact that it is smaller than might be desired (51 hospitals and about 425 outpatient clinics and health centers). These factors are aggravated by the lack of many essential, high-technology medical services at its component hospitals, health centers, and clinics. Nevertheless, these facilities are usually very well run within their limitations, such as the facts that the population being served lives mostly on reservations that are located in isolated rural areas and that transportation difficulties arise when patients must be moved to distant, private-sector health providers for services that are otherwise unavailable to them.

The problems of Indian Health Service health care delivery, as well as some of the solutions, are exemplified by the Navajo reservation, with a population of more than 200,000. This reservation, on which live the members of the largest American Indian tribe, is located on an area about the size of West Virginia and sprawls over parts of Arizona, New Mexico, and Utah. The reservation's Indian Health Service component is divided into 8 of the 137 service units found in the United States. It contains hospitals with a total of about five hundred beds as well as numerous clinics and other health centers.

Problems of overcrowding and the already mentioned lack of high-technology health services necessitate the expensive transfer of many Navajo Indian patients to private-sector facilities. A partial solution to this logistics problem is the use of a relatively economical ambulance service operated by the Navajo tribe. Other problems include the high incidence of heart disease, alcohol-related deaths (from cirrhosis of the liver, for example), homicide, suicide, and diabetes that consume much of the resource base of the Navajo reservation service units. Present solutions include using both Medicare and Medicaid revenue obtained for qualifying Indians. In the long run, increased budgets for the Indian Health Service and additional hospital facilities will be required.

Another severe problem is the high turnover and shortage of nurses and other essential health care professionals. Permanent nursing positions in the Indian Health Service, for example, are reported to be only 75 to 80 percent filled. It has been noted by upper-level Indian Health Service administrators that increasing staff salaries will only partly solve the problem. Rather, the problem is viewed as being largely attributable to both geographic and professional isolation. Complicating the issue still more are the existing decreases and the expected ending of some federal programs that pay all of the educational costs of physicians and nurses in return for a term of practice in the underserved regions of the United States, including Indian reservations. This is particularly problematic because a large percentage of the Indian Health Service professional staff comes from this source (the National Health Service Corps, NHSC). Even in the best of times, however, only 5 to 10 percent of NHSC physicians have remained in the Indian Health Service for even one year beyond the time required by their scholarship program obligations. A positive change is the increased number of Indians entering and projected to enter the system as professional staff.

Identifying Indians to Be Served. Estimates of the percentage of American Indians who are being treated by the Indian Health Service vary from 60 to about 80 percent, depending upon the source of the estimate of the total U.S. Indian population. One basis for counting the Indian population is self-assessment of being an Indian via the U.S. Census. Another approach is based on the percentage of Indian blood possessed by a person. The Indian Health Service itself is not concerned with quantifying the amount of Indian blood in the people it serves. Rather, service at one of its facilities depends on being recognized as an Indian by a contemporary Indian tribe. Requirements for this recognition vary from tribe to tribe, but they often consist of being of one-fourth Indian blood. Indian Health Service facilities are not limited to reservation-based Indians, although most facilities are located on or near reservations. One reason that the service provides care for both reservation and nonreservation Indians is that many tribes count individuals as members regardless of their formal place of residence.

Special Health Needs. The American Indian population has traditionally exhibited a significantly greater incidence of infant mortality as well as adult deaths from a number of diseases than seen in the general U.S. population. These problems have been attributed to Indian families' generally lower incomes as well as to their poorer nutrition and living conditions. Inroads had been made, however, in most of these areas by the end of the twentieth century.

For example, there has been a drop in infant mortality from 22.2

per 1,000 live births to 8.7, a rate very near that for the "U.S., all races" category. Improvement of both health services and living conditions has also diminished the absolute numbers of deaths from the main diseases that kill modern Indian adults. Contemporary deaths from accident, alcoholism and related problems, diabetes, homicide, influenza/pneumonia, suicide, and tuberculosis still exceed those in the "all races" population.

The Indian Health Service has attempted to diminish the extent of these health problems in a variety of ways. Among efforts directed toward accident reduction is an injury prevention program that includes motor vehicle aspects such as child passenger protection, the promotion of seat belt use, and the deterrence of drunk driving. Furthermore, educational programs on such topics as smoke detector use and drowning protection are widespread.

Another aspect of disease prevention among Indians is a widespread nutrition and dietetics program in which clinical nutrition counseling and general health aspects are promoted. This aspect of Indian Health Service activity is viewed as possessing a very high potential for success, having had a large number of contacts per year with patients. Also important is the provision by the Indian Health Service of modern sanitary facilities for many Indian homes. Between 1960 and 1991, almost 200,000 homes were provided with modernized sanitary facilities by the service. This assistance has included water and sewage facilities, solid waste disposal, and the development of local organizations to maintain the new systems. Yet much more help is needed in these ventures. In 2001, an article on the Indian Health Service's Sanitation Facilities Initiative reported that after ten years of funding, nearly 30,180 Indian homes still needed either a safe water supply or an acceptable sewage disposal system. In some cases the homes lacked both of these initiatives.

Shamanic and Modern Health Care. A particularly intriguing aspect of modern medical treatment is the combination of conventional Western treatment with the activities of the traditional tribal shaman. This combination of treatments may be found in many Indian Health Service facilities and elsewhere. Its use is partly attributable to the fact that shamanic treatment is comfortable to many Indians. Many of today's physicians find that the shamanic ceremonies and medicinal treatments are a useful complement to their ministrations. These procedures are deemed to be particularly important in resolving mental health problems, but they have also found wide utility in problems ranging from heart disease to dermatitis to cancer.

Sanford S. Singer

Sources for Further Study

Gregg, Elinor D. *The Indians and the Nurse.* Norman: University of Oklahoma Press, 1965. Points out problems, shortcomings, strengths, and other interesting aspects of federally funded care of American Indians from 1922 to 1937. Provides much insight into physicians, nurses, and Indian patients.

Hammerschlag, Carl A. *The Dancing Healers: A Doctor's Journey of Healing with Native Americans.* San Francisco: Harper & Row, 1988. Various aspects of a psychiatrist's experience with Indian healing are described. Examples of syntheses of Indian and Western medicine that produce useful, interactive processes are carefully explored.

Hultkrantz, Ake. *Shamanic Healing and Ritual Drama: Health and Medicine in Native North American Religious Traditions.* New York: Crossroad, 1992. A detailed survey of Indian practice and belief in health, medicine, and religion. Both the historical and modern aspects of shamanic ritual are covered. Also included is a copious set of valuable references.

Kane, Robert L., and Rosalie A. Kane. *Federal Health Care (with Reservations).* New York: Springer, 1971. Indian Health Service strengths, problems, and shortcomings are described knowledgeably. Included are the capacity to respond to patient needs and conflicts engendered when health providers and consumers have different cultural backgrounds. Kane was a director of the Indian Health Service Navajo service unit at Shiprock, New Mexico.

Rhoades, Everett R., ed. *American Indian Health: Innovations in Health Care, Promotion, and Policy.* Baltimore: Johns Hopkins University Press, 2000. A comprehensive review of the health and health care of Native Americans.

Torrey, E. Fuller, E. F. Foulkes, H. C. Hendrie, et al. *Community Health and Mental Health Care Delivery for North American Indians.* New York: MSS Information Corporation, 1974. This interesting multiauthored book covers mental health problems of North American Indians. It includes articles on general problems, cultural conflicts, alcoholism, drugs, suicide, and Indian mental health care needs. Shamanic aspects are also described.

Trafzer, Clifford E., and Diane Weiner, eds. *Medicine Ways: Disease, Health, and Survival Among Native Americans.* Walnut Creek, Calif.: AltaMira Press, 2001. An examination of the thought and practice of health care in the Native American communtiy.

U.S. Department of Health and Human Services. Indian Health Service. Division of Program Statistics. *Trends in Indian Health, 1989-.* This report briefly describes the Indian Health Service and its history and gives many modern statistics about Indian health care. Included are organizational data, handy health statistics, and statistics on many related issues.

U.S. Office of Technology Assessment. *Indian Health Care.* Washington, D.C.: Government Printing Office, 1986. This substantive book covers, in depth, many aspects of Indian health care. Included are the federal-Indian relationship, a population overview, American Indian health status, the Indian Health Service, selected special health topics, and extensive references.

See also: Alcoholism; Disease and Intergroup Contact; Medicine and Modes of Curing: Pre-contact; Religious Specialists.

Medicine and Modes of Curing: Pre-contact

Tribes affected: Pantribal
Significance: *Traditional American Indian cultures had a number of explanations of illness and approaches to healing, including medicinal, ritualistic, and supernatural approaches.*

During the prehistoric period, Native American groups had adequate medical systems for successfully treating illness and disease, consisting of a corpus of time-tried explanations and therapeutic procedures that were inextricably related to the notion of supernatural and natural causes. The cause, diagnosis, and prognosis of all illnesses and diseases were explained by a definite classification that was usually unique to a particular group.

Medical Systems. Most external injuries, such as fractures, dislocations, wounds, bruises, skin irritations, snake and insect bites, and even occupationally related deaths, were considered to have been caused by natural means. Many internal illnesses and psychological afflictions, however, were diagnosed as being the result of sorcerers who were capable of manipulating supernatural malevolent powers, resulting in maladies that could be treated only by medical practitioners, or shamans, who possessed special benevolent religious powers and abilities.

Indigenous medical systems resulted from a group's particular adaptation to a certain environment—its wide variety of medicinal as well as noxious plants. It was not unusual for Native Americans to learn medical procedures from the close observation of certain animals. For example, in the early spring, when deer go from browsing to grazing, they will develop diarrhea, and they consume clay to correct this condition. Similarly, clay eating, or geophagy, was universally utilized by Native Americans for curing diarrhea. Clay was also applied externally for certain dermal eruptions, as clay effectively absorbs liquids.

Hunters and gatherers were more concerned with illness than with the advent of death because of their need to maintain a high degree of mobility in order to exploit the animal and plant foods that were located in different areas, according to elevation and time of year. Consequently, illness could debilitate a group's strategies for obtaining food. Because of this concern, Native Americans developed extensive and successful methods of interpreting and treating different afflictions by the use of medical practitioners.

Shamans. The principal medical practitioner was the shaman, a man or woman who had acquired supernatural curing power through a variety of ritualized procedures, but more often through the vision quest, dreaming, receiving a sign, inheritance from a kinsperson, survival of an illness, and less frequently, resurrection after "death." The supernatural power to cure could be general or specific to certain maladies, and usually one's tutelary spirit was associated with curing a particular illness. For example, bear power was most effective in treating burns, heron power to retrieve a lost soul.

Shamans maintained their power through frequent renewal rituals such as sweating, dreaming, reciting special curing songs, isolation, fasting, and continually revitalizing their medicines and paraphernalia through purification. Usually, during an annual rite, shamans would publicly demonstrate their powers to the congregation; this was an occasion when one's power could be stolen by a more powerful individual. The practitioner's life was further burdened by almost continual stress in observing strict behavioral and dietary taboos, which, if violated, could mean the shaman's loss of power or even illness and possibly death.

The curing knowledge and skills of a shaman were sometimes acquired through serving an apprenticeship to a known shaman or to an established practitioner of one's family who would serve as a sponsor and guide during the often long and arduous training period. Shamans tended to work individually but sometimes required the assistance of herbalists, women who usually had a more complete knowledge of local plants and their medicinal uses and

A medicine man, Little Big Mouth, near Fort Sill, Oklahoma, during the late nineteenth century. *(National Archives)*

properties than did men. Often esoteric medical knowledge was jealously guarded.

Shamans were respected and even feared, for a person who could cure was also believed capable of sorcery. If a patient died, the attending shaman could be accused of being the sorcerer. Medical practitioners were sometimes physically different because of blindness, minor congenital defects, or permanent injuries. They were also considered psychologically different from others because of their ability to perform shamanistic rites such as soul-flight, physical and spiritual transformation, legerdemain, ventriloquism, glossalalia (nonmeaningful speech or "speaking in tongues"), and various prophetic skills.

Causes of Illness. Native Americans were not disease-free. They experienced mostly gastrointestinal problems, arthritis, pneumonia, and some endemic maladies. Therefore, illnesses and injuries attributable to natural causes were well understood and could be treated by an elderly, more knowledgeable kinsperson. Supernatural maladies and death were believed to be caused by moral transgression, unfulfilled dreams, misusing one's power, sorcery (as in soul loss, spirit intrusion, or object intrusion), and, in some cases, poisoning.

Spiritual or supernatural illnesses were invariably thought to be caused by a sorcerer who had successfully manipulated an individual's soul or tutelary spirit because the victim had offended or humiliated someone—or simply because the sorcerer was malicious. A person who was greedy, selfish, boisterous, or malicious was subject to being sorcerized. Consequently, the fear of sorcery was an effective means of social control, not only because of the dire consequences but also because one was not always certain who was a sorcerer.

Illness could be self-induced through breaking a taboo or by not informing a person who was to suffer an illness or some misfortune, as revealed in one's dream. If one had such a prophetic dream, and if the person in the dream was not properly warned, it was common for the dreamer to experience that specific misfortune. In fact, many Native Americans, upon awakening in the morning, revealed their dreams to an elderly member of the family who would interpret the dream's significance and prescribe appropriate behavior to prevent misfortune.

It was not unusual for an aged or sick shaman to give up his or her curing power through a special ritual, one that ensured the particular power would be acquired later by another person. It also freed the aged shaman from further responsibilities and possible maladies. Illness or even death could occur if one failed to acknowledge that one possessed curing power and should fulfill the obligations of this responsibility.

Women sometimes became shamans after menopause, when they could receive obstetrical power for assisting as midwives in difficult deliveries, prolapse, uterine hemorrhaging, or cases of malposition. Female shamans were knowledgeable about abortives and contraceptives, and they instructed the new mother about postnatal dietary and behavioral taboos. They often instructed a menarcheal girl about pertinent taboos associated with being a woman. They administered decoctions, roots, powders, and other medicines for dysmenorrhea and other female disorders, even when fecundity was thought to be a problem. Female shamans were, on occasion, sought for empowering courting flutes or providing love incantations or medicines.

Universal to Native Americans was the strict observance of dietary and behavioral taboos that surrounded an individual's death, for if the survivors violated purification rites intended to prevent spiritual contamination, failed to accord the deceased certain respect, mentioned the name of the deceased, or dreamed improperly of the dead person, or if the widow or widower married too soon, then a specific illness would beset the offender, inflicted by the dead person's ghost.

Nor was it unusual for a person who had not accorded proper respect through the strict observance of taboos associated with killing an animal to become ill. For example, a man who killed a bear had to sing the death song of the creature and, for a prescribed period, abstain from sexual relationships and eat a restricted diet. If the hunter was remiss, the dead bear might appear in the man's dream and pull back its scalp, which could result in the hunter losing his mind and being condemned to endless wandering and continual hunger.

Curing Rituals. Treatment of supernatural illnesses depended upon an impressive array of medicines, cures, and ritual therapies that required the intervention of a shaman. These rituals were shamanistic performances that included dancing, singing, drumming, and the use of religious paraphernalia that were personal and power-associated. Medical knowledge was jealously guarded, for it was feared that a shaman could lose his or her power if the knowledge were divulged.

An important aspect of treating supernatural illnesses was the group medical inquest, or therapeutic interview, a collective ceremony in which the patient and shaman were joined by family and friends, and on occasion the entire village. This collective psychodrama functioned to integrate the group and to reinstate a moral order. It was an effective therapeutic session that publicly permitted shamans to demonstrate their power and ability. Shamans were sometimes attended by a medical chorus who chanted curing songs and played percussion and wind instruments which were believed to facilitate a shaman's power flight in seeking a vision or recovering a lost soul.

The group medical inquest also afforded the patient a managerial role, expiated guilt through oral catharsis, facilitated group confession of moral transgressions, and provided an opportunity for others to make confessions of transgressions that would prevent them from becoming ill. These rituals invariably lasted until the patient was completely rehabilitated, which meant that the practitioner and his or her entourage would reside temporarily with the patient, noting reasons for illness and anxiety.

Shamans effectively utilized various prophetic rituals and interpreted signs to ascertain the diagnosis and prognosis of illness, and even the specific cause. The offending sorcerer could be identified and might later participate in removing the malevolent power that was causing the affliction. Often a shaman's prophetic abilities in foreseeing medical problems were enhanced by the use of drugs, tobacco, fasting, spiritual transformation, hypnosis, dreaming, trances, and the use of musical instruments and singing. Some groups had prophetic devices such as special tule mats, sand paintings, smoke, or a container of water, or they had tutelary spirits that would communicate the needed information.

Prior to a curing ceremony, it was not uncommon to tie a shaman's hands and feet securely with rawhide and place him behind a hide screen. Immediately he would throw the loose rawhide over the screen. To demonstrate their power before curing, shamans might also perform different proofs of ordeal, such as withstanding excruciating pain or demonstrating unusual manipulative skills. For example, shamans might dramatically plunge an arm into boiling water or hold a hot stone to show the patient and group they were impervious to pain because of their power.

During curing ritual shamans often had to be protected as their personal powers might be elsewhere seeking the cause of a patient's malady. Temporarily without power, shamans were be-

Traditional Indian Medicines Still Used			
Plant	*Symptom*	*Preparation*	*How Used*
Black spruce	Cough	Soft inner bark	Chewed
Devil's club	Aching muscles	Boiled	Drunk
Fireweed	Swelling	Large infusion steamed	As poultice
Lichen	Ulcers	Mixed with other herbs	Chewed
Sage	Colds	Boiled	Inhaled
Soapberry	Diarrhea	None	Eaten
Spruce needles	Eye infection	Needles boiled	As eye wash
Spruce pitch	Infected wound	Applied directly	As poultice
Strawberry leaf	Ensure safe pregnancy	Dried and boiled	Drunk
Strawberry root	Diarrhea	Boiled	Drunk
Tamarack bark	Stomach trouble	Beaten, tea added	Drunk
Wild rhubarb	Arthritis	Boiled as tea	Drunk
Wild rhubarb	Infected wound	Pounded root	As poultice
Willow leaves	Insect stings	Chewed and applied	As poultice

Source: Duane Champagne, ed., *The Native North American Almanac.* Detroit: Gale Research, 1994. Primary source, Medical Services Branch, Alberta Region, health and Welfare Canada.
Note: A partial listing of herbal medicines still used today in Canada.

lieved susceptible to danger, since their power could be lost or taken by a more powerful person. On occasion, the shaman may have been required to have a power duel with the malevolent power, a struggle which was evident by the practitioner's unusual behavior when he or she was thrown about or lifted into the air. A shaman of lesser power could be killed by the illness when it was removed from the patient, particularly if the shaman used a sucking tube.

Medicines. Through continual observation and long use, Native Americans developed an extensive materia medica, estimated to have been approximately fifty-four percent chemically active. It was constituted from geological, floral, and faunal substances. These compounds and simple medicaments were administered to most internal and external afflictions by shamans who were knowledgeable of the intended effect.

Medicines were administered in the form of poultices, salves, expectorants, vermifuges, emetics, cathartics, astringents, febrifuges, poisons, anesthetics, stimulants, narcotics, diuretics, and infusions. Most medicines were acquired locally, but some were obtained through trade.

John Alan Ross

Sources for Further Study

Corlett, William Thomas. *The Medicine-Man of the American Indian and His Cultural Background*. Springfield, Ill.: Charles C Thomas, 1935. A book that explains the cultural significance of medicines and their ritual application, particularly the role of the shaman.

Radin, Paul. *The Story of the American Indian*. New York: Boni & Liveright, 1927. An early but significant recognition of Native American medical systems that explains the role of ritual in treating psychosomatic illnesses.

Ross, John Alan. "Indian Shamans of the Plateau: Past and Present." *Medical Journal* 62, no. 3 (1989). An article dealing with aboriginal and syncretic medicine in the Plateau, which is representative of many Native American groups.

Stone, Eric. *Medicine Among the American Indians.* Clio Medicia 7. New York: Hafner, 1962. A comprehensive text explaining indigenous Native American medical systems that contains an extensive bibliography.

Vogel, Virgil J. *American Indian Medicine.* Norman: University of Oklahoma Press, 1970. This excellent book is the most definitive study of Native American medicine because of extensive research, references, and readability for the nonspecialist. It is illustrated and stresses the significance of medicinal plants. Contains a comprehensive bibliography.

See also: Disease and Intergroup Contact; Medicine and Modes of Curing: Post-contact; Religious Specialists.

Medicine Bundles

Tribes affected: Pantribal
Significance: *A medicine bundle is a physical token of an individual's, clan's, or nation's relationship to the spiritual world and its power.*

A medicine bundle is a collection of objects that have connection with sacred power. The objects may include artifacts such as the carved stone statue of the Kiowas (known as the Tai-me), gaming dice, or whittled sticks, as well as natural or found items such as feathers, smooth stones, naturally occurring crystals, and herbs and sweet grasses collected for the bundle. Whatever the contents, the bundle is always carefully arranged, whether bound by string and tied with special knots or rolled into a bark or buckskin container. Sweet grass, sage, and other aromatic herbs are renewed periodically. The bundle may be inherited from clan or family, may be given by a mentor to a disciple, or may be constructed according to directions received in a vision. In any case, the bundle represents and contains great power: It is the physical embodiment of the spiritual power of the owner, whether shaman, warrior, or priest.

Helen Jaskoski

See also: Bundles, Sacred; Clans; Ethnophilosophy and World-view; Medicine and Modes of Curing: Pre-contact; Religion; Religious Specialists.

Medicine Wheels

Tribes affected: Pantribal
Significance: *A medicine wheel is a circle of iconic stones used as a teaching tool.*

The medicine wheel is a sacred, powerful teaching circle. There were numerous medicine wheels composed of stones laid out by the indigenous North Americans, some of which are still extant. The most famous, found in the Bighorn Mountains in north central Wyoming, was used by a number of different tribes, including Crow, Cheyenne, Arapaho, and Lakota. It is a circle 80 feet in diameter with twenty-nine spokes of numerous limestone slabs, with three small outer circles, two outer vessel shapes, and one inner vessel shape, all placed at about 8,700 feet in altitude on Medicine Mountain. One of the spokes points to the place on the horizon where the sun rises at summer solstice. Another spoke points to Arcturus rising at spring equinox. The Department of the Interior wishes to turn this site into a tourist attraction and build a visitor center, picnic area, and campground. Tribes have petitioned the government to declare twelve days on both sides of equinoxes and solstices limited to tribal use of the site. The tribes also want the protected area around the medicine wheel enlarged so that the habitat within three miles of the wheel is undisturbed.

Glenn J. Schiffman

See also: Architecture: Plains; Religion; Sacred, the.

Menses and Menstruation

Tribes affected: Pantribal
Significance: *Indigenous tribal peoples have viewed menstruation as an important phenomenon, meriting ritual treatment.*

Menstruation occasioned widely varied responses and rituals by indigenous tribal peoples. Older women in Mesoamerican groups tried to keep a girl's first menstruation secret from the men in the tribe, but tribes in the intermountain basin, the Yukon, and Canadian Subarctic regions treated the girl as dangerous to the welfare of herself and the group and constructed elaborate rules she had to follow to prevent contaminating others. Other tribes, especially in Northern California and Apache territory, celebrated the onset of a girl's puberty as a milestone of maturation with a great feast. Some groups on the Northwest Coast, to safeguard a young woman's virginity, cloistered her from her first menstruation onward in part of the dwelling until her marriage.

Believing that a menstruating woman possessed supernatural powers that might harm her or her tribe, most tribal peoples required her to go into seclusion, avoid contact with men, and undergo special diets (often abstaining from eating meat) and baths. Often an older woman supervised her, but some customs dictated that the menstruant remain alone. Watchers scrutinized the woman to see how well she adhered to these prohibitions; some groups viewed these as tests that predicted a woman's future behavior. In some practices she could not touch her hair or skin for fear of self-contamination. At the end of the seclusion, usually the woman underwent a ritual bathing and received new clothes.

Even those tribal groups that did not insist on strict cloistering demanded that a menstruating woman keep clear of cooking areas and away from any task necessary to tribal survival. Many tribal groups assumed that a menstruating woman would scare off game animals during the hunt or diminish a warrior's medicine during warfare. After Cheyenne chief Roman Nose was fatally wounded during the Battle of Beecher's Island in 1868, for example, either he or others in the tribe blamed his wound on his having eaten food that a menstruating woman had prepared or touched.

European American settlers and missionaries did not find these indigenous menstruation customs strange. Although most European American groups did not force menstruating women into seclusion or insist they refrain from cooking, menstruation was the subject of certain cultural taboos. Many men thought a menstruating woman unclean morally and physically and sometimes shunned her. She was often treated circumspectly, for fear she possessed special magic or linkage with the Devil.

Thomas L. Altherr

See also: Children; Puberty and Initiation Rites; Rites of Passage; Women.

Metalwork

Tribes affected: Hopewell prehistoric tradition, Northeast tribes (especially Cayuga, Iroquois, Onondaga, Seneca), Southwest tribes (especially Navajo, Zuñi)
Significance: *Copper and, more recently, silver, have been used extensively for Indian ornamentation.*

The earliest examples of metals being used in North America date to around 4000 B.C.E. In the Great Lakes region, pieces of native copper were gathered and hammered into lance points and decorative or ritual objects. Archaeologists have discovered necklace beads composed of thin copper strips and fish-shaped pieces fashioned from the same metal during this era. These so-called Old Copper culture people did not practice true metallurgy, since the native metal was simply beaten and treated as a malleable stone. Copper ornaments and weapons produced by cold hammering, and some engraved sheets of silver of the Hopewell people, have also been found that date to the Common Era. The use of copper for personal ornamentation is one of the most striking differences between North American tribes and the pre-Columbian cultures of South and Central America, where gold was extensively used. Most North American tribes lacked any effective metalworking skills until after contact with other cultures, whereas the sixteenth century Spanish explorers of the New World found well-developed metalwork skills in Mexico and Central America.

By the seventeenth century, Northeast tribes, such as the Seneca, Cayuga, and Onondaga, hammered, shaped, and cut European silver coins for jewelry. The more intricate techniques of silverworking were introduced to the Southwest Navajo by Mexican silversmiths during the early second half of the nineteenth century. Later, the Zuñi (Pueblo) learned the craft from the Navajo. The Navajo style was distinguished by die-stamp designs that showed off the metal itself. Zuñi work was more intricate in detail, and die work was rarer.

Indian silversmiths produce work of extraordinary variety and beauty that reflects the unique creativity of Indian art. Bracelets, rings, earrings, necklaces, bow guards, concha belts, and buttons are only a few of the objects that, through the years, have been cre-

A depiction of an Indian blacksmith shop. *(Library of Congress)*

ated from hand-wrought silver. Turquoise, which was frequently used in ornamentation long before the introduction of silversmithing, has also featured prominently in Indian silverwork. Although commercial imitations of Navajo and Zuñi work have been mass-produced for the tourist market, they are unable to reproduce the beauty of authentic hand-made pieces.

Nicholas C. Thomas

Source for Further Study
Dubin, Lois Sherr. *North American Indian Jewelry and Adornment: From Prehistory to the Present*. New York: Henry N. Abrams, 1999.

See also: Gold and Goldworking; Ornaments; Silverworking; Turquoise.

Midewiwin

Tribes affected: Fox, Iowa, Menominee, Miami, Ojibwa (Chippewa), Ponca, Winnebago
Significance: *Midewiwin refers to a secret society and set of rituals that transferred knowledge of healing rites, herbal medicines, and moral codes to succeeding generations.*

The Midewiwin, also called the Grand Medicine Society, was both a secret society and a series of initiation and healing ceremonies. In tribal myths, this knowledge and power were given by the Great Spirit through an intermediary during a time of trouble and death. A central symbol is the white shell, representative of one which appeared to the Ojibwa from the eastern sea and led them west. Simultaneously with the shell, rules for moral living were given. The songs, rites, and stories of tribal origins are recorded in picture writing on birchbark scrolls. These scrolls are one of the few examples of Indian writing north of Mexico.

To join a society, a man or woman had to be recommended by a member. If accepted, they paid a fee and were assigned a teacher.

There were eight degrees of instruction, each of which required separate initiation rites. At the higher levels, persons were taught the use of herbal medicines and poisons. At each level, a Mide bag (medicine bundle) made of bird or animal skin containing the elements associated with that degree was presented.

In the central ceremonies, usually celebrated in the spring and lasting several days, initiates were ritually shot with pieces of white shell from a Mide bag, after which they feigned death. The fragments were then removed by Mide leaders, reviving the initiates to new life, both moral and spiritual.

The Midewiwin powers of healing and code for living were believed to guarantee a long life. The power of the Midewiwin was considered so great that members resisted Christian conversion. Eventually, however, legal and cultural pressures led to a decline of the practice. With the renewal of Indian culture that began in the 1960's, movements such as the Three Fires Society have revived the practice of the Midewiwin. Similar practices are found in the shell society of the Omaha and the Navajo chantway rituals.

Charles Louis Kammer III

See also: Medicine and Modes of Curing: Pre-contact; Medicine Bundles; Religious Specialists; Secret Societies.

Midwinter Ceremony

Tribes affected: Iroquois Confederacy (Six Nations)
Significance: *The Midwinter Ceremony was, and is, the pivotal event of the annual Iroquois ceremonial cycle; eight days of thanksgiving, propitiatory, and curing ceremonies traditionally began five days after the first new moon after the Pleiades were directly overhead at sunset.*

The Midwinter Ceremony, sometimes called the New Year Ceremony, is the biggest annual ceremony in Iroquois culture. Although the ceremony is still important today, this article will discuss it in the past tense to emphasize that the discussion concerns the ceremony as it existed before it was somewhat modified by contact with European culture. The Midwinter Ceremony began at dawn of the first day with shamans entering the village compounds beating on drums. The ashes of each hearth were swept to find glowing coals, which were brought to the longhouse where the ceremony was held. Here a new fire was kindled. Hearth fires for the new year were kindled from this fire.

The villagers assembled were congratulated for having survived to participate in another Midwinter Ceremony. The Thanksgiving Address, a cosmological statement of profound holistic knowledge, was then offered. Fifty-three songs accompanied the Thanksgiving Prayer.

Next the children born since the Green Corn Ceremony of midsummer were given clan names. Other events included washing with fire; the rite of personal chant; and a dream-guessing festival to initiate new members into the established medicine societies and to purge living souls of bad thoughts and spiritual tortures. The Iroquois put much faith in the sacred quality of dreams.

One popular event of the Midwinter Ceremony was the gambling game. One moiety of four clans played against the other moiety for personal power and certain political and ceremonial rights in the coming year. The game did not end until one moiety controlled all 108 dice. This ritual reflected the game of dice played between Creator and Dead Earth for the right for life to exist on earth. Then the Great Feather Dance was conducted, with its many songs, interspersed with pauses for praying and rejoicing that life continues.

Another key ceremony was the arrival of the Husk Face Society, men who imitated women, acted as clowns, and prophesied an abundant corn harvest in the coming year. The last ceremony of the Midwinter Ceremony was the sacrifice of the white dog. The spirit of the dog served as messenger to the Master of Life, conveying the good wishes and thankfulness of the people.

The Midwinter Ceremony was ordained first by the Peacemaker, and mnemonics for its recitation are found on wampum belts. The prophet Handsome Lake adjusted the Thanksgiving Prayer to fit the needs of the 1800's, and that version is the one in use today.

Glenn J. Schiffman

Sources for Further Study

Cornelius, Carol. "The Thanksgiving Address: An Expression of the Haudenosaunee Worldview." *Akwe:kon Journal* 9, no. 3 (Fall, 1992).

Henry, Thomas R. *Wilderness Messiah: The Story of Hiawatha and the Iroquois*. New York: Bonanaza Books, 1955.

Josephy, Alvin M., Jr. *The Indian Heritage of America*. New York: Alfred A. Knopf, 1968.

Morgan, Lewis H. *League of the Ho-de-no-sau-nee, or Iroquois*. Rochester, N.Y.: Sage and Brothers, 1851.

Spencer, Robert F., Jesse D. Jennings, et al. *The Native Americans*. 2d ed. New York: Harper & Row, 1977.

Tooker, Elisabeth. *The Iroquois Ceremonial of Midwinter*. Syracuse, N.Y.: Syracuse University Press, 2000.

_____, ed. *Native North American Spirituality of the Eastern Woodlands*. New York: Paulist Press, 1979.

See also: False Face Ceremony; Games and Contests; Husk Face Society.

Military Societies

Tribes affected: Primarily Plains tribes
Significance: *The main function of military societies was to enculturate young men into the ways and ethos of warfare.*

Military societies, or sodalities, were made up of men from different bands within a tribe. They were most common, and highly developed, in the Plains. These voluntary societies were often age-graded, with a person usually gaining greater status with age.

Sometimes one could shift membership and allegiance to another society. Some tribes, such as the Blackfeet, had as many as seven military societies. The societies' leaders were the main war chiefs of the tribe, who would have an entourage of subchiefs, messengers, and "ambassadors." There was often competition between the societies in games, physical endurance, and military deeds. Each fraternity, though fundamentally alike in their internal organization, had its own sacred and profane paraphernalia, war and dance songs, power bundles, rattles, pipes, emblems, and dress. Many societies were totemic by name and origin, which was sometimes reflected in dances and in art form upon shields, horses, and even a member's body.

The main functions of these societies were to enculturate young men into the ways and ethos of warfare; to embody the concepts of self-control, bravery, and honor; to exercise social control during communal bison hunting; to police tribal ceremonies; and to accord status to a society's members.

John Alan Ross

See also: Secret Societies; Societies: Non-kin-based; Warfare and Conflict.

Missions and Missionaries

Tribes affected: Pantribal
Significance: *Missionaries and their missions provided American Indians with their first concentrated contact with white culture. Missionaries helped implement the policies of assimilation, agrarianism, and cultural extermination.*

From the 1500's, when Spanish and French explorers brought Roman Catholic priests to North America, until the 1950's, missionaries influenced both American Indians and U.S. policy toward Indians. Missionaries taught English, built schools and churches, and created pantribal connections. They also, however, spread disease and forced assimilation and Christianization on Indians. Most missionaries were well-meaning, but their efforts were often misguided. Some were so convinced of the correctness and superiority of their own culture and belief system that they tried to suppress and destroy those of the Indians. Missionary work supported by various denominations continues today, but since the 1950's, missionaries have been more sensitive than their predecessors to Indian culture. Missionaries and their missions remain controversial in most American Indian communities today.

Sixteenth Century Through Eighteenth Century. Missionaries first entered North America through the Spanish Empire in Mexico and through French trading posts in Quebec. The Spanish viewed Christianization as their holy duty to God and used it to rationalize conquest. State-sponsored Catholic missionaries developed missions in New Mexico, Texas, Arizona, and California. They provided protection, food, and shelter to the weaker tribes, such as the Pueblo Indians, while being constantly threatened by the stronger tribes, such as the Apaches and the Navajos. This system suffered a setback in the 1680 Pueblo Revolt (also known as Pope's Revolt), when tribes rose up and chased the missionaries and the Spanish settlers out of New Mexico. The Spanish reestablished the missions within fifteen years.

The French allowed Catholic missionaries into their territory, but they were not state-sponsored as they were in the Spanish Empire. Jesuits attempted to Christianize the Hurons, but instead they brought smallpox, which decimated the tribe. This upset the tribal balance of power, and the Iroquois attacked and killed off most of the Hurons. The Jesuits retreated and simply kept missions at trading posts until the 1790's.

The English Protestants also saw Christianization of the Indians as part of their role in North America. In the seventeenth century, John Eliot of Massachusetts established praying villages where Indians lived "as white men": They wore English clothes, learned farming techniques, and became Christians. As disease decimated many of the Northern Woodlands tribes, the remaining members joined the praying villages for survival. The villages appeared to be successful at attracting converts. Though many of the Indian residents did convert, most died from diseases spread by the whites within the praying villages.

David Brainerd, an Eliot student, began a mission among the Cherokee in Tennessee. The Cherokee used the mission to learn English and to learn about white culture. The high attendance rate made the school appear to be a success, which inspired other Protestant groups to send missionaries among the Indians. All these early missionaries—Spanish, French, and English—believed in the power of Christianity, the importance of sedentary farming, and the necessity of extinguishing Indian culture.

Nineteenth Century. Mission work exploded with the development of large missionary societies between 1830 and 1850. Presbyterian, Methodist, Baptist, and Catholic societies sponsored hundreds of missionaries, both male and female, to work with Indians. Missionaries built schools and churches to attract Indians to Christianity and white civilization. They expected Indians to convert in large numbers and to support their own missions financially (as the natives of India and Africa had done). Despite these efforts, the Indians showed little interest in converting to Christianity.

In the 1850's, the missionary societies grew impatient with the lack of progress. They accepted money from the American government to help support their missions. In return, the government demanded that the missionaries increase their efforts to Christianize and "civilize" the Indians. Money was supplied to help assimilate all Indian groups to sedentary farming and Christianity. This method was a general failure, perhaps most conspicuously with Plains and Northwest Coast groups.

By the 1870's, missionary societies lost patience with the lack of success and cut off funding for missionaries. Individual missionaries became responsible for their own financial support. Many entered into agreements with the U.S. government that tied them to conversion quotas. The government wanted a certain number of "pacified" Indians in exchange for its invested dollars. Additionally,

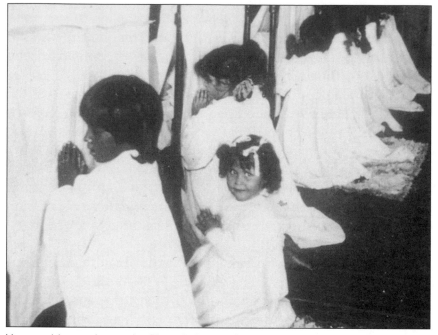

Young girls praying at the Phoenix Indian School in the early twentieth century. *(National Archives)*

missionaries wrote pamphlets and books about the "wretched condition" of specific Indian groups. These writings influenced public views of the condition of the American Indian. Many of these missionary works formed the basis for anthropological studies of the Sioux, the Cheyenne, the Navajo, the Salish, and other native groups.

Despite their funding problems, missionaries continued their program of assimilation, agrarianism, and cultural extermination. The height of this policy occurred during the 1870's when the government's "peace policy" allowed missionaries to administer the Bureau of Indian Affairs (BIA). At this time, residential schools became popular. Missionaries removed Indian children from their parents and sent them away to be acculturated into white society. Missionaries forbade the children to speak their own language, wear their own clothes, or practice any aspect of their own culture.

At this point, missionary and government policy coalesced into one united front against Indian culture. By the end of the nineteenth century, missionaries had fallen out of favor with the government, which saw their attempts at fostering assimilation as failures. Few Indians had converted to Christianity; most had developed a resentment of missionaries and saw them as agents of cultural genocide. However, missionaries remained part of Indian policy through the 1950's. They ran schools, wrote reports, and continued to act as agents and intermediaries for the government.

Positive Contributions. Though missionaries generally attempted to destroy Indian cultures and societies in their efforts to help Indians, they made some positive contributions. First, education and acculturation provided Indian groups with a common language—English. Second, the residential school system provided a common experience for native leaders and gave them the opportunity to meet people from different tribal groups. Finally, education created bicultural natives who understood their own culture and white culture. This development helped many tribal groups in their legal battles against white governments.

C. L. Higham

Sources for Further Study

Beaver, Robert Pierce. *Church, State, and the American Indians*. St. Louis: Concordia, 1966.

Berkhofer, Robert, Jr. *Salvation and the Savage*. Lexington: University Press of Kentucky, 1965.

Devens, Carol. *Countering Colonization: Native American Women and Great Lakes Missions, 1630-1900*. Berkeley: University of California Press, 1992.

Grant, John Webster. *Moon of Wintertime: Missionaries and the Indians of Canada in Encounter Since 1543*. Toronto: University of Toronto Press, 1984.

Higham, C. L. *Noble, Wretched and Redeemable: Protestant Missionaries to the Indians in Canada and the United States, 1820-1900*. Albuquerque: University of Mexico Press, 2000.

Kelley, Robert. *American Protestantism and United States Indian Policy*. Lincoln: University of Nebraska Press, 1983.

See also: Boarding Schools; Children; Disease and Intergroup Contact; Education: Post-contact; Praying Indians; Religion.

Mississippian Culture

Significance: *A maize-based economy that dominated the Eastern Woodlands and built its largest city, Cahokia.*

"Mississippian" describes hundreds of Native American societies that populated the river valleys and the drainage system of the Mississippi River from about 750 to about 1500 C.E., a period of some forty generations. This period is the last prehistoric period in the Eastern Woodlands culture pattern. The Mississippian Culture Complex included six major areas: Oneota, around the Great Lakes; Fort Ancient in present-day Ohio; the Caddoan Mississippian, with a ceremonial center at Spiro, now in Oklahoma; Plaquemine Mississippian, with a center in Nunih Waya in present-day Mississippi; the Middle Mississippian area, with centers in Cahokia (Illinois) and in Moundville, now Alabama; and the South Appalachian Mississippian culture centered around Etowah in present-day Georgia.

The immediate source of this cultural pattern is not clear; however, between 800 and 1100, there were dramatic developments taking place in the area. Not just a time of change in the style of artifacts, the Mississippian period saw a new way of life with new kinds of technology and a new relationship to the surroundings. It has been said that the period was the closest to being a time of cultural revolution that the prehistoric Central Valley had experienced up to that time.

Chief among the developments of the period was a turning away from the traditional cultivation of native plant crops. A single species of corn, the nonindigenous maize, came to dominate both the fields and the lives of the Mississippian peoples. The Northern Flint variety of maize, an eight-rowed maize that matured more quickly and was more frost-resistant than earlier ten- to twelve-row varieties, thrived in some of the country's richest farmland. This development led to radical changes in the social and political fabric of the people. Maize would become the staple of the Oneota people on the Great Lakes, the Iroquoian Confederacy to the northeast, the people along the middle Ohio River Valley, and those in the river valleys to the southeast and in the Midwest.

Later, maize would be just as important in the lives of the Creek and Choctaw to the south, and the Mandan and Pawnee people in the Great Plains area. The Mississippians also cultivated two other crops, beans and squash, that along with maize formed what the Iroquois called the Three Sisters, crops available in quantities sufficient to provide the main food supply. These crops were supplemented by game and fish.

As these proliferating societies were connected by the common denominator of maize, there developed a need for more centralized authority and more concentrated social controls. Agricultural surpluses were needed for redistribution of food. One change led to others, and the people responded to the challenge by reorganizing their settlements into hierarchical arrangements. That is, the arrangement of housing gave greater distance between nobles and commoners.

The hub of much of this reorganization was under way by about 950, when the city of Cahokia in present-day Illinois emerged as a center of urban expansion. Cahokia was located north of the Central Valley, within what is called the American Bottom region just opposite what would become St. Louis, Missouri. Within a century, thousands of families poured into the area, making Cahokia the largest city north of Mexico. It is the largest archaeological site in the eastern United States. Its dispersed community covered an area of almost five square miles, and the population has been estimated at approximately thirty thousand.

The walled city of Cahokia was characterized by the presence of more than one hundred mounds of various sizes, shapes, and functions distributed in a pattern that indicates an organized community, perhaps arranged around plazas. The majority of the mounds were platform mounds, on which various kinds of structures were built. The greatest of the mounds, now called Monk's Mound, was originally taller because there was a conical mound atop it; it now is approximately 100 feet high and extends 1,037 feet north to south and 790 feet east to west. On some of the flat-topped mounds, palaces for the living ruler and housing for the new nobility, perhaps as much as 5 percent of the population, had been constructed. Thus, the elite literally towered over everyone and everything in the Cahokia area.

Not all the mounds were used as sites for palaces of royalty; some were burial mounds, and the burial offerings in the mounds reveal much about the extensive communication that the Mississippians had with other people on the Atlantic coast. The best-known of the burial mounds at Cahokia is the one now labeled Mound 72. This mound provides extensive information about the major trade contacts of the Mississippians. In it was found copper from Lake Superior and mica from the southern Appalachians. Examination of the style and content of arrow points has indicated sources in Wisconsin, Tennessee, east Texas, and eastern Oklahoma. In other locations in Cahokia, conch shells indicated contacts with people living along the Atlantic Ocean.

The Cahokian aristocrats presided over complex ceremonies and rituals that were at the center of the Mississippian's life. The sense of community was closely related to long-term political cycles. As long as chiefs were particularly effective, the people gladly accepted their rule and united as a regional community. When a chief died, the huge community became fragmented into several townships. The more social and political ranking increased, the more important ceremony and sacrament became to the people. These ceremonies expressed obligations to ancestors, celebrated successful harvests, hunts, and warfare, and involved elaborate death rituals in homage to social leaders.

The religious system that evolved is called the Southern cult, the Southern Death Cult, or the Southeastern Ceremonial Complex. It included a network of artifacts and motifs. Ceramics modeled on animal and human forms could be found throughout much of the East during Mississippian times. Some of the important motifs included crosses, human hands with eyes or crosses on the palms, winged or weeping eyes, human skulls, long bones, dancing men in elaborate costumes, arrows, and symbols of the sun. Also important were animal symbols such as the feathered serpent, woodpecker, falcon, raccoon, and eagle. These symbols are found on pottery and on shell and copper ornaments. The objects are associated with the burial of high-status personages, mostly at major centers such as Cahokia, and the distribution of particular styles is outside regional boundaries.

Although Cahokia and other great Mississippian centers were already in decline prior to Hernando de Soto's arrival in North America, their ultimate collapse is associated with the appearance of Europeans in their territory. Disease in epidemic proportions overtook people in the surviving towns, and by 1500, the complex political and social mores that defined the Mississippians were greatly diminished. Constructed public works such as the mounds and palisades were no longer built. Burial rituals for ancestors and support for royalty ended.

Nevertheless, many of the Mississippian beliefs lived on among southeastern tribes of later generations, such as the Cherokee, Creek, Choctaw, and Chickasaw. For example, the *puskita*, or Green Corn ceremony, shows the influence of the fertility rituals associated with the maize crop. Another ceremony of the Southern Cult, the Black Drink, also survived. The drink, made from roasted leaves of the sassina shrub, was taken with great ceremony and in the belief that the drink conferred spiritual purification upon all participants. Rich in caffeine, the drink was believed to clear the minds for debate and to cleanse and strengthen the bodies of warriors for battle.

Victoria Price

Sources for Further Study

Ballantine, Betty, and Ian Ballantine, eds. *The Native Americans: An Illustrated History*. Atlanta: Turner, 1993. Chapter 6 of this comprehensive treatment of Native American history discusses the emergence and demise of the Mississippian Culture Complex, in which the Indian confederacies of the southland were rooted.

Kehoe, Alice B. *North American Indians: A Comprehensive Account*. 2d ed. Englewood Cliffs, N.J.: Prentice-Hall, 1992. Systematically traces the Americas' earliest humans and discusses the people of each of seven geographical areas. Maps, charts, and recommended lists.

Morse, Dan F., and Phyllis A. Morse. *Archaeology of the Central Mississippi Valley*. New York: Academic Press, 1983. Places the complex origins of the Cahokia site in the context of the entire Mississippian complex. Focuses on environmental adaptation and ceramics and other important artifacts.

Pauketat, Timothy R., and Thomas E. Emerson, eds. *Cahokia: Domination and Ideology in the Mississippian World*. Lincoln: University of Nebraska Press, 1997. A collection of essays that explore religion, social organization, subsistence, trade, and mound construction in Cahokia.

Silverberg, Robert. *Mound Builders of Ancient America: The Archaeology of a Myth*. Greenwich, Conn.: New York Graphic Society, 1968. A comprehensive study of various mound-building prehistoric societies. Discusses the emergence, triumph, and deflation of the myth that the Mound Builders were a lost race.

Smith, Bruce D., ed. *Mississippian Settlement Patterns*. New York: Academic Press, 1978. Discusses a number of Mississippian settlement patterns, including those of Cahokia and the American Bottom.

See also: Black Drink; Corn; Culture Areas; Green Corn Dance; Mounds and Moundbuilders; Ohio Mound Builders.

Moccasins

Tribes affected: Pantribal

Significance: *Animal-skin moccasins, comfortable and practical, were the type of American Indian footwear most widely worn in North America.*

The word "moccasin" is an Anglicization of the Natick term *mohkussin*, which is derived from the Algonquian word *maxkeseni*. Moccasins are soft leather shoes or slippers made of animal hide and worn throughout the Americas in areas where animal skins are used in the making of clothing and footwear.

There are many styles of moccasin. Although this type of footwear is widely used, particulars regarding materials, construction, styles, and decoration are tribe-specific. The hides of deer, elk, moose, buffalo, and other large game are most often used, although in the Arctic sealskin is preferred. On the Northwest Coast, footwear is most often made of cedar and other vegetable fibers.

Moccasins can be cut low, in the form of a slipper; cut to medium height to make an ankle-high shoe; or made in the form of a boot that can be tied as high as the thigh. Some are slipped on, some use laces, while others are tied with straps. Moccasins are often decorated with beautiful designs using porcupine quills or beads of various kinds.

Michael W. Simpson

See also: Dress and Adornment; Hides and Hidework.

Mogollon Culture

Significance: *Along with the Anasazi and Hohokam cultures, the Mogollon peoples created pueblo dwellings and a complex social order.*

The pre-Columbian Mogollon cultural tradition of the Southwest (distributed throughout central New Mexico and extending into eastern central Arizona and northern Mexico) is a subcultural variant of the "Pueblo Complex," which includes two other great traditions: Anasazi (of the Colorado Plateau) and Hohokam (central and southern Arizona, extending into the Sonoran Desert of northern Mexico). The Mogollon cultural complex and its Southwestern counterparts are among the most notable cultural developments in North American prehistory. Classic Mogollon culture reached its pinnacle at approximately 1200. By 1250, however, Mogollon culture as a cohesive tradition began to fall apart.

Diagnostic Mogollon culture traits first appear during a transitional phase from the older and more generalized Cochise period (7000 B.C.E. to 1000 C.E.). Distinctively Mogollon culture came to dominate the core area of what is now central New Mexico by 750 C.E. This transition is characterized by a gradual shift away from an exclusively hunter-gatherer and foraging way of life to one dominated by domestication of plants, primarily maize, squash, and beans. Other traits include the presence of circular and semicircular house pits, brown and red pottery, tightly stitched basket weaves, cotton textiles, and distinctive burials. Through time, there was also a tendency toward increased sedentary settlement; but, unlike their highly sedentary neighbors—for example, the Anasazi and Hohokam—the Mogollon maintained numerous seasonal village sites and periodically shifted residence according to the availability of water and wild food resources.

The florescence of "classic" Mogollon culture (roughly 900 to 1200 C.E.) is identified by the presence of multiple-room, pueblo-style dwellings, large and extensive settlements, polychrome pottery, advanced textile weave patterns, intensive agricultural systems, and indications of a complex social and political order.

Excavations carried out in the Mogollon area suggest that long-distance trade was an important component of the Mogollon economy. Materials that originated in regions as far away as the Mississippi Valley and Mesoamerica (particularly southern and central Mexico) have been found at Mogollon sites. For example, pipe stone sourced to the Mississippi and Wisconsin areas has been found at numerous Mogollon sites, while copper bells, shell beads, and a wide variety of effigy designs are most likely of Mexican origin.

Anthropologists and archaeologists who have worked on interpreting Mogollon artifacts have speculated that Mogollon society showed some signs of class or status differences. For example, some burial sites contained numerous and sumptuous grave goods, while others were sparse or contained only skeletal mate-

Area of the Mogollon Culture

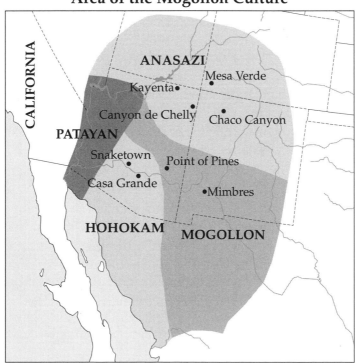

rial with no grave goods present at all. These scholars have also speculated that these class differences indicate a general cultural evolutionary pattern favoring increases in intensive economic productivity. To maintain such economic systems, more centralized political authority must have become increasingly important so that various subsistence, trade, and construction projects could be effectively organized and conducted. Despite such archaeological evidence, an exact reconstruction of Mogollon society can never be made; it is sufficient, however, to acknowledge that Mogollon society must have been relatively complex, bordering on large-scale.

To understand what the Mogollon political system must have been like, anthropologists have looked at modern horticultural populations to provide a working analogy. The concept of a chiefdom has been used to describe sociopolitical structuring at this level. A chiefdom, as defined by anthropologists, refers to a sociopolitical system that depends on the redistribution of goods through a local chief or set of subchiefs. Chiefs found in contemporary horticultural societies enjoy higher status than other members of society but have little explicitly recognized political power. Their real power typically rests on their ability to redistribute goods effectively, often during festivals or ceremonies, and their ability to persuade or influence decision making through speeches. It is possible that Mogollon leaders operated in much the same way as their modern counterparts.

Equally problematic have been attempts to reconstruct a tenable picture of Mogollon religion. Numerous artifacts suggesting religious themes have been found, but without specific ethnographic or historical data to indicate their actual cultural functions, interpretations have been highly speculative. Although few specific aspects of Mogollon religion can be described, there are some continuities between historical Southwestern Native American populations and religious traits that occur in earlier Mogollon contexts. Perhaps the most conspicuous is the kiva. Kivas are cylindrical, subterranean structures used primarily for purposes of carrying out religious ceremonies. Kivas are present at all significant late-period Mogollon sites and are still in use throughout much of the Native American Southwest. In addition, various general characteristics of contemporary Southwest practices suggest some general features of Mogollon religion. For example, among contemporary Zuñi and Acoma peoples, religion is integrated closely with other aspects of life; planting corn is considered a religious activity. Calling for rain by appealing to kachinas or nature spirits is also highly religious. Kachina symbols appear as art motifs in the Mogollon area, possibly as early as 1100 C.E. Moreover, the ritual cycles of the contemporary Acoma and Zuñi are closely tied to the annual growing cycle. It is likely that the Mogollon ritual cycle followed the same basic annual pattern, although contemporary researchers cannot describe in detail how these rituals were conducted.

From about 1200, and continuing into the fourteenth century, the Mogollon area, along with the neighboring Hohokam and Anasazi areas, experienced a period of rapid decline. Many of the large pueblo sites were abandoned, and much of the artistic splendor of the classic period disappeared. Archaeologists analyzing various types of artifactual remains (material culture, paleoclimatological, and human osteological data) have generated four basic theories to explain the decline. Some archaeologists have suggested that Mogollon decline resulted from severe changes in climate. These researchers have pointed out that tree ring and pollen data show that after 1200, the Southwest became much more arid than it had been previously. Researchers speculate that the Mogollon subsistence economy could not withstand this shift in climate and eventually collapsed. Other scholars have suggested that Mogollon society fell apart as a result of internal cultural disintegration. Some artifactual material suggests that Mogollon cultural institutions were highly inflexible and fragile, and may have become too disconnected from practical economic concerns. Still others have indicated that warfare may have delivered the final blow. The presence of Athapaskan-speaking groups (Navajo and Apachean), who were latecomers in the Southwest, offers evidence of cultural conflicts that, these researchers posit, might have permanently disrupted the Mogollon way of life.

Most scholars, however, take a synthetic or systemic view of Mogollon decline, believing that the combined forces outlined in all of these theories caused the decline. Some of this latter group of scholars have downplayed the idea of decline and inferred that the Mogollon tradition did not disappear, but became fragmented and subsequently evolved into the various contemporary Native American traditions now found in central New Mexico and eastern Arizona.

Whatever may have stimulated their decline, it is accurate to say that the Mogollon have had a significant impact on modern views of pre-contact Native American societies of the Southwest and in North America in general. These were not simple societies, but complex, long-held traditions that rival any found in other parts of the world. Although it is difficult to measure precisely the impact Mogollon culture has had on contemporary Southwest native traditions, or the impact it has had on contemporary Euro-Americans, its influence is felt. Many Native American groups in central and southern New Mexico still make pottery, jewelry, and textiles that resemble Mogollon forms. Euro-Americans also have felt this influence when they visit ancient Mogollon sites, buy artwork, or observe native ceremonies as they continue to be practiced.

Michael Findlay

Sources for Further Study

Binford, Sally R., and Lewis R. Binford, eds. *New Perspectives in Archaeology*. Chicago: Aldine, 1968. A comprehensive overview of scientific approaches to archaeology. Includes many references to Southwest prehistory.

Cordell, Linda S., and George J. Gumerman, eds. *Dynamics of Southwest Prehistory*. Washington, D.C.: Smithsonian Institution Press, 1989. Contains a variety of high-quality articles on Southwestern prehistory.

Gladwin, Winifred, and Harold S. Gladwin. *Some Southwestern Pottery Types*. Series III. Glove, Ariz.: Gila Pueblo, 1933. An overview of ceramic types for most Southwestern cultural traditions.

Martin, Paul. "Prehistory: Mogollon." In *The Southwest*. Vol. 9 in *Handbook of North American Indians*, edited by Alfonso Ortiz. Washington, D.C.: Smithsonian Institution Press, 1979. A detailed article on the archaeology of the Mogollon culture area.

Plog, Stephen. *Ancient Peoples of the American Southwest*. New York: Thames and Hudson, 1997. An examination of the Anasazi, Hohokam, and Mogollon cultures.

Reid, Jefferson, and Stephanie Whittlesey. *Grasshopper Pueblo: A Story of Archaeology and Ancient Life*. Tucson: University of Arizona Press, 1999. Grasshopper Pueblo is a prehistoric ruin that was the home to a Mogollon community. The daily life of this ancient community has been deduced from the artifacts found in the more than 100 rooms that have been excavated at this site.

Snow, Dean R. *The Archaeology of North America*. New York: Chelsea House, 1989. A detailed, in-depth overview of North American archaeology. Includes a notable section on Southwestern archaeology.

See also: Anasazi Civilization; Architecture: Southwest; Arts and Crafts: Southwest; Culture Areas; Hohokam Culture; Political Organization and Leadership; Pottery; Religion.

Money

Tribes affected: Pantribal

Significance: *A variety of monetary systems were developed by American Indians for economic and ceremonial purposes; although these systems differed from European coinage systems, the two shared many features.*

Money can be defined as a medium of exchange that is used by common consent to pay for goods and services. Money has certain defining criteria: value (worth and desirability), standardization (which may be established by authority or custom), durability, portability, divisibility (it can be separated into parts), stability (its value is relatively constant), and cognizability (it is known or recognized). Barter, on the other hand, need only involve mutual consent involving an exchange between two parties. Money came into being when certain items became desirable and symbolized wealth.

By these criteria, Indians clearly had money, although coinage was entirely unknown. This money assumed many different forms and, unlike European systems of coinage and currency, was often intimately involved with myth and religion. Shells symbolized water (the Haida believed the first people came from a shell; to the Omaha shells embodied the Great Spirit). Shells also symbolized fecundity, birth, good luck, and health. Red ochre, traded by the Apaches and Mojaves, symbolized blood or earth's life substances. Stones were thought to resemble animals and had healing powers. Feathers represented the wind, soul, and rain. With the advent of trade with whites, money became more secularized, as tools, weapons, cloth, and blankets became valued exchange media. For several centuries sacred and secular monies existed side by side and sometimes were combined into a single medium.

In southern and central California, golden orange magnesite cylinder beads were most valued and white clam or snail shell discs less so. These materials were ground and shaped to a uniform size and appearance and polished on deerskin to give them a beautiful shine. At one time a necklace of 160 clam shell beads was worth about one dollar; as it circulated eastward, its value and desirability increased significantly. In contrast, an average two-inch-long piece of finished magnesite was worth about eight hundred clam shells. Woodpecker scalps, the shells of haliots, olivella, abalone, and dentalia, and obsidian blades also had monetary value. These monies were used for a variety of purposes, such as purchase of staples and goods, bride buying, "blood money" indemnification, atonement for religious trespass, and ornamental symbols of wealth and status.

Dentalium, a type of shell, was the exclusive medium on the Northwest Coast. For the Chinook, the *hiaqua* consisted of no more than twenty-five shells to the fathom (six feet). *Kop kop* consisted of smaller shells strung together with broken ones and shells of poorer quality and was used as small change. Dentalium eventually gave way to blankets, which were acquired from whites in exchange for beaver fur. The Tlingit used sea otter and caribou skins as money.

Laurence Miller

See also: Blankets; Shells and Shellwork; Trade; Wampum.

Morning Star Ceremony

Tribe affected: Pawnee
Significance: *The Morning Star Ceremony, a sacred Pawnee ritual, was intended to ensure the abundance of corn and buffalo.*

The Morning Star Ceremony was one of the most sacred Pawnee rituals. Its central act was the raiding of another village, the capture of a young girl, and her sacrifice at the rising of the Morning Star (Mars or Venus). Tied to a wooden scaffold, she was killed by an arrow through the heart. Her blood was included in a burnt offering of buffalo meat. The many songs sung during the ceremony indicate its purpose was to ensure the growth and abundance of corn and buffalo. The Skidi Pawnee of the central Plains were the last group to practice this ritual.

For the Pawnee, the Morning Star (a young warrior) and the Evening Star (a young woman) were the parents of a daughter who was the mother of the first humans (the son of the Sun and Moon was the father). The stars entrusted humans with sacred bundles that became the focus of Pawnee ceremonies.

The ceremony itself was orchestrated by the caretaker of the Morning Star bundle. It began when a young warrior underwent purification rituals and prepared special materials. He was equipped with objects from the bundle, including an otter-fur collar, a hawk, an ear of corn, and a sacred pipe. After observing the rising of the Morning Star, he undertook the raid and brought back an adolescent girl to sacrifice. Preparations included the procurement of buffalo meat. The sacrifice commenced with sacred songs and dances extending over four days. During this time, the victim was treated well and instructed to eat with a special horn spoon and bowl. She was then dressed in ritual clothing and fixed to a scaffold made of several different kinds of wood. After her death, male members of the village (including children) shot arrows into her body as part of their contributions to the ritual.

John Hoopes

See also: Buffalo; Corn; Music and Song.

Mosaic and Inlay

Tribes affected: Aztec, Carib, Chichimec, Maya, Mixtec, Navajo, Olmec, Pueblo, Tlingit, Zapotec, Zuñi

Significance: *Mosaic and inlay were used for decorative purposes by Indians prior to European contact and continue to be used by modern Indians.*

Mosaic is an art form using small pieces of stone, glass, tile, or other materials such as feathers and straw to form a decorative design or picture. Used for such things as masks, jewelry, and architecture, mosaic art was common among the Indians of Mesoamerica, the Southwest, and the Northwest.

In Mesoamerica, mosaic and inlay were used by the Maya Indians for funeral masks—small pieces of turquoise, jade, red and white shells, and mother-of-pearl were glued to a wooden base and buried with the deceased. The Mixtec Indians made ceremonial shields by covering a ceramic base with cut and polished turquoise stones. They also covered the interior and exterior of buildings with precisely patterned tiled mosaics. The Zapotec Indians decorated their cultural center with stone mosaics in zigzag patterns. The Aztecs made feathered mosaic shields for their commanders and chiefs. Ceilings, floors, walls, pavements, and walkways were often covered with tiled mosaics. Some exterior walls had patterns inlaid on them using cut stones that were cemented in the walls like bricks.

In North America, the Tlingit Indians of the Northwest made headdress frontlets and hats carved out of cedar and inlaid with abalone shells. In the Southwest, the ancient Anasazi were known to have made turquoise mosaic pendants. The Pueblo and Zuñi made jewelry and pendants with colored shell mosaics. After the Spanish conquest, the Pueblo made crosses with inlays. The Navajo are known for making silver and turquoise jewelry, such as squash blossom necklaces, bracelets, and small silver boxes, using turquoise stones inlaid in polished silver forms. Modern Zuñi jewelry uses mosaic patterns of stones and shells in turquoise and white, red and black.

Turquoise was the most commonly used stone in mosaic design and inlay in the Southwest and Mesoamerica because of its availability and also because of its mystical association with both the sky and water. In the Northwest region, abalone shell was most commonly used for inlay.

Diane C. Van Noord

See also: Feathers and Featherwork; Metalwork; Shells and Shellwork; Turquoise.

Mother Earth

Tribes affected: Pantribal

Significance: *The original people of the Americas viewed Mother Earth as the source of all life. This personification of the regenerative and provident attributes of nature has its roots in animism.*

Animists believe that all things are alive and related. Everything that exists is further defined by its relationship to all other things. In many mythopoeic oral traditions throughout the Americas, all things receive their life from the earth itself. Plant and animal life as well as the elements and forces of nature are the source of human life. Human beings are seen as the spiritual guardians and stewards of the natural world. They are the children of Mother Earth and must treat her in ways that show respect and honor.

Numerous ceremonial and ritual means can be used to address Mother Earth—such as the sweatlodge ceremony and prayer—in order to ensure her continued beneficence. It is thought that when people cease to use such means to express their respect and gratitude for her blessings all life will be destroyed and human life on this planet will come to an end.

The spiritual traditions which have their roots in the natural world see all things as part of the sacred web of life. Spiritualism is seen as the highest form of political consciousness. Those who honor Mother Earth live in accordance with traditions that sustain life. Traditional native peoples and their belief in Mother Earth are seen as the primary sources of knowledge that can reverse the destructive materialistic worldview and processes of Western civilization.

Michael W. Simpson

See also: Ethnophilosophy and Worldview; Religion; Sacred Narratives; Sacred, the.

Mounds and Mound Builders

Tribes affected: Northeast and Southeast tribes (prehistoric and historic)

Significance: *Various groups of American Indians built earthen mounds at different time periods in different locations, which served different cultural functions; the American Indian construction of these mounds was not fully accepted until 1894.*

Earthen mounds are located in the eastern United States from the Gulf of Mexico to the Great Lakes, with concentrations in the Midwest along the Ohio and Mississippi River drainages. These mounds were constructed by a number of different Native Ameri-

Areas of Mound Building

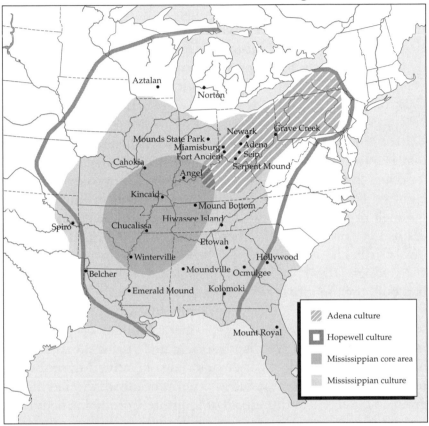

The earliest of the Ohio River Mound Builders, the Adena Indians, are thought to have lived between 700 B.C.E. and 200 C.E. The Adena gave rise to the Hopewell Indian culture, also centered in the valleys of the Ohio River and its tributaries, which is recognized from around 100 B.C.E. until about 400 or 500 C.E. The Hopewell developed vast, nearly continentwide, trading networks. Some researchers posit that Hopewellians were ancestral to the Iroquois. The last North American mound-building culture, the Mississippian, was centered along the Mississippi River, at Cahokia, where East St. Louis, Illinois, now stands. It developed around 700 C.E. and flourished until after 1500. Many scholars believe that the Mississippians were direct ancestors to the Cherokee, Sioux, and other American Indian tribes.

can groups during several different time periods, and they were used for a range of functions. In some cases, Indians built conical mounds to inter their dead, while in other locations or time periods, they constructed flat-topped pyramidal mounds to serve as the foundations for important buildings such as temples or chiefly residences. Some of the better-known mound sites are Cahokia, near St. Louis, Missouri (with a florescence between 1050-1250 c.e.), Moundville, Alabama (a dominant center from 1250 to 1500 c.e.), and those associated with the Hopewell culture (circa 200 b.c.e.-400 c.e.), centered in the Ohio Valley.

When these mounds were first noted by Europeans in the late eighteenth century, they stimulated acrimonious debate concerning their origins, namely whether Indians, their ancestors, or others had constructed them. These arguments continued unabated until Cyrus Thomas' *Report on the Mound Explorations of the Bureau of Ethnology* (1894), which demonstrated that Native Americans had built the mounds.

There are several underlying factors that explain why it took scholars so many years to accept the aboriginal origins of the moundbuilders. First, the dispute originated during the early colonial period, when settlers' understanding of Native American culture was based on their interactions with socially disrupted Indian groups no longer continuing all of their pre-Columbian activities. Second, based on these data, and on racist beliefs concerning Native Americans, it seemed unlikely to them that the Indian ancestors of these groups would have possessed the technological skills to construct the mounds. In addition, in some instances, Native American land rights could be denied if it could be demonstrated that earlier, more "civilized" people had once inhabited the area. European Americans also may have desired to construct a heroic past for members of their own cultures, which may explain the proliferation of hypotheses proposing that various early European groups built the earthen monuments. For example, in 1787, it was suggested that the Ohio Mound Builders were Danes, while an 1812 work opted for the Welsh. Caleb Atwater's article "Description of the Antiquities Discovered in the State of Ohio and Other

Western States" (1820) went so far as to propose Hindu builders. Others, such as E. G. Squier and E. H. Davis, in their *Ancient Monuments of the Mississippi Valley* (1848), favored Mayan or Aztec construction, believing them to be of a different, more evolved "race" from the local Indians.

Granted, there were a few dissenters from the prevailing views of the time, but these dissenting voices did not affect general public opinion. By the 1880's, the United States Congress became involved in the controversy, and it provided funds to the Smithsonian Bureau of Ethnology, directed by Major John Wesley Powell, to investigate the mounds. Powell appointed Cyrus Thomas to lead the Division of Mound Exploration. With the publication of Thomas' 1894 report, the "Mound Builders controversy" was effectively quelled, and a Native American origin for these constructions was accepted.

Susan J. Wurtzburg

Source for Further Study
Woodward, Susan L., and Jerry N. McDonald. *Indian Mounds of the Middle Ohio Valley: A Guide to Mounds and Earthworks of the Adena, Hopewell, Cole, and Fort Ancient People.* 2d ed. Blacksburg, Va.: McDonald & Woodward, 2002.

See also: Astronomy; Effigy Mounds; Ohio Mound Builders; Serpent Mounds.

Music and Song

Tribes affected: Pantribal
Significance: *Music has always played an important role in American Indian culture; singing, in particular, is essential in many ceremonies, including religious rituals, as well as at social gatherings.*

When Europeans first encountered the natives of North America, they found a culture vastly different from their own. Because this culture was considered "primitive" and was thus branded inferior, there was little attempt to understand the culture of the "savages" at first. American Indian music was often described as atonal chanting, and it was assumed that Indian songs, like other aspects of their culture, were less advanced than those of the Europeans. This attitude persisted well into modern times. As American Indians began the attempt to reclaim their cultural heritage, and scholars began taking this culture seriously, it was found that American Indian music, song, and dance were complex; moreover, they varied greatly among the assorted cultures of North America.

Indian Concept of Music. One of the major reasons that early settlers and explorers found American Indian music so difficult to comprehend was that the Indians had a completely different concept of music in general, and singing in particular. The Indians use songs for specific purposes, often of a religious nature. There are songs to appease the spirits, songs for success in hunting and fishing, songs in preparation for war, and songs celebrating victory in war. There are also personal songs composed by individuals who have had visions.

Indian cultures have never codified music as European cultures have. Undoubtedly, musical styles changed over the centuries before the Europeans' arrival, but modern researchers are at a loss to trace prehistoric developments of this sort, as none of the American tribes developed written languages or a system of describing specific tunes in a permanent manner.

Possibly the most essential difference between the European and American Indian cultures when it comes to music is that, in Indian cultures, virtually everyone may participate in music and singing. There is no group of professional composers or performers. In this sense, all Indian music is folk music. There has never been a difference between popular or folk songs, religious music, and "serious" music, as there has been in Europe and in the cultures the Europeans brought to North America.

The Indian Scale. As a general rule, Indian singing is accompanied only by percussion instruments or is unaccompanied. For this reason, a song does not have to be "in tune" in the sense that a specific scale must be used at all times. A common scheme is a steady fall in pitch during the song, though this is far from universal. (Some tribes play flutelike instruments made of hollowed wood or reeds, but these have a very limited range in pitch and are not used to accompany songs.) The result of this situation is that many Indian songs sound discordant to people used to European musical traditions. A song may not even come close to the harmonic patterns to which white cultures are accustomed. It is therefore impossible to play American Indian music on an instrument that is limited to the twelve-tone chromatic scale that has played an essential role in European music at least since the time of the ancient Greeks. It is also impossible to use standard musical notation to record tunes accurately.

Religious Songs. To the American Indian, all music has a strong supernatural element. This aspect can also be found in Christian cultures; hymns are an important part of church services, for example, and there is considerable popular music based on religious themes. Yet this element is far more essential to American Indian songs. Music is considered a gift of the gods and is vital to almost all religious ceremonies. The songs involved are not hymns as such; rather, they are specific to a particular spirit or aspect of nature.

One very common type of religious song is essentially a prayer. Many songs in many tribes are named after animals and are intended to appease the spirit controlling the animal, thus giving the hunter or fisherman a greater chance of subduing his prey. The Inuits (Eskimos), for example, are greatly dependent on the sea for their survival. In their boats, they sing specific songs for whales, seals, fish, and other potential food sources. The Plains Indians have songs for buffalo, deer, and other game.

Another type of religious singing is the chanting of spells to cure disease. An Indian with a serious disease is often considered to be possessed by an evil spirit, and the proper chant may drive out this spirit. When other remedies, especially herbal treatments, are used, the songs still play a vital role. The herbs must be sung over to ensure their potency.

There are also songs to control the forces of nature. In arid areas, there are many songs to appease the rain spirits and cause much-needed rain. In areas subject to flooding, there are songs to appease the water gods and lessen the rain. There are songs to ensure crop fertility as well.

Finally, some religious songs are used as a celebration of religious events rather than as an invocation. These songs are usually of an individual nature, composed and sung by a person who has had a vision. These are personal songs, owned by the singers. The Navajo have a strong tradition in this regard. Personal songs are considered a form of wealth.

Secular Songs. American Indians have never separated the religious and secular sides of life to any great extent. Most modern Christians, Jews, and Moslems worship once a week, and may say prayers at other special times. During the rest of the week, they work in secular occupations that have no relation to their worship.

In American Indian cultures, the case is vastly different. Everything on earth is controlled by spirits, and every facet of life has a religious aspect. For this reason, there is really no way of speaking of secular songs in a strict sense of the term. Not all songs are related to specific religious rituals, however, and spirits may not be mentioned in them at all. There are, of course, love songs, sometimes related to courting rituals but often made up simply to express affection. In essence, they are not much different from the love songs that are sung in European cultures. There are also lullabies to put children to sleep and children's songs for pure entertainment.

An unusual aspect of some Indian songs is the use of nonsense syllables (vocables). Often these meaningless syllables are inserted into a song to fill out a necessary rhythm, but sometimes entire songs have no concrete meaning whatsoever. It is difficult to explain this, except that it is not limited to American Indian cultures. From the "tra-la-las" of traditional European songs to the "doowahs" of 1950's rock and roll songs, other cultures have often used this device. Its use in American Indian songs, however, may have a somewhat deeper meaning.

The very fact that not all Indian songs have literal meaning suggests that the act of singing is enjoyed for its own sake and is not always a prayer or a prelude to war or hunting. A comparison can be made to European culture's development of instrumental music unaccompanied by singing; a Beethoven sonata has no concrete meaning. American Indians have developed very little in the way of instrumental music, apart from percussion accompaniment to singing. The singing of nonsense songs may be an indication that music for music's sake is a universal enjoyment.

Song and Dance. A virtually universal aspect of American Indian song is its relationship to dance. With rare exceptions, songs are accompanied by body movements, often highly ritualized body movements specific to a particular song. One major reason for this is the close ties both singing and dancing have to religious rituals.

This is another great difference between the European and American Indian cultures. There was probably religious dancing at some time in ancient Europe, as it seems to be a nearly universal aspect of cultures around the world. Many centuries ago, however, dancing in Europe became strictly a social event, and most dancers did not sing at the same time. Among American Indians, dance still retains its religious aspect and is often accompanied by songs. Both the dance steps and the songs can be extremely complex and are often performed in elaborate sequences. There are dance/song cycles in many areas, especially among the Navajos and a number of Plains tribes. In some cases, hundreds of songs with their related dance steps must be sung in a specific sequence to fulfill a religious obligation.

Modern Changes. Like virtually all aspects of American Indian society, Indian songs have been somewhat altered by contact with white culture. The traditions are still very much in evidence, but in many cases they have lost their original significance. Many modern American Indians have adopted the Christian religion and no longer sing and dance to appease spirits. At important tribal ceremonies, there may be Christian hymns intermixed with ancient tribal songs.

It is difficult to assess fully the influence of white culture on Indian music, at least partly because the only written records of Indi-

These drummers and singers provided the important song element at a pow-wow in Springfield, Missouri. *(Unicorn Stock Photos)*

ans in the earliest days of contact were written by whites, who did not understand the cultures they were facing. Yet one particular modern development must be considered. In the 1960's, American folk music changed drastically in many ways. There was a movement toward increasing social and political meaning in a genre that was once mostly concerned with romance, religion, and historical events. American Indians were among the many who used this vehicle to express their concerns. Usually these songs were written in English so that they could reach as wide an audience as possible.

The "protest songs" written and sung by American Indians are in some ways fundamentally different from those written by white Americans. They often speak of love of the earth, of ancient traditions and ceremonies, of a return to the land. They rarely have the angry tone that so many songs protesting ill conditions have. Rather, they tend toward a longing for a return to basics, for a recapturing of a lost world. The most common tone is one of sadness.

This development suggests a true resurgence of the ancient uses of song among the Indian cultures. Even if they are sung in English, to the accompaniment of electric guitars or even orchestras, the lyrics often involve some use of a native language and are essentially born of the same thoughts and feelings that inspired the ancient songs.

Musical Accompaniment. Indian songs are almost always accompanied by drums of various sorts. The particular musical instruments involved will be discussed below, but it is essential here to stress that tonal instruments are rarely used while singing is going on. As discussed above, this has meant that Indian song is not necessarily confined to a particular scale.

Drumming, however, is a common accompaniment of singing. It does not provide an exact rhythm for the song. One of the most disturbing aspects of American Indian music for someone used to the European tradition is that the singers may not follow the rhythm of the drums; it is completely acceptable to be "off the beat."

Drums. The musical instrument most often associated with American Indians is the drum. Drums are almost always used to accompany singing and dancing and have also been used as a form of communication, with a sort of "Morse code" utilized to send messages over long distances.

One common type of drum is a hand drum, which can be carried about by an individual and played while dancing. The materials used in construction vary according to the materials available. Most often the body of the drum is made of hollowed wood, but woven baskets are used in some areas, and hollowed gourds are used in the Southwest. The head is generally the hide of an animal, most often a deer.

Another type of drum is a large drum around which several people are seated; they play it together. This may be made by simply planting stakes in the ground and stretching a hide over them, or a large wooden structure may be made. In modern times, wooden or metal washtubs have sometimes been used. Water drums are made from hollowed logs that are partially filled with water. The water greatly increases resonance, and the sound of such a drum can be heard for miles.

Drums are frequently decorated in elaborate fashions. The paintings are often filled with religious symbolism; beads and leather thongs are often added. The proper spirits must be invoked for many ceremonies, and, since drums are so heavily involved, one of the ways to invoke the spirit is by drawing or painting the appropriate pictures on the drum.

Indians place a somewhat greater importance upon drumsticks than European cultures do. Although in many cases the drumsticks are merely twigs, quickly discarded, in other ceremonies, the drumsticks may be decorated, covered with leather, and have particular ceremonial meanings. A decorated drumstick can be a sign of prestige in certain tribes. There are other percussion instruments used in Indian music, including poles or planks around which a number of players are seated, and stretched hides with no drum body attached.

Wind Instruments. Some Indian tribes have used flutes and whistles to produce music. The most common sort of flute is much like a recorder; it has a few holes to vary pitch and is blown through the top end. It may be made of clay, wood, or reeds, again depending upon available materials. Whistles are far simpler and are used more often as signals than for playing music. They are used by men courting women, by shamans invoking spirits, or by war parties passing signals.

Wind instruments are not generally used as an accompaniment to song. While they may have variable pitch, they are made individually from natural materials and are far from standard in their scales. Flutes and whistles are used alone or in concert with percussion instruments.

Rattles. Rattles are nearly universal instruments among North American Indian tribes. The most common type of rattle is a hollow object filled with pebbles, bits of clay, or seeds. This sort of rattle is very important in many tribal ceremonies and is an essential component of many medical treatments.

In many areas, the body of a rattle is a hollowed gourd. In some places, rawhide is shaped into an appropriate receptacle. Like drums, rattles are often painted and decorated. Rattles are also made by suspending small objects so that they clash together.

Marc Goldstein

Sources for Further Study

Bancroft-Hunt, Norman. *People of the Totem*. New York: G. P. Putnam's Sons, 1979. A description of the Northwest American Indian culture, including a study of their history, ceremonies, music, and contemporary conditions.

Butree, Julia M. *The Rhythm of the Red Man*. New York: A. S. Barnes, 1930. A descripton of Indian rituals, especially music and dance, including step-by-step instructions for a number of songs, dances, and rituals followed by a variety of tribal groups.

Densmore, Frances. *The American Indians and Their Music*. New York: Woman's Press, 1936. A comprehensive guide to American Indian music, song, and dance. Includes an overview of Indian culture and specific discussions of songs, musical instruments, and dances.

Lassiter, Luke E. *The Power of Kiowa Song: A Collaborative Ethnography.* Tucson: University of Arizona Press, 1998. An examination of how song is created, understood, and its purpose to individuals.

Nettl, Bruno. *Folk Music in the United States.* 3d rev. ed. Detroit: Wayne State University Press, 1976. A general overview of American folk music, from prehistoric times to the 1970's, including a long and comprehensive chapter on American Indian music, both as discussed by the first European settlers and as it exists in contemporary times.

Spencer, Robert F., Jesse D. Jennings, et al. *The Native Americans.* New York: Harper & Row, 1977. An encyclopedic discussion of American Indian culture, from prehistory to modern times.

See also: Dances and Dancing; Drums; Feasts; Flutes; Hand Tremblers; Medicine and Modes of Curing: Pre-contact; Pow-wows and Celebrations; Religion.

Names and Naming

Tribes affected: Pantribal
Significance: *Indian names were often descriptive of a person's unique trait or of a significant action or event in his or her life.*

At the time of first contact with Europeans, North American Indians generally used a single name for an individual, rather than attaching a surname as was the European fashion. Indian names were often descriptive of some action or trait or of some occurrence in the life of the bearer. The translations were deemed "colorful" by Europeans, although mistranslations were common, such as the case in which a name meaning "Young Man Whose Very Horses Are Feared" was mistranslated as "Young Man Afraid of

His Horses." These names were not static throughout life, but could change many times between birth and late adulthood. Various tribes followed different naming practices. Usually Indians did not name themselves but were given names by parents, shamans, or other members of their tribal group. Some names could be inherited from a dead ancestor, and were bestowed following the prevalent line of descent, either matrilineal or patrilineal. It was considered improper for an Indian to mention his or her own name, and husbands and wives generally did not use their proper names when speaking to each other.

When an Indian child was born, naming might be delayed from a few days to a few months. This often paralleled the intensification of pregnancy taboos surrounding the mother, which were extended after the baby's birth. Baby names were not considered particularly important or anticipatory of an individual's character or performance in later life. When the baby was given the name of a dead ancestor, some tribes believed that the ancestor's spirit entered into the child. (Inuit parents refrained from slapping or verbally abusing their children, fearing that the ancestor's spirit would be offended and depart the child's body, resulting in the child's death.)

Some tribes gave children derogatory or unflattering nicknames, with the intent of encouraging them to seek accomplishments that would bring the bestowal of an appropriate new name. Common occasions for the bestowal of new names included the onset of menses for girls, success in hunting or warfare for boys, or the acquisition of a supernatural power during the vision quest for both genders. For boys, initiation into a sodality (a club or organization for men), also served as an occasion for a new name. When names were inherited from living relatives, such as a father, the boy might be prevented from assuming the name until he had attained a status in warfare or hunting comparable to that of his father.

Older men past the age of active hunting and warfare would often turn their attentions to civil and religious affairs and would assume new names related to their activities. Some names were taboo and were never used, such as the names of certain animals. Many tribes did not speak the name of a deceased member for fear of attracting the departed's spirit back from the other world, but when a living person was given the name, the taboo was lifted.

Belief in the power of a name was strong. The origin of this belief can be traced to ancient tales of the beginnings of the people, when the spoken word could be made manifest within the creation. Among the Apaches, use of a person's name called forth obligations that were almost impossible to ignore. If a warrior was about to be left behind in battle, he could call out the name of a companion, and that warrior was honor-bound to return and attempt to rescue him, even if such action meant his own certain death.

Modern American Indians choose names in many different ways. Surnames are common—often tying the bearer to parents, famous ancestors, or perhaps identifying clan affiliation. Others have adopted or been given names from the mainstream American culture that do not reflect their Indian heritage.

Patricia Masserman

See also: Children; Ethnophilosophy and Worldview; Puberty and Initiation Rites; Rites of Passage.

Native American Church

Tribes affected: Pantribal
Significance: *From its beginnings in the late nineteenth century, the Native American Church has been a unifying force for scattered Native American peoples.*

The collection of teachings that became the doctrine of the Native American Church had their beginnings in the 1880's, probably among the Kiowas and Comanches living in Oklahoma. The church emphasizes the brotherhood of all American Indians. Among the main themes of the church's ethical code are mutual aid among members, a strong family, self-reliance, and the avoidance of alcohol.

The Native American Church was chartered as a Christian church in 1918. At that time, American Indians of every tribe were still reeling from the devastating effects of three centuries of contact with European American culture. Indians had been subjected to slaughter, enslavement, forced labor, the destruction of food supplies, the confiscation of land, forced dispersal, catastrophic depopulation, and forced religious conversion. Yet American Indians in the late nineteenth and early twentieth centuries created a monotheistic church with discernible and complex doctrines, ethics, and rituals; a strong sense of morality; a body of symbolically rich origin legends; and an individualistic approach that emphasized profound original spiritual experiences.

The ceremony that was to become central to the Native American Church was first described by anthropologist James Mooney in 1892. Its form was similar to that of present-day meetings. After 1900 the ceremony spread rapidly throughout tribal North America. Opposition to its spread came from traditional tribalists, Christian missionaries, and Indian agencies. Wherever the church entered a tribe, it rejected both significant belief aspects of that tribe and the dominant white culture. In 1918 it was chartered as a legal church. Anthropologists helped write the articles of incorporation and appeared before judicial and legislative bodies in defense of the church, shrewdly aided by insightful Indians who included Christian elements to make the chartering process more amenable to legislatures.

The ingestion of peyote is part of the ritual of the church (the church has sometimes been called the Peyote Church). Peyote produces an altered state of consciousness. To the Native American Church, peyote is both a teacher and a healer. The use of peyote is strictly limited to the church's ceremonies, and other use is vigorously opposed. Nevertheless, the use of peyote has at times made the church controversial among Indian leaders and organizations. Jesus is seen as a deified spirit with whom church members can communicate. Today church members find the universalism of

Christian ideology acceptable, but it is rare to find Christian symbols in the ceremony. Some songs still appeal to Jesus for health and help. Christian sin, judgment, and redemption are not found in Native American Church doctrine.

By 1947 the Native American Church was a widely prevalent religion among the Indians of the United States and had assumed the proportions of an intertribal religion. In 1960 the church was believed to have about 200,000 members, or half the population of adult Indians. Since U.S. law classifies peyote as a psychotropic drug and prohibits non-Indian use, non-Indian participation is minimal. The Native American Church continues to exist as an important pan-Indian movement uniting diverse cultures in common goals.

Glenn J. Schiffman

Sources for Further Study

Evans, Sterling, ed. *American Indians in American History, 1870-2001: A Companion Reader.* Foreword by Donald L. Fixico. Westport, Conn.: Praeger, 2002.

LaBarre, Weston. *The Peyote Cult.* 1938. Reprint. Hamden, Conn.: Shoestring Press, 1964.

Laney, John H. *On the Symbolism of the Native American Church of North America.* Zurich, Switzerland: C. G. Jung Institute, 1970.

Shonle, Ruth. "Peyote, the Giver of Visions." *American Anthropologist* 40 (1932): 698-715.

Slotkin, James. *The Peyote Religion.* Glencoe, Ill.: Free Press, 1956.

Smith, Huston, Reuben Snake, and Walter B. Echo-Hawk, et al., comps. and eds. *One Nation Under God: The Triumph of the Native American Church.* Santa Fe, N.Mex.: Clear Light Publishers, 1996.

Swan, Daniel C. *Peyote Religious Art: Symbols of Faith and Belief.* Jackson: University Press of Mississippi, 1999.

See also: Peyote and Peyote Religion; Religion.

Ohio Mound Builders

Significance: *The earliest "architects" in North America built elaborate burial sites.*

When a large number of human-made burial mounds were found in the Ohio River drainage and other parts of eastern North America in the nineteenth century, the ancestors of native North Americans seemed an unlikely source for their grandeur, at least to the European mind. Various non-Indian Mound Builders were hypothesized: the lost tribes of Israel, the Vikings, and other Old World groups. This oversight of Native Americans is surprising, given the high culture developed by the Native Americans in Mexico and Peru. In fact, other hypotheses suggested that the Mound Builders were an offshoot of, or ancestral to, these Middle American cultures. Few explanations allowed for a relationship to North American Indians. Late in the nineteenth century, however, careful studies by the Smithsonian Institution's Bureau of Ethnology demonstrated that the mounds were built by ancestors of the historic North American tribes.

How did the builders of such elaborate structures, presumably sedentary agriculturalists of high culture, develop? How did they give rise to the more mobile, and seemingly less highly cultured, natives encountered by the pioneers? These questions cannot be answered definitively, but much is known about the Mound Builders, and reasonable hypotheses for their origin and relationship to the historic Indian tribes have been developed.

Most evidence suggests that the original natives of North and South America were members of Siberian tribes that crossed the Bering Strait from Siberia to Alaska some time after fifteen thousand years ago. This was during the early stages of the last glacial retreat, when the Bering Strait was dry land. These tribes were big-game hunters who moved south into North, Central, and South America as the ice sheets melted. These people, called Paleo-Indians, moved into the eastern part of North America and came to live in sparse, wide-ranging populations in the forests that developed there after the glacier melted.

Archaeologists recognize a second Native American culture, the Archaic, beginning about eight thousand years ago. Directly descended from Paleo-Indians, the Archaic Indians are thought to have given rise to the Mound Builders around 700 B.C.E. Some late Archaic woodland groups buried their dead in small, natural hills, and a few built small burial mounds, the presumed progenitors of the more elaborate burial mounds built by the Woodland Indians. The larger burial mounds are widespread throughout eastern North America but are centered in the Ohio River drainage.

The earliest of the Ohio River Mound Builders are called Adena Indians and are thought to have lived between 700 B.C.E. and 200 C.E. Their culture is characterized by the development of fiber-tempered pottery, domestication of several kinds of native plants, and the development of elaborate rituals and practices for burying their dead, including the mounds in which they were buried. They also worked stone to make pipes and various ornaments. In addition to cultivating plants, they gathered wild plant products and hunted available animals. They used a spear-throwing device called an "atlatl" (developed by Archaic or late Paleo-Indians) to produce greater flight speed in their spears. They added burials to individual mounds through time, and were more sedentary than their Archaic predecessors. There is evidence that trading networks developed between the Adena people and contemporaneous American Indian cultures.

The Adena gave rise to the Hopewell Indian culture, which was also centered in the valleys of the Ohio River and its tributaries. The Ohio Hopewell culture is recognized from around 100 B.C.E. until about 400 or 500 C.E. The Hopewell tradition is characterized by advanced pottery production and stoneworking, more intensive cultivation of native plants, some cultivation of corn (*Zea mays*, ultimately obtained from Mexico), and more elaborate funeral procedures and burial mounds.

Although corn was grown by the Hopewell people, it was not the staple it became in Middle American and Mississippian cultures. Instead, corn seemed to be grown more for symbolic and religious ceremonies. There is some anthropological evidence that the Hopewell people's more diversified diet, based on the cultivation of several native plant species and supplemented by hunting and gathering, produced a healthier population than did the corn-intensive diet of the Mississippians.

The Hopewell Indians also developed vast, nearly continent-wide, trading networks. This trade may have been associated with another cultural development that differentiates the Hopewell from the Adena. Researchers have hypothesized that some Hopewell men obtained privileged positions in society due to their trading skill and trade contacts. These men were buried with more elaborate material goods and in larger and more complex mounds than were other members of the population. As a result, Hopewell burials suggest a class structure not seen in the more egalitarian Adena burials.

Adena and Hopewell mounds were built by people carrying baskets full of dirt from a source region, called a borrow pit, and depositing the dirt on the growing mound. Large mounds with many burials were built in stages, with one set of burials superposed upon an earlier group. Many artifacts, presumably prized possessions and tools needed for the next life, were buried with the dead. More of these are found in Hopewell burials than in Adena burials. The Hopewell differentiation of class, and contrasting Adena egalitarianism, are hypothesized on the basis of such artifacts and specific conditions of the burials.

Hopewell characteristics are all elaborations of Adena characteristics. It is impossible to determine the point in time at which the Adena culture ended and the Hopewell began; instead, there is a lengthy transition period. Clearly, the Hopewell tradition is a continuation of the Adena culture.

The Hopewell culture peaked in the Ohio River Valley around 200 c.e., and their mound-building activities, at least, disappeared between 400 and 500 c.e. Numerous hypotheses have been proposed for the decline of Hopewellian peoples, at least as Mound Builders. The theories range from an environmental catastrophe,

brought on by larger population concentrations and intensive agriculture, to changes in trade balances that brought an end to the
Hopewell people's strategic central position between the northern
and southern and between the eastern and western sources of raw
materials and finished goods.

The last North American mound-building culture, the Mississippian, was centered along the Mississippi River, at Cahokia,
where East St. Louis, Illinois, now stands. It developed around 700
C.E. and flourished until after 1500. Adena and Hopewell mounds
were primarily burial mounds, but many Mississippian mounds
were platforms upon which temples, houses, and other structures
were built. Many scholars believe that these Mississippian Mound
Builders were descendants of the Hopewell, through intermedi-
ates who, for unknown reasons, abandoned mound-building activities. Many also believe that the Mississippians were directly ancestral to the Cherokee, Sioux, and other historic American Indian
tribes. Some researchers posit that Hopewellians were ancestral to
the Iroquois.

The Ohio Mound Builders maintained a developing culture for
more than a millennium and played a central role in North American prehistory for much of that time. Their descendants gave rise
to the prehistoric Mississippian culture and to historic Indian
tribes. In addition, North American archaeology traces its professional roots to the exploration of their mounds.

Carl W. Hoagstrom

Sources for Further Study

Fagan, Brian M. "The Eastern Woodlands." In *Ancient North America: The Archeology of a Continent*. 2d ed. New York: Thames and
Hudson, 1995. Describes the Mound Builders and their place in
prehistory. Chapter 2 gives a brief history of the European
Mound Builder hypothesis. Illustrations, maps, index, bibliography.

Romain, William F. *Mysteries of the Hopewell: Astronomers, Geome-
ters, and Magicians of the Eastern Woodlands*. Akron, Ohio: University of Akron Press, 2000. An analysis of the Hopewell and

their achievements in astronomy, geometry, and measurement.

Shaffer, Lynda Norene. *Native Americans Before 1492: The Mound-building Centers of the Eastern Woodlands*. Armonk, N.Y.: M. E. Sharpe, 1992. Explores Mound Builder cultures and the interactions and interrelationships between those cultures and other Native American cultures. Illustrations, maps, index, bibliography.

Silverberg, Robert. *The Mound Builders*. Athens: Ohio University Press, 1970. Discusses the European-Mound-Builder-race hypothesis and its demise. Also describes the American Indian Mound Builder cultures. Illustrations, maps, index, bibliography.

Snow, Dean R. "The Nations of the Eastern Woodlands." In *The Archaeology of North America*. New York: Chelsea House, 1989. Outlines the prehistory of the Mound Builders. Chapter 1 covers the Mound Builder mystery and its importance in American archaeology. Illustrations, maps, index, glossary, bibliography.

Thomas, Cyrus. *Report on the Mound Explorations of the Bureau of Ethnology*. 1894. Reprint. Washington, D.C.: Smithsonian Institution Press, 1985. Describes the Bureau of Ethnology's mound work. The introduction to the 1985 edition adds historical perspective. Illustrations, maps, index.

Webb, William S., and Charles E. Snow. *The Adena People*. Knoxville: University of Tennessee Press, 1974. Descriptions of the mounds, pottery, pipes, and other artifacts of the Adena and Hopewell people. Illustrations, maps, index, bibliography.

Woodward, Susan L., and Jerry N. McDonald. *Indian Mounds of the Middle Ohio Valley: A Guide to Adena and Hopewell Sites*. Blacksburg, Va.: McDonald and Woodward, 1986. A guide to Adena and Hopewell sites that can be visited by the public. Illustrations, maps, index, lists of pertinent topographic maps and publications.

See also: Culture Areas; Effigy Mounds; Mississippian Culture; Mounds and Moundbuilders; Serpent Mounds.

Okeepa

Tribe affected: Mandan
Significance: *The Okeepa was a Mandan summer ceremony conducted to reestablish the tribe's ties with nature.*

The Okeepa was a ceremony conducted by the Mandans, a semi-nomadic tribe living in the northern Great Plains. It was a ritual held during the summer that was seen as a means to renew the life of the tribe and to reestablish the tribal relationship with nature. The specific purpose of the Okeepa was to appease the spirits of the waters, which Mandan legend claimed had once covered the earth in a flood. Tribal members took part in the ceremony by impersonating certain animal spirits, such as the snake or beaver. Other members were painted to represent day and night.

The main action, however, centered on two young men who dangled in the air, hung by ropes stuck into their flesh with pegs. After a certain period of time they were lowered to the ground. They then had to make their way to a masked warrior, who would proceed to cut off one or two of their fingers.

At the conclusion of this grueling experience, the two men ran a circle around the outside of the medicine lodge. Participants sometimes collapsed and had to be dragged. Any young man who excelled in withstanding the ceremony was considered a good candidate for future leadership positions.

Ruffin Stirling

See also: Religion; Sun Dance.

Olmec Civilization

Significance: *One of the earliest advanced civilizations on the North American continent.*

Olmec civilization is considered to be one of the oldest civilizations of native North America. Recognition and identification of Olmec culture are based exclusively on archaeological evidence, since no direct descendants of Olmec civilization have ever been identified. The Olmec heartland included the present Mexican states of Veracruz, Tabasco, and Chiapas, along the southern and western edge of the Gulf of Mexico, but Olmec influence extended across most of southern Mexico and northern Central America. The term "Olmec" is drawn from the Aztec language Nahuatl and loosely translates as "the rubber people," in reference to the production of rubber in the Olmec heartland.

Evidence of Olmec culture first appears about 1500 B.C.E. in the state of Tabasco. The area consists of flat, swampy coastal floodplains crossed by rivers draining from highland mountains to the south into the Gulf of Mexico to the north. Seasonal flooding and the lush tropical environment permitted the development of agriculture and the exploitation of domesticated plants, particularly corn, which led to the development of sedentary societies and advanced forms of social and political organization.

At sites such as San Lorenzo Tenochtitlán, the Olmec constructed large earthen platforms more than 3,000 feet long, 1,000 feet wide, and 150 feet high, upon which were erected ritual and ceremonial structures of stone and more perishable materials such as wood or plaster. These platform complexes served several purposes, including residences for elite Olmec families and rulers, gathering places for public ceremonies, and burial sites for Olmec royalty. At the site of La Venta, the Olmec constructed conical pyramids in the center of their platform complexes, perhaps meant to imitate mountains or volcanoes not found in the immediate Olmec area. The earthen platforms consisted of layers of worked colored stone laid out in large plazas and covered with as many as a dozen sequential layers of sand and earth piled one on top of the other to construct the platforms. The complexity suggests that the process of construction was as important as the final structure.

Platforms were engineered and constructed to control water flow throughout the structure. Elaborate drainage systems, composed of sections of carved stone, channeled water throughout the platforms, diverting it for waste runoff and public hygiene and creating decorative and sacred ponds and streams of fresh water within the platform complexes. The scale and complexity of the earthen platforms, along with the evidence of extensive farming and agriculture, suggest that several thousand people may have used or occupied the sites at one time. At least ten large-scale Olmec sites have been identified in the Olmec heartland. Advanced systems of political organization must have been in place to enable the assembly and management of the workforce necessary to construct such elaborate complexes. It is also significant that the Olmec created their buildings and monuments without the wheel, domesticated animals, or metal tools, none of which was used by any Mesoamerican peoples.

Most information regarding Olmec culture that does not come from their architecture is drawn from their remaining artworks. Although the Olmec probably created a wide variety of art forms, such as paintings and textiles, most of these forms have not survived in the archaeological record. What has survived in great abundance is Olmec stone sculpture, and the remaining carved stone images convey a great deal of information about Olmec beliefs. The Olmec were extremely adept at working very hard types of stone, particularly volcanic basalt and jade, neither of which occurs naturally near the Olmec heartland sites. Large basalt boulders, some more than ten feet tall and weighing several tons, were transported as much as sixty miles from volcanic mountain ranges such as the Tuxtla mountains; sacred green jade was imported from areas of western Mexico or eastern Guatemala and Belize.

The basalt boulders were carved into a variety of shapes, usually human but occasionally representing animals or mythological deities, probably originally intended to be displayed in the open plazas of the earthen platforms. Many of the large carved boulders were intentionally defaced or broken and buried within the platforms during Olmec times, suggesting that either the Olmec or a foreign people symbolically killed the sculptures before abandoning the sites.

One of the most common types of boulder sculptures is a series of human heads carved in a lifelike, naturalistic style. Although the specific identity of the subjects is not clear, evidence suggests that the heads portray either former Olmec rulers or defeated enemies. Facial features vary noticeably from one head to the next, suggesting individualized depictions, and each wears a distinctively different type of skullcap or helmet. The caps may represent royal headdress or a type of headgear worn by participants in a ball game similar to modern-day soccer. The losers of this game, which was played on stone, I-shaped courts throughout ancient Mesoamerica, were ritually sacrificed, usually by decapitation. Portions of the ball game may have developed in the Olmec heartland, since that is the source of the rubber used for the ball itself. Regardless of the specific identity of the stone heads, the size and degree of naturalism attest the Olmec sculptors' ability to manipulate large, hard stone for artistic purposes. Smaller stone objects, such as jewelry, ritual implements, and burial offerings, were carved from other hard stones, including jade. The color green was probably considered sacred, and jade was much valued by all pre-Columbian societies. Humans and animals were common subjects, and implements such as ax heads were frequently formed in the shape of humans, suggesting a spiritual tie between the function of the object and its symbolic imagery.

Olmec art reveals much about Olmec political and religious beliefs. Olmec sites were probably governed by elite royal families and kings. Warriors and human prisoners are frequently depicted in Olmec sculpture, suggesting that the Olmec practiced formalized warfare and related forms of human sacrifice. They worshiped a pantheon of natural spirits, chief among which were powerful animals such as the cayman or alligator, the eagle, the shark, and, perhaps most important, the jaguar. The Olmec were

similar to most Native American cultures in that the most important religious figures in Olmec society were the shamans, or curers,
who were believed to be able to change into animal forms at will
and communicate directly with the supernatural world. Olmec
sculpture frequently depicts shamans in the act of such transfor-
mations.

Between 1000 and 300 B.C.E., Olmec influence stretched far beyond the Olmec heartland. Carved jade and ceramics in Olmec
style have been found in central and far west Mexico, and Olmec-
style rock carvings, paintings, and earthen platforms occur in areas
south of Mexico City. Large Olmec-style carved boulders and upright stones occur along the southern Pacific coast of Guatemala
and El Salvador during this period, and Olmec ceramics are found
as far east as eastern Guatemala and Belize. The evidence suggests
that the Olmec were interacting with a large number of non-Olmec
cultures throughout the area at this time. After 500 B.C.E., early examples of hieroglyphic writing, similar to the later hieroglyphic
writing of the Maya, appear in a few isolated examples of Olmec
art, but these cases are rare, and Olmec civilization appears to have
declined before the writing system was fully exploited.

After 300 B.C.E., Olmec culture disappears from the archaeological record. Several later Mesoamerican cultures, particularly the
Maya of Guatemala and the Yucatan peninsula, inherited and continued many aspects of Olmec style and culture, and the Maya, in
fact, seem to have considered the Olmec as their divine ancestors.

James D. Farmer

Sources for Further Study

Benson, Elizabeth P., ed. *The Olmec and Their Neighbors: Essays in
Memory of Matthew W. Stirling*. Washington, D.C.: Dumbarton
Oaks Research Library and Collections, Trustees for Harvard
University, 1981. Collected papers focusing on shared artistic
influences between Olmec and neighboring or later Mesoamer-
ican cultures.

Coe, Michael D. *America's First Civilization*. New York: American
Heritage, 1968. One of the earliest comprehensive treatments of

Olmec art and culture. Coe was the first scholar to interpret Olmec culture as the precursor to later, more widely known Mesoamerican cultures such as the Maya.

Coe, Michael D., and Richard A. Diehl. *In the Land of the Olmec.* Austin: University of Texas Press, 1980. Extensive report of archaeological investigations at the Olmec site of San Lorenzo Tenochtitlán between 1966 and 1968. Includes numerous detailed maps and line drawings and illustrations of stone monuments from the site.

Coe, Michael D., and Rex Koontz. *Mexico: From the Olmecs to the Aztecs.* 5th ed. New York: Thames & Hudson, 2002. An exhaustive introduction to Mexico's early history and peoples.

Pina Chan, Roman. *The Olmec: Mother Culture of Mesoamerica.* Translated by Warren McManus. New York: Rizzoli International Publications, 1989. Well-illustrated volume of Olmec art. Presents a thorough summary of Olmec art, archaeology, and culture by a noted Mexican and pre-Columbian scholar.

Sharer, Robert J., and David C. Grove, eds. *Regional Perspectives on the Olmec.* New York: Cambridge University Press, 1989. Discusses Olmec culture in the broader context of greater Mesoamerica. Scholarly treatment of Olmec cultural interaction with other pre-Columbian cultures.

Stuart, George S. "New Light on the Olmec." *National Geographic* 184, no. 5 (November, 1993): 88-115. Discusses up-to-date interpretations of Olmec culture and art, including previously undocumented monuments and controversial translations of Olmec hieroglyphic writing. Includes artists' reproductions of Olmec lifeways.

See also: Agriculture; Ball Game and Courts; Corn; Culture Areas; Mayan Civilization; Political Organization and Leadership; Religion; Sculpture.

Oral Literatures

Tribes affected: Pantribal

Significance: *With no written languages, American Indian peoples transmitted their ideas from one generation to the next through storytelling; the surviving legends link Indian history to the present.*

Among peoples who do not have a written language, cultural traditions and philosophies are transmitted orally. In traditional American Indian cultures, senior members of a tribe used storytelling to pass ideas, events, and value systems to the next generation. Oral storytelling differs greatly from written literature because stories are slightly varied with each telling. Storytellers have individual styles and preferences; they can exaggerate some aspects or eliminate ideas altogether. With each generation, stories are altered to fit the present situation.

Geographic Influence. Legends of American Indians relate closely to all elements of the natural environment. Tribes occupied a wide range of geographical landscapes, with some Indians living in desert conditions, others by the sea. Some tribes occupied wooded mountains where rivers and waterfalls were plentiful; others existed on dusty plateaus. In Indian tales, regardless of the environment, all parts of the natural landscape—pebbles, trees, mountains, rivers, shells—pulsate with life. Humans, animals, vegetation, and landforms are all interrelated.

The Supernatural. Indian stories are religious experiences that include taboo, ritual, and magic. Natural elements are often personified during the course of a storyline. Mountains, rocks, and rivers may be given human characteristics and feelings, while humans may be turned into fish, stars, or mountains. Just as quickly, these elements may return to their former states. Some characters are permanently assigned natural forms. For example, troublemakers may become mountain peaks as lessons for future rascals. Legends also set human lovers as stars in the sky, destined to chase each other for eternity. Indian tales are filled with an interweaving of supernatural and natural elements.

Story Structure. There is often a circular element to the progression of Indian legends and stories that is different from the linearity of European storylines. The time progression reflects the Indian belief that all reality is cyclical. The repetitive circular patterns allow listeners to hear subtle variations on themes, which promotes both the remembrance and the understanding of oral legends.

Those accustomed to European storylines have at times criticized Indian legends as chaotic or incomplete. They claim that recognizable beginnings and endings are missing. Indian stories are not intended to be evaluated by Western logic, however; oral stories are often told in chains, with one image or character triggering another story. The chain often reaches back in time. Many tales are not intended to be isolated from previous episodes; instead, these stories are parts of a progression. The knowledge of past legends may be needed to understand a particular story. Moreover, certain words may have meaning only if previous tales have been heard. For example, the word for "sun" may represent the name of a sun god who is present in a whole line of stories. Without knowledge of the full significance of the word "sun," listeners may misinterpret a particular story. Indian legends are not isolated stories for entertainment but are part of a lifetime collection which educates tribe members about religion, the supernatural, and living in harmony with nature and with other humans.

Many Indian tales center on celestial elements that are used to inspire appropriate behavior and to punish unacceptable actions and attitudes. They also attempt to explain the mysterious nature of the skies.

Sun and Moon. The sky held great significance for American Indians. They studied the stars carefully to determine when their crops should be planted and harvested. They followed the sun's placement in the sky as an indication of the seasons. This fascination with the heavens is reflected in Indian legends. The sun is seen as the great fertilizing agent of the universe. Although the Juchi, Cherokee, and Inuit regard the sun as female, most tribes give male attributes to the sun. In many tales, the sun makes love to mortal women who then give birth, not only to humans, but to animals. In a Brule Sioux tale, the male sun removes an eye and throws it into the wind, where it becomes the moon woman. The sun directs the moon maiden to walk along a bridge of lightening so that she can roam the earth. Man and woman then come together on Earth and through mutual understanding and caregiving join their bodies to people the earth.

In one Winnebago myth of the sun's creation, the orb is reduced to a small object that is snared by Little Brother. The reward for his great power in bringing light to his tribe is that humans would thereafter be chiefs over animals. The Inuit tell about a brother raping his sister. After the rape, the sister runs, lighting her way with a torch. Her brother, who carries a torch of his own, follows, but falls in the snow, where his torch turns from flames to embers. A large windstorm lifts the brother and sister into the sky, where he is turned into the moon and she into the sun. They are always far away from each other, with the sun coming out only after the moon is gone. The Cherokee give female qualities to the sun, which is stolen by Grandmother Spider and brought to her people along with fire. The Zuñi tell about Coyote, the trickster, who steals the sun and moon from the kachinas (supernatural intermediaries). Coyote is greedy, wanting the box of light for his own. Because of his curiosity, Coyote disobeys the chief and opens the box to examine the light. The moon and sun escape into the sky, and cold comes to the world.

The Stars. The Plains tribes were primarily nomadic hunters and gatherers; they relied greatly on the stars to indicate direction, time, and the seasons. These Indians considered the celestial bodies supernatural beings and often told stories of various stars taking human form. The Blackfoot explain the origin of the North Star in this way: A young maiden looks longingly at the Morning Star and wishes that she could have that star for her husband. In time, the Morning Star appears on Earth as a handsome youth who takes the maiden to the house of his parents, Sun and Moon. The maiden is married to Morning Star and lives a life of ease in Sky Country; however, her curiosity and disobedience result in her son being turned into a star. This star, the North Star, never moves and is called the Fixed Star by the Blackfoot and the Star That Does Not Walk Around by the Omaha.

The seven stars of the Pleiades hold great significance for many cultures. This small cluster of stars helps define the calendar and signals coming events. The disappearance of the Pleiades tells the Tapirape Indians that the rainy season will soon end. The Zuñi of New Mexico use the Pleiades to determine when planting should begin. The Cherokee of the Southeast give special significance to the Pleiades because there are seven stars in the group. Seven is a sacred number because it represents seven directions—north, south, east, west, up, down, and center.

Many Indian legends incorporate the Pleiades. The Onondaga of the Northeast tell of seven children who neglect their chores and dance throughout each day. After several warnings from the elders, these children become so lightheaded that they drift into the sky, never to return. The Shasta, from the forested lands of Northern California, tell how the greed and selfishness of Coyote, the trickster, lead him to kill Raccoon. As punishment, the children of Raccoon kill all Coyote's children, except for Littlest Coyote, who is not selfish. Raccoon's children and Littlest Coyote run away to Sky Country to be protected from the selfishness of Coyote. They become the Pleiades.

Earth. Many tribes have myths which explain the emergence of the earth. Many explanations describe a watery primordial environment from which mud is brought up to make the earth. Some tribes describe life in the interior of the world. These inhabitants dig their way up from the center of the world until the top layer, earth, is reached. Earth is that environment which is in light. Indians of the Northwest tell of entering a hole in the sky in order to emerge on the earth. From the California region and the Southwest come tales about the original world parents, Earth and Sky. Many myths have the creation of Earth eliminating the darkness of the universe.

The Cherokee describe an Earth suspended in delicate balance, which humans must maintain for survival. The earth floats on waters and is tied to the ceiling of the sky by four ropes connected to the sacred four directions. If the ropes break, the world will tumble, carrying all living things to death. The earth will then be like a submerged island, covered with water. This tale also incorporates the supernatural, for sorcerers and shamans are called upon to put the sun higher so that the earth will not be too hot for human survival.

The Hopi tell a tale about two goddesses who cause the waters of the world to recede eastward and westward until dry land appears. To bring light and warmth to this land, the sun removes his skin of gray fox and dons a yellow skin to brighten the sky. The two goddesses then create a little wren out of clay. Animals and humans are later brought to life, always in pairs. Humans feed mostly on rabbits and deer, which leads to many quarrels. In frustration, the goddesses leave to live in the middle of the ocean.

Humans. Human creation myths seek to answer mysteries about the human condition. Humans are generally created from supernatural beings, from natural elements, or from animals. In most tales, animals and plants precede the creation of humans.

A number of legends have the first woman of Earth impregnated by a sunbeam, a salmon, or the west wind. For some tribes, the first human is a child endowed with supernatural powers. The Sioux tell of Stone Boy, who brings sacred ceremonies and prayers to his tribe by building the first sweatlodge for purification. The Brule Sioux, however, say that the first human is an old woman who has sacred medicinal powers. Many legends have women as the first humans, for women are associated with fertility, conception, and pregnancy. In some stories, the first humans are twins, born of a supernatural god. In others the trickster, Coyote, is given credit for breathing life into humans. The deceitful side of humans is the result of having been created by Coyote.

The Modoc tell about Kumush, Old Man of the Ancients. He and his daughter descend into the underground, where spirits gather to sing and dance. Darkness permeates the underworld, and after a week, Kumush longs for light. When he returns to the upper world, he takes some underground spirits with him to people his world. To feed these people, he supplies fish and beasts, roots and berries. He then designates certain roles for the people: "Men shall fish and hunt and fight. Women shall get wood and water, gather berries and dig roots, and cook for their families."

In human creation myths, the earth and the universe are often seen as neverending circles within which humankind is just another animal. Because all elements of nature are related, animals are often responsible in whole or in part for the creation of humans. In a tale from the White River Sioux, a rabbit comes across a clot of blood and begins to kick it around as if it were a ball. The movement of the clot brings it to life in human form. At times, the processes and rhythms of nature bring life to humans. The Penobscot tell of a young man "born from the foam of the waves, foam quickened by the wind and warmed by the sun." The same legend tells of a girl born after "a drop of dew fell on a leaf and was warmed by the sun."

Some stories explain the different races. The Pima tell how Man Maker uses clay to mold human images and then places them in an oven. When he removes the various forms, they have different shapes and colors. He saves the forms that please him best; the others are sent to live in various places across the water. The Modoc explain that Kumush, Old Man of the Ancients, gathers bones in the underworld and selects certain ones to make Indians to reside in particular places. He makes the Shastas brave warriors, the Klamath easily frightened, and the Modoc the bravest of all.

Love. Indian love stories teach responsibility and commitment to loved ones. The characters are often given tests to demonstrate the strength of their commitments. In some tales, battles are fought between two men for the love of a young maiden. These contests are fought until death, a death in the name of love. Legends of love also weave the natural and supernatural together. In various stories, human lovers are transformed into stars; a whale takes a human wife; a man marries the moon; and a wife follows a butterfly man. These tales also include traditions that had significance in the courting process. The Keres Pueblo tell a story about men and women who try to live apart. The tale illustrates that women depend on men for survival. A legend of unselfishness comes from the Multnomah; it concerns a maiden who shows great love for her people by sacrificing her life to the spirits so that all those suffering from sickness will be cured. She jumps from a cliff as the moon rises over the trees. Today, her spirit, dressed in white, exists in the waters of Multnomah Falls.

Death. American Indians believe that accepting death is an affirmation of life. Crazy Horse claimed that being willing to die was a way of honoring the human spirit. Indian tales reveal not only human death but also the crumbling of cultures and nations. The end, however, makes way for the arrival of the new. The Caddo explain that people must die because the earth is too crowded. To ease the pain of losing loved ones, a medicine man sings songs that call the spirits of the dead to come and reside with those still living. The Haida tell of a great flood which takes the lives of many people. Survivors drift in the waters until they reach mountain peaks sticking out of the ocean. The tribes are dispersed in this way. The Wishram tell of an Indian hunter who kills more elk than is needed for food. In doing so, he also kills his guardian elk. Because his guardian spirit no longer exists, the young brave dies in the Lake of the Lost Spirits. From the Brule Sioux comes another story which teaches that humans must live in balance with nature. In the worlds before this world, people did not know how to act properly, so Creating Power used fire, earthquakes, and floods to destroy the previous worlds. He then remade the world and populated it with people of understanding and speech. He told the people that they must live in harmony with one another and with all living things.

All Indian legends teach the need for balance between living creatures and natural phenomena. When greed and egotism cause humans to treat nature or other people abusively, then the offenders are punished. By weaving natural and supernatural elements into every story, Indians pass on models of behavior that reflect harmony between physical and spiritual realms.

Oral storytelling gives importance to the elders in a tribe, for they are respected for their wisdom. They are the transmitters of traditions and history. Through their art, they preserve culture.

Linda J. Meyers

Sources for Further Study

Bemister, Margaret. *Thirty Indian Legends of Canada.* Vancouver, British Columbia: J. J. Douglas, 1973. Most of these stories are taken from their original sources. A pronunciation guide to vocabulary is included.

Erdoes, Richard, and Alfonso Ortiz, eds. *American Indian Myths and Legends.* New York: Pantheon Books, 1984. This collection of 166 Indian legends covers a wide range of native people of North America. An appendix gives background on sixty-eight tribes from North America. A fine bibliography is included.

Kroeber, Karl, comp. and ed. *Traditional Literatures of the American Indian: Texts and Interpretations.* 2d ed. Lincoln: University of Nebraska Press, 1997. A collection of essays that provide an introduction to the analysis and understanding of Native American oral literatures.

Kroeber, Theodora. *The Inland Whale.* Bloomington: Indiana University Press, 1959. This collection of nine California Indian legends is followed by a thorough discussion of each piece. A discussion is also offered about qualities of Indian stories and about the place of oral literature in the study of comparative literature.

Monroe, Jean Guard, and Ray A. Williamson, comps. *They Dance in the Sky.* Boston: Houghton Mifflin, 1987. This collection of star myths comes from North American Indians who lived all across the United States. The selections are arranged geographically. Included are a glossary and suggested further readings.

Ywahoo, Dhyani. *Voices of Our Ancestors*. Boston: Shambhala, 1987. This book does not include stories but is a discussion of the philosophy behind many Cherokee traditions. Ywahoo discusses oral teachings rather than oral stories.

See also: Ethnophilosophy and Worldview; Oratory; Religion; Sacred Narratives; Wampum.

Oratory

Tribes affected: Pantribal
Significance: *In traditional American Indian cultures, which had no written languages, the ability to speak effectively was a respected trait and a necessary one. Oratorical skill is still highly valued today.*

The ability to speak powerfully and persuasively is a talent every culture admires. For Native Americans, oratory is an extremely important element of ceremonial and nonceremonial life. Before the invasion of North America by Europeans, most native peoples had no written language, so human experience was memorized and transmitted orally from one generation to the next. The information handed down included family and tribal histories, mythology, craft techniques, and the content and syntax of rituals and ceremonies. Many tribes honored articulate speakers with leadership, since oratory was seen, along with dreaming, as a spiritual power. Most tribes developed both understandings of what made oratory effective and formal rituals surrounding the practice of it.

Perhaps the most concise division of the types of Native American oratory comes from A. LaVonne Brown Ruoff's book *American Indian Literatures* (1990), in which the author suggests that Native American oratory may be ceremonial, nonceremonial, or a mixture of these two. Donald M. Bahr, in *Pima and Papago Ritual Oratory* (1975), uses a more complex system for categorizing such orations ritual oratory, preaching, and songs and stories.

Ceremonial or ritual oratory occurs in sacred situations. These addresses may be directed toward the powers of nature or to the tribe itself, and may take the form of prayer or the tale of a hero's journey. Nonceremonial oratory, or preaching, takes place in public settings, such as at parties, political events, battle sites, and council meetings. In his essay "The Plains Indian as a Public Speaker," Theodore Balgooyen writes, "Public speaking was associated with nearly every kind of public ceremony and was an important means of settling political and legal questions. Every respected warrior was expected to speak on matters of policy if he had a strong opinion."

In daily practice, oratory took many forms. In the Southwest, tribal leaders often gave a sermon each morning from the top of a hut or mound. In rituals of mourning and celebration, leaders and warriors were often moved to eloquence as they expressed sorrow, hope, and thanksgiving for all that the Great Spirit had done. The most commonly collected examples of native oratory are speeches given at tribal councils and U.S. government forums in which Native Americans struggled for peace and for their rights. Children and adults learned history and geography from tribal storytellers, as well as tribal values and the original meanings behind customs and ceremonies.

The right to speak publicly, Ruoff notes, was generally restricted to men, but there have been numerous exceptions, including Chief Viola Jimulla (Yavapai), Sarah Winnemucca (Paiute), Celsa Apapas (Cupeño), Warcaziwin (Sioux), and Gertrude S. Bonnin (Sioux name: Zitkala Sa). Over the past several decades, particularly, the status of women as orators has grown significantly.

A variety of techniques can be identified in Native American oratory, whatever its context. One of the most common tropes is repetition. By repeating key words or phrases, the orator is able to emphasize certain themes and is able to make each speech more memorable for his or her listeners. For example, when Creek leader Tecumseh confronted Governor William Henry Harrison about his violation of various agreements, he frequently referred to Harrison as "brother." This was ironic, because Tecumseh was notifying Harrison that if he did not make amends with the Indians, they would declare war. By repeatedly calling his potential enemy "brother," Tecumseh suggested that his people wanted peace and he reinforced the idea that European Americans and Native Americans were equal.

Another technique which Bahr describes is the "there was/he did" technique. This device operates as a form of parallel construction, in which one section—the *there was* line—"states the existence of a thing," while the following section—the *he did* line—"tells what was done to it." Using this technique, an orator was able to construct long chains of events, thus forming a logical and descriptive narrative.

Other oratorical techniques used by Native Americans include the careful use of rhythm, metaphor, assonance, and alliteration. These techniques, which can help make speeches more easily understood and remembered, were common among all tribes, and they remain in use by Native American orators today.

Kenneth S. McAllister

Sources for Further Study

Clements, William M. *Oratory in Native North America*. Tucson: University of Arizona Press, 2002.

Gustafson, Sandra M. *Eloquence is Power: Oratory and Performance in Early America*. Chapel Hill: University of North Carolina Press, 2000.

See also: Kinship and Social Organization; Music and Song; Oral Literatures; Political Organization and Leadership; Wampum.

Ornaments

Tribes affected: Pantribal
Significance: *In traditional Indian cultures, people decorated their bodies as well as objects such as garments, weapons, and pouches.*

Ornaments among North American native cultures were as diverse in type as the peoples that produced them. Decorations were added to possessions as well as to the human body, serving various purposes from helping in functional activities to beautifying an individual to visually delineating status, gender, or age.

Indigenous mineral and animal materials were often formed into ornaments. Eagle talons, bird feathers, sea otter and beaver teeth, molted puffin beaks, bone, and ivory are some examples of varied animal parts used as objects of enhancement. Precious stones and reworked silver, copper, lead, brass, and steel were made into jewelry, bells, tacks, hairplates, and buttons, and they were inlaid into functional objects. Archaeological remains have revealed that some ornaments were of specific rare materials, including circular shell gorgets (throat protectors) with incised figures from the Mississippian period; turquoise and shell jewelry and feather pendants from the Hohokam and Anasazi of the Southwest Desert cultures; and ivory clothing toggles from prehistoric Arctic sites.

Because of the portability and rarity of such objects, they were used as trade items and gifts among many native cultures. Coastal peoples traded shell jewelry for goods from inland tribes, while Mesoamerican Indians traded jade and turquoise for desired objects from northern peoples.

Many ornaments took the form of functional objects that went beyond their aesthetic role, such as the beaded pouches, painted bark bags (parfleche), and embroidered porcupine quill garments of the Plains Indians; California Pomo Indian baskets with feathers or beads tightly woven into or attached to the surface; or the snow goggles, fishing equipment, and engraved ivory pipes of the Inuit and Aleut. For example, Aleut men's bent-wood fishing visors were individually painted and lavishly adorned with colorful beads, carved ivory amulets, and sea lion whiskers. The form of the visor kept the sun out of a fisherman's eyes while the embellishments ensured a successful hunt by protecting the wearer and attracting the desired prey with the beauty of the object.

Ornamentation of a highly personal nature among some American Indians consisted of permanent body adornment in the forms of lip labrets made of bone and ivory; ear bobs and nose plugs of metal, ivory, shell, and precious stones; and tattoos. Objects and designs of this type, which are physically incorporated into a wearer's body, defined indelible status within the culture. Cultural affiliation and status were also evident in decoration applied to architecture and transportation as seen in the surface painting and/or carving on canoes, houses, and tipis.

Patricia Coronel and Michael Coronel

See also: Dress and Adornment; Feathers and Featherwork; Headdresses; Quillwork; Parfleche; Shells and Shellwork; Silverworking.

Paints and Painting

Tribes affected: Pantribal
Significance: *Painting has been a primary American Indian art form for thousands of years and is used for social, historical, and decorative purposes.*

American Indian painting reaches back to the earliest known inhabitants of the Americas. Some of the earliest paintings are called pictographs, which simply means paintings or drawings on rock. These drawings and paintings were highly symbolic and stylized and can be seen even today in certain areas, especially the Southwest of the United States.

Before the coming of the Europeans, many different forms of painting were in existence. Painting was prevalent in the Plains and East in the form of painting on animal skins and tattooing, in the Northwest Coast on wooden poles and masks, and in the Southwest and Mexico on pottery, rock, and adobe walls. These different forms of painting had primarily religious, decorative, and historical purposes, with the emphasis on content rather than form.

Styles of painting varied among tribes and regions and were based on such factors as tribal experience and available materials. Designs were generally two-dimensional and geometric, or linear, showing simple frontal and profile figures and shapes or geometric patterns. Designs developed as a result of visionary experiences were painted on shields, tipis, and clothing

An Apache youngster with his face and legs painted. *(National Archives)*

and were believed to give protection. Symbolic painting, which was more stylized and abstracted than representational, was often used for ceremonial mural and sand painting, rock art, heraldics, pottery, masks, and body painting. Representational painting was commonly used for historical purposes such as the recording of events and for calendrical use.

The choice of medium was determined by what was available in the natural world in a given geographic area. Pigments were made from mineral, and sometimes vegetable, sources, with the most common colors being red, yellow, dark brown, and white. Paint colors sometimes symbolized the four cardinal points as well as the zenith and the nadir, with the specific colors for each point tribally determined. The colors themselves were believed to have special attributes or magical powers. By 1300 C.E., polychrome rather than monochrome paints were being used. Painting was done with a stylus made of bone or wood, with brushes made of animal hair, or simply with the fingers and hand.

Contemporary American Indian painting uses modern materials and reflects both the preservation and adaptation of traditional subject matter and styles. Since the late 1800's, painting has changed in purpose, reflecting European influence in materials, marketing, and attitude. The emphasis shifted to the individual artist from Indian painting as an ethnic or folk art, and artists began to sign their names to their work. As an art form, painting continues to be a primary means of expression for American Indians and is pursued as a profession by many Indian painters.

Diane C. Van Noord

See also: Art and Artists: Contemporary; Dress and Adornment; Grooming; Petroglyphs; Pottery; Sand Painting; Symbolism in Art; Tattoos and Tattooing.

Pan-Indianism

Tribes affected: Pantribal
Significance: *American Indians have long attempted to balance tribal loyalties and affiliations with the possibilities and benefits afforded by intertribal unity; during the latter half of the twentieth century, Pan-Indianism has become a hotly contested issue.*

Since the 1960's American Indians have become increasingly politicized and reform-minded. This mobilization has occurred along three lines: tribal, pantribal, and Pan-Indian. Tribal activity currently focuses on organizations or actions by and for members of a specific tribe. This type of movement usually concentrates on the protection or expansion of a single tribe's rights or opportunities. Pantribalism occurs when two or more tribal entities unite in pursuit of a mutually beneficial goal. The Council of Energy Resource Tribes (CERT) is an example of such activity. Tribal and pantribal mobilizations are distinct from the Pan-Indian movement, which promotes the universality of the Indian experience and emphasizes ethnic identification rather than tribal affiliations. According to Vine Deloria, Jr., a nationally recognized authority on Indian rights, in his work *The Nations Within: The Past and Future of American Indian Sovereignty* (1984), "the tribes are concerned with the substance of Indian life while the ethnics [Pan-Indianists] look to the process."

Historical Background. The Pan-Indian movement had its inception during the opening decades of the nineteenth century. The first definable Pan-Indian action occurred during the War of 1812 at the instigation of the Shawnee chief, Tecumseh, and his brother, a revivalist religious leader named Tenskwatawa (the Shawnee Prophet). Urging the various tribes at the frontier to put aside their differences and to oppose the encroachment of the U.S. government, Tecumseh proclaimed in 1810, "The only way to stop the evil is for the red men to unite in claiming a common and equal right in the land, as it was at first and should be now—for it was never divided but belonged to all." The Pan-Indian activity during the remainder of the nineteenth century focused on a combination of strategies and objectives guided largely by religious inspiration. The most notable of these mobilizations remains the Ghost Dance revivals of the Great Plains fostered by the Paiute spiritual leader Wovoka.

At the beginning of the twentieth century, this movement acquired different direction and form. The focal point shifted from religious revival toward political and civil equity and more formal organization. In 1912, for example, a group of Indians drawn together by common experience founded the Society of American Indians. This group continues its commitment to collective action and its promotion of a variety of Pan-Indian and pantribal activities. One such organization was the National Congress of American Indians (NCAI), founded in 1944 by the Indian employees of the Bureau of Indian Affairs. Its primary purpose remains the lobbying for American Indian causes and rights.

Developments Since World War II. In the 1960's and 1970's, distinctions between pantribal and Pan-Indian mobilizations became more pronounced. Government programs and policies aimed at termination of tribal status gave the movements greater impetus. The general atmosphere of protest and reform during the 1960's and early 1970's radicalized the behavior of Indian reformers. An early indicator of the growing schism and changes in tactics was the founding of the National Indian Youth Council in 1961. Frustrated by the "poetic" responses of the older, more established Pan-Indian organizations, a group of younger, more radical leaders led by Clyde Warrior, a Ponca, and Melvin Thom, a Paiute, formed a new organization. They urged their audiences to come to grips with the continued paternalism of the federal government and its failure to correct dire social and economic conditions confronting Indians everywhere. Their cause, according to Thom, was "a Greater Indian America." This action also foreshadowed the development of the Red Power mobilizations of the 1970's and the constituency within which they would find their base.

The movement particularly attracted the interest of urban Indians, whose identification was ethnic rather than tribal in nature. Many often felt alone because they could not document at least one-quarter Indian heritage. These "mixed-bloods" did not come under any recognized tribal jurisdiction and, furthermore, were not recognized by the U.S. government. Nevertheless, they identified themselves as Native Americans if not members of a specific tribal nation. Their sense of alienation and isolation was therefore great, and Pan-Indianism answered a need.

Among the most important and visible organizations of the next generation of organizations was the American Indian Movement (AIM), founded in 1968 in Minneapolis by Dennis Banks, George Mitchell, and Clyde Bellecourt of the Chippewa (Ojibwa), and Russell Means, a Sioux. This group advocated a much broader range of tactics to accomplish their purpose. In addition to legal re-

A sign urging support of the American Indian Movement in New York City. *(Library of Congress)*

course, they employed protest demonstrations, sit-ins and occupations, and occasional violence to promote their causes. Two of the most memorable of these activities were the occupation of Alcatraz Island in 1969 and the violent stand-off at Wounded Knee in 1973. The founding of the International Indian Treaty Council and the Women of All Red Nations represents institutional outgrowths of the AIM mobilization.

In 1977, a contingent of Indians from North and South America presented the United Nations with their Great Law of Peace, which warned against the ill effects European colonialism on the earth's people and environment. A year later, in 1978, a watershed event in the Pan-Indian movement occurred when thousands of Native Americans began a five-month demonstration by walking from the former Indian-occupied Alcatraz Island in San Francisco Bay to Washington, D.C., where on July 15, 1978, they camped on the Mall in an attempt to persuade Congress not to pass legislation that would weaken Indian rights. During this period, dubbed the Longest Walk, many participants found new spiritual meaning in their status as Indian people, and one Buddhist monk on the walk called for a New Age of peace. Pan-Indianism thus has a definite spiritual and religious aspect, which rejects Christianity as a colonial force and embraces old Pan-Indian traditions such as the Sun Dance.

Pros and Cons of Pan-Indianism. The movement has also discovered some limitations, especially with regard to goal setting and continued competition with traditional tribal organizations. The strongest supporters of the Pan-Indian mobilization remain urban Indians whose tribal affiliations have eroded. In large and often hostile cities, Indians of various tribes find it easier to identify with one another than with the larger communities that surround them. They acknowledge a common ethnic origin and welcome partnerships across tribal lines. This tendency places them at odds with many tribalists, who are more traditional in their approach and perceive this blending as a dilution of their identities. Pan-Indianists have also realized that defining themselves, their ideals, and their objectives in the abstract is much simpler than developing specific plans of action. All but the broadest of their objectives involve groups too specific to be truly considered Pan-Indian in nature. Nevertheless, Pan-Indianism, despite its flaws, has played and important role and continues to do so, in that it has brought to national attention common issues of Native Americans that might not have received as much attention from the activism of individual nations.

Martha I. Pallante, updated by Christina J. Moose

Sources for Further Study

Barsh, Russel Lawrence, and James Youngblood Henderson. *The Road: Indian Tribes and Political Liberty.* Berkeley: University of California Press, 1980.

Cowger, Thomas W. *The National Congress of American Indians: The Founding Years.* Lincoln: University of Nebraska Press, 1999.

Deloria, Vine, Jr., and Clifford M. Lytle. *The Nations Within: The Past and Future of American Indian Sovereignty.* New York: Pantheon Books, 1984.

Johnson, Troy R. *The Occupation of Alcatraz Island: Indian Self-Determination and the Rise of Indian Activism.* Foreword by Donald L. Fixico. Urbana: University of Illinois Press, 1996.

Johnson, Troy R., Joane Nagel, and Duane Champagne, eds. *American Indian Activism: Alcatraz to the Longest Walk.* Urbana: University of Illinois Press, 1997.

Josephy, Alvin M., Jr., Troy Johnson, and Joane Nagel, eds. *Red Power: The American Indians' Fight for Freedom.* 2d ed. Lincoln: University of Nebraska Press, 1999.

See also: Ghost Dance; Political Organization and Leadership; Repatriation; Urban Indians.

Parfleche

Tribes affected: Plains tribes

Significance: *Widely used within and outside the Plains, parfleches were both practical devices for storing and transporting food and clothing and objects subject to sophisticated ornamentation.*

A parfleche is a rawhide storage container that was used primarily among Plains tribes to store dry meat, pemmican, or clothing. It was made of a single sheet of hide folded into an envelope, with leather laces passed through holes in flaps to keep it closed. Often parfleches were made in pairs. Variant types of rawhide containers formed into a box shape and often referred to as parfleches were manufactured by tribes who had contact with Southern Siouan groups. The Iowa, Oto, Ponca, and Santee (Sioux) cut pieces from a large hide and then bent, folded, and sewed them together in a box. The Sauk and Fox, Kickapoo, and Menominee used a single piece of buffalo rawhide and folded and bent it into a box. Parfleches were widely diffused outside the Plains area partly through friendly visits during which gifts were exchanged and trade occurred.

Women manufactured parfleches and applied incised or painted designs to them. There were distinctive tribal variations in designs with symmetrical geometric designs consisting of straight lines, triangles, rectangles, and diamonds predominating, although the Blackfoot often integrated some curved lines. Patterns were sometimes incised. In this method the artist scraped away portions of the rawhide, leaving lighter and darker shading. Designs were also painted onto the rawhide, with colors derived from iron-containing clays that yielded yellow, brown, red, and black, with some green and blue. Parfleches were useful, compact storage containers that were well-adapted to the mobile Plains lifestyle; they also served decorative purposes and were often prominently displayed in the tipi and reflected the industriousness of the women.

Carole A. Barrett

See also: Arts and Crafts: Plains; Hides and Hidework; Ornaments; Paints and Painting.

Pemmican

Tribes affected: Pantribal
Significance: *A winter food, pemmican was used throughout the climates of North America where winter resources were limited.*

Pemmican is a winter food. The word *pemikan* is of Cree origin, from *pimii*, meaning grease or fat. The usage of pemmican was universal throughout the temperate climates of North America where winter resources are limited.

Pemmican was prepared by North American indigenous peoples from a variety of ingredients. The primary ingredient was strips of dried lean meat (or fish). The type of meat used varied from one locale to another—elk and venison in the woodlands, buffalo on the Plains, and salmon on the Northwest Coast. The meat was ground or pounded into a powder. It was sometimes mixed with ground seeds or nuts of various kinds, depending on availability.

The dry ingredients are moistened slightly and then combined with fresh berries or other fruit and animal fat. The specific ingredients vary depending upon locale and availability. When the mixture is thoroughly combined and of the correct consistency, it is shaped into cakes by hand. The cakes are then set aside to dry. They are stored for later use as a winter food, to supplement the diet, or as emergency rations when other foods are not available.

Pemmican is a nutritious and palatable food. It combines proteins, carbohydrates and sugars, and animal fat in such a way as to fulfill minimum energy requirements in winter. It stores well and can be used by village dwellers as well as hunters and travelers on expeditions.

Michael W. Simpson

See also: Buffalo; Food Preparation and Cooking; Salmon; Subsistence.

Petroglyphs

Tribes affected: Pantribal

Significance: *Indian designs carved on rock represent a rich legacy of Native American culture, expressing myth, history, and ethnic identity.*

Petroglyphs are designs that have been pecked, abraded, or incised into a rock's surface, frequently by direct percussion with a hammer stone or indirect percussion with a chisel. These are different from pictographs, which are images painted on rock surfaces. There are petroglyphs that have also been painted, but this is rare.

Petroglyphs are found throughout the continental United States, Alaska, and Hawaii. Some of the densest concentrations in the entire world occur in California, the Southwest, the Great Basin, and the Columbia Plateau. The content of petroglyphs includes images of animals, humans, plants, cultural items, and geometric designs. They are portrayed in an array of styles, from realistic to curvilinear or rectilinear abstract.

Ever since English settlers of the Massachusetts Colony first noticed petroglyphs at Dighton Rock in the 1600's, a persistent question has been, "Who made them?" A number of fanciful explanations have been put forward through the years; they have been attributed to Egyptians, Phoenicians, Iberians, and many other Old World groups, and even to extraterrestrials. None of this is

Tsagiglalal, a guardian spirit, is depicted in this Nez Perce petroglyph. *(Library of Congress)*

supported by the evidence, which has firmly established that Native Americans were the makers.

This is known partly because living Indian traditions regarding petroglyphs still exist today. Petroglyphs do not involve a hieroglyphic system or even a pictorial version of a sign language system. No one can walk up to a cliff face and "read" petroglyphs like a book. Contemporary traditions, then, give valuable insight into another common question, "Why were they made?"

The evidence shows they were made for a wide variety of cultural purposes. The Hopi identify images at the Willow Springs site near Tuba City, Arizona, as clan symbols made by members on journeys from their mesa villages to sacred salt deposits. In Northern California, so-called "baby rocks" of the Pomo and "rain rocks" of the Hupa, Karok, and Tolowa reflect a concern with human fertility and world renewal. Rites of passage for Interior Salish youth included portraying dream quest visions on the rocks, while nearby, petroglyphs were seen carved at Fort Rupert on the Northwest Coast in the context of a Hamatsa ritual.

Even where passing time and memory have erased cultural links, purpose is sometimes evident. For example, spiral petroglyphs on Fajada Butte carved by the Anasazi of Chaco Canyon have been shown to be astronomical calendars, recording the movement of the sun and moon. Evidence belies a common claim that this art is idle "doodling" or prehistoric graffiti. Exceptions occur, but the vast majority of it reflects a purposeful, patterned expression of the makers' values, priorities, and worldview.

The most difficult question to answer is, "When were the petroglyphs made?" Relative and absolute dating methods have shown some to be recent, while others date back to the time of the first people in the Americas. The richness of such a legacy for all people should lead to its preservation and protection. A growing awareness of this fact was symbolized by the inauguration of Petroglyph National Monument near Albuquerque in 1990, the first national monument in America to be dedicated to a purely cultural resource.

Gary A. Olson

Sources for Further Study

Diaz-Granados, Carol, and James R. Duncan. *The Petroglyphs and Pictographs of Missouri*. Tuscaloosa: University of Alabama Press, 2000.

Lenik, Edward J. *Picture Rocks: American Indian Rock Art in the Northeast Woodlands*. Hanover: University Press of New England, 2002.

Mancini, Salvatore. *On the Edge of Magic: Petroglyphs and Rock Paintings of the Ancient Southwest*. Foreword by Eugenia Parry Janis. San Francisco: Chronicle Books, 1996.

Moore, Sabra. *Petroglyphs: Ancient Language, Sacred Art*. Santa Fe, N.M.: Clear Light Publishers, 1998.

See also: Anasazi Civilization; Bragskins; Hohokam Culture; Pictographs; Symbolism in Art.

Peyote and Peyote Religion

Tribes affected: Pantribal

Significance: *Since the late nineteenth century, peyote has played a central part in an American Indian religious movement; peyote is viewed as a spiritual teacher, and its use forms a part of a long, complex ceremony.*

To the American Indians who practice peyotism, peyote is considered a spiritual being. This is a concept which defies accurate definition in Western terms. Indians describe peyote iconically and refer to it as "medicine"; it is used as a sacrament. The ritualistic use of peyote in a religious setting to communicate with and be instructed by "spirit" is accepted as a way to "return to the source."

Peyote itself comes from a type of cactus with the scientific name *Lophophora williamsii*, a small, spineless cactus with a rounded top. The parts of the cactus that contain peyote are referred to as "buttons." A peyote button contains more than fifty alkaloids, one of which, mescaline, induces a state of consciousness that can be likened to a healing or religious experience. There is no evidence that peyote is addictive or harmful.

Peyote Religion. The religion, often called peyotism or the peyote cult, is at the center of a pan-Indian movement. The religion has doctrine, an ethical code, unique rituals, and origin legends. Fire, water, the medicine, the eagle, and a drum are the central symbols. Precise rituals involve long, extensive prayer meetings and require knowledge of many songs with repetitive, chanted musical bridges. The peyote religion, referred to formally as the Native American Church of North America (NAC), is pan-Indian, both geographically and tribally. It appeared suddenly after 1880 and spread rapidly.

The origin of the peyote religion as practiced in North America is unknown. James Slotkin (*The Peyote Religion*, 1956) describes twenty-nine different traditions of origin. The ritual of the modern Native American Church is very different from the pre-Columbian and Mexican Indian use of peyote. Peyote reveals itself to the Indian people as a transformer which is integratable and renewing. After 1880, tribal religious traditions, devastated by the relentless encroachments of European Americans, opened to the inevitability of profound change. The church origin legends reflect the devastation suffered by the old ways and depict the need for transformation in the Indian psyche.

Origin legends and doctrinal formulations are of secondary importance to Indians, who are more concerned with original religious experiences. If there is doctrine, it can be said that God put humankind on Earth for a purpose, and it is up to humans to learn that purpose directly from God on "the peyote road" via the mediation of peyote, prayer, and focus or awareness. People should then fulfill that purpose via a moderate lifestyle, outlined by Slotkin as "care of one's health and welfare, care of family, brotherhood, self-reliance, and by belief in the power of peyote to 'teach one how to live.'"

Church Ritual. Church members describe their religion and ritual as uniquely Indian. Some standards seem to have developed, leading to various forms referred to as Kiowa-Apache, Southern Plains, and Oklahoma Fireplace. A number of elements, however, are consistent at every meeting since James Mooney's description of a peyote ceremony in 1892. At all the fireplaces the door opens east, and the roadman, or church leader, sits opposite the door. The meeting (as the church services are called) opens with the placing of the Chief Peyote on the altar and closes with the Chief's removal. The most common form for the altar is a crescent or "half moon," shape. There are five officers, or roadcrew, who have various formal functions in the ceremony: roadman, drummer, cedarman, fireman, and dawn woman. Each one at some point during the meeting will offer a "prayer smoke"—each will roll tobacco in a corn husk and pray with this smoke communicant.

All movement during the meeting is clockwise. The drum is a water drum made from a six-quart metal pot into which are placed water and four coals from the fire. The vessel is then covered with a hide, usually deerskin, and tied with a long rope which wraps around seven stones pocketed in the hide so that the rope makes a seven-pointed star, seen as the morning star, around the bottom of the vessel. The fireman, aside from keeping a ritually constructed fire going through the night, maintains a poker or burning stick from which all "prayer smokes" are lit. Other ritual paraphernalia invariably found at meetings are a bone whistle, gourd rattles, a beaded staff, sage, feather fans, and corn husks and tobacco used in making the hand-rolled prayer smokes. There are always four stages to each meeting: opening, midnight, morning, and closing ceremonies. Particular songs are sung in conjunction with these stages no matter which tribe or fireplace is holding the ceremony, because these particular songs were given through the origin story. Four foods—meat, berries, corn, and water—are also always a part of the ceremony.

Some details of the four stages vary with each roadman. The reason is that peyote teaches a roadman his way; this is a mark of the church's and the religion's vitality. These variations come from prayer, searching, and the medicine. A roadman's ceremony is called his Fireplace.

The ritual is only sketched here; it is extremely complex, more complex than most Christian ceremonies. Meetings usually last a minimum of twelve hours, and the roadman is in control of all of it and aware of the psychological state of every member of the meeting throughout. The ceremony often has aspects of a long, soul-searching journey through the night for each of the participants. It is understood to be a prayer meeting from beginning to end. Church members come to a sacred area, concentrate on its transcendental center or source, and sit with their peers in community to receive healing and instruction.

Glenn J. Schiffman

Sources for Further Study

LaBarre, Weston. *The Peyote Cult*. 1938. Reprint. Hamden, Conn.: Shoestring Press, 1964.

Laney, John H. *On the Symbolism of the Native American Church of North America*. Zurich, Switzerland: C. G. Jung Institute, 1970.

Martin, Joel W. *The Land Looks After Us: A History of Native American Religion*. New York: Oxford University Press, 2001.

Ross-Flanigan, Nancy. *Peyote*. Springfield, N.J.: Enslow, 1997.

Shonle, Ruth. "Peyote, the Giver of Visions." *American Anthropologist* 40 (1932): 698-715.

Slotkin, James. *The Peyote Religion*. Glencoe, Ill.: Free Press, 1956.

Steinmetz, Paul B. *Pipe, Bible, and Peyote Among the Oglala Lakota: A Study in Religious Identity*. Reprint. Syracuse, N.Y.: Syracuse University Press, 1998.

Swan, Daniel C. *Peyote Religious Art: Symbols of Faith and Belief*. Jackson: University Press of Mississippi, 1999.

See also: Native American Church; Pan-Indianism; Religion.

Pictographs

Tribes affected: Pantribal

Significance: *"Pictograph" literally means "picture writing" and refers to any image intended to communicate a thought, idea, belief, or record of events. Pictographs were widely used by native people in the Americas, and they appear on cave walls, rocks, skins, bone, bark, pottery, sticks, and later cloth and paper. They extend from historic times into the early twentieth century.*

Communication. Artistic skill was not an important factor in picture writing, and since pictographic images were intended to communicate and to be widely understood by large groups of people they generally employed conventionalized characters so that they could be easily read. Pictographic drawings often portrayed information from standard angles of vision, often the side or profile, and used certain signs that were widely understood by a tribal group. Among various groups of people, colors often have symbolic meaning and these too were used in pictographs to convey meaning through the drawings. As an example, among the Algonquian and Iroquoian tribal groups, white symbolized peace, so white was used on wampum belts to designate that a fair and open path lay between two enemies. Since the images were easily understood by a group of people, information was shared, communicated, and kept within the tribe.

Mnemonic Uses. Some pictographs existed as mnemonic devices and attempted to remind people of a particular order or pattern to some activity. Among the Ojibwa, for example, there was a medicine society known as the Mide for which rounds of ceremonial songs had to be sung in a precise manner with no variations. Therefore, the Ojibwa created song records drawn on flat strips of birchbark. Each character on the birchbark corresponded to a phrase in the song. When the singer saw a picture of a human figure arising from a double circle, which represented his sleeping place, he was prompted to sing, "As I arise from sleep." These birchbark pictorial hymnals ensured that the songs would retain their power from generation to generation.

Geographic Directions. Pictographic representations were also used by a variety of tribal groups to communicate information about their geographic location or intended destination. Messages were left at a campsite or other obvious place, and some picture drawings were sent to another group.

Personal Histories. Personal records depicting an individual's exploits were quite common, particularly among Plains Indian men. The warrior ethic defined the male role among the Plains tribes, so a system of recording personal achievements and events connected with warfare became highly developed. These records were kept by each warrior, usually on buffalo robes, tipi liners or covers, and other personal objects generally known as bragskins. Bragskins were highly conventionalized so that they could easily be read by any tribal member. A tied horse's tail, for example, denoted war.

Accounting Records. Once they began to engage in trade with non-Indians, many tribes kept records of economic transactions or statistical data in pictographic form. One such record, from the Abenaki tribe, is a drawing of a man, really not much more than a stick figure, shooting a rifle at a deer. On the next line is an indication that the man shot three deer: three hides accompanied by six lines and circles, indicating that he received two dollars for each hide, for a total of six dollars. These accounting records are succinct and communicate the exchange easily to those familiar with the drawings' conventions.

Census Data. Pictographs also recorded census data, particularly in early periods of contact with Euro-Americans, when numbers of people became important in negotiating with government officials. Pictographic census records typically list and identify all male heads of families. For example, one Oglala census record pre-

Prehistoric pictographs on sand rocks in Adamana, Arizona. *(National Archives)*

pared by Red Cloud in the nineteenth century depicts a conventionalized profile of a man's head and then a line that extends upward from the head; the name of the person is designated by a pictographic rendering. For instance, Spotted Elk is represented as a speckled elk. During the treaty period, many of the men signed treaties using these name glyphs, which functioned as their signatures.

Histories and Chronologies. A number of tribal groups kept chronological records of their bands in pictographic form. Among the Teton Sioux, these were known as wintercounts, and their purpose was to record the most important event that had occurred to a band in a yearlong period. The drawings in the wintercounts were terse, serving as mnemonic devices; however, they could be read easily and became ways of preserving band histories.

During the latter half of the nineteenth century and extending into the early twentieth century, some of the Plains tribes developed a pictographic convention that had the explicit purpose of narrating a particular event in the history of the tribe through pictures. These records were narrative and contained significant detail of an event. As animal hides became scarcer, many of these pictographic accounts were recorded in ledger books on paper. Red Horse, a Miniconjou Lakota, produced forty-one drawings in which he detailed what he saw and experienced at the Battle of the Little Bighorn (1876). His pictures provide a sense of the action and tumult of the battle, as well as the stress and overwhelming defeat of the soldiers. Red Horse's account survives as a rare and important history of this key battle from the viewpoint of a Native American survivor.

Amos Bad Heart Bull, an Oglala, kept a pictographic record of his people in a ledger book. Rather than provide insight into a single event, Bad Heart Bull maintained a chronology of events important in the history of his people. In a series of drawings depicting the death of Crazy Horse (1877), for example, he records a pictorial narrative that locates the event and identifies the major participants.

Current Use. Pictographs functioned to give permanence to certain important concepts and events that otherwise would have existed only in oral forms among American Indian people. Although their function as devices to communicate thoughts, ideas, and beliefs disappeared in the early twentieth century as they were replaced by alphabetic writing and reading, much contemporary Indian art recognizes the importance of picture writing among tribal people and employs pictographic imagery.

Carole A. Barrett

Sources for Further Study

Blish, Helen H. *A Pictographic History of the Oglala Sioux.* Lincoln: University of Nebraska Press, 1967.

Mallery, Garrick. *Picture-Writing of the American Indians.* New York: Dover Publications, 1972.

Szabo, Joyce. *Howling Wolf and the History of Ledger Art.* Albuquerque: University of New Mexico Press, 1994.

Tillett, Leslie. *Wind on the Buffalo Grass: Native American Artist Historians*. New York: DaCapo, 1976.

See also: Bragskins; Paints and Painting; Petroglyphs; Sacred Narratives; Symbolism in Art; Tattoos and Tattooing; Walam Olum; Wampum; Wintercounts.

Pipestone Quarries

Tribes affected: Plains, including Blackfoot, Crow, Iowa, Mandan, Oto, Pawnee, Ponca, Sioux

Significance: *The quarries, located in southwest Minnesota, were being worked in the seventeenth century with metal tools acquired from European traders.*

From the beginning, the area was considered a sacred place where peoples from various tribes could quarry stone in peace. The quarry contains a soft pink or red stone called catlinite, named for George Catlin, who visited the quarries in the 1830's. (He sent a sample for analysis to a friend in Boston who then named it for Catlin.) The catlinite, or pipestone, was formed when clay was pressed between layers of sand deposited when the area was an inland sea; pressure and chemical reactions then created thin layers of pipestone sandwiches between thicker layers of quartzite. The layers of quartzite must be removed to obtain the pipestone, which gets its pink or red color from traces of iron.

The earliest diggers were the Iowa and Oto. By the 1700's, the Dakota Sioux had acquired a monopoly, trading pipestone extensively throughout North America. The stone, prized for its color and softness, was ideal for carving ceremonial pipes, including calumets, called "peace pipes" by Europeans. Pipes were so valuable that a finely carved pipe could bring a horse in exchange. By 1851, the Dakota, through treaties, had lost rights to the quarries. Until 1926, the Yankton Sioux struggled to maintain control, losing title through a Supreme Court ruling. In 1937, an act of Congress created the Pipestone National Monument. All native peoples were granted access to the quarries. By the early 1950's, pipe carving and work in the quarries had all but ceased. The revival of tribal traditions and arts has led to a resurgence of carving, however, and the quarries are again actively used.

A variety of legends surrounds the site, each attesting its sacredness. In one account, an Omaha Indian woman followed a sacred white bison whose hooves turned the rocks red. In another, borrowed by Henry Wadsworth Longfellow for *The Song of Hiawatha*, the Great Spirit (Kitchi Manitou), in the form of a bird, calls the people together. Drawing out a piece of red stone, He fashions a pipe and begins to smoke. He tells the people that the red rock is their flesh and is to be used only for making ceremonial pipes. Yet another legend traces the quarries' origins to a time when people from many tribes were fleeing a flood. Unable to escape, all perished but a single young woman. The bodies of the dead became the pipestone. The communal origins of the site meant that all peoples were free to use it in peace.

Today an interpretive center housing displays of carvings and quarrying techniques is on the site and open to public view.

Charles Louis Kammer III

See also: Arts and Crafts: Plains; Calumets and Pipe Bags; Tobacco.

Pit House

Tribes affected: Southwest tribes
Significance: *Pit houses are among the earliest types of structures known to have been built in the Americas.*

Pit houses (or pithouses) are the earliest recognizable form of architecture adopted by semi-sedentary cultures in the southwestern United States and northern Mexico. Pit houses appear with the Hohokam culture in Arizona as early as 300 B.C.E., and with the

Anasazi Basket Maker culture of southwestern Colorado by 200 C.E. Associated with the introduction of domesticated crops and pottery, pit houses remained the principal architectural form until approximately 700, when they were replaced by masonry and/or adobe Pueblo-style architecture.

Pit houses consisted of excavated earthen pits, between 2 and 5 feet deep and 10 and 25 feet in diameter, usually lined with adobe or stone slabs. The pit was covered with a domed log roof topped with thatch and earth or adobe. Early varieties were round in plan; they were entered through a lateral doorway at the east end and contained a small smoke hole in the roof above a central fire pit. In later versions, plans were generally square, the lateral entrance decreased in size, sometimes becoming a mere air vent, and the smoke hole was enlarged to become the primary means of entrance via a ladder. Primarily single-family dwellings, pit houses could be found as isolated units or grouped into village clusters of a hundred or more, though rarely were they organized into formal village plans. Later versions may have combined domestic and ritual functions, since many examples contain ceremonial features such as the *sipapu*, symbolizing the mythological hole of emer-

Pit house

gence (according to Hopi mythology), and surrounding benches, features commonly associated with later Pueblo kivas. Pit house prototypes associated with Archaic hunter-gatherers have been found in Canada and eastern Siberia.

Beginning around 700, pit houses apparently evolved into two distinctly different and more specialized forms: the square, above-ground Pueblo style room-blocks which served primarily utilitarian functions, and the round subterranean kivas, which served more religious or esoteric functions.

James D. Farmer

See also: Anasazi Civilization; Architecture: Southwest; Hohokam Culture; Kivas; Pueblo.

Plank House

Tribes affected: Auinault, Bella Coola, Chehalis, Chinook, Coast Salish, Coos, Haida, Hupa, Karok, Klamath, Klikitat, Kwakiutl, Nootka, Takelma, Tillamook, Wivot, Yurok

Significance: *Large plank houses were widely used in the Northwest Coast culture area, where there were abundant forests to supply the material.*

Plank houses of the Northwest were usually built of white cedar. An oblong or rectangular area was cleared and the earth removed. The area could be from 10 to 30 feet long or more, from 6 to 20 feet wide, and 1 to 3 feet deep. Vertical posts were sunk into the ground, or log walls were built around the shallow pit and were capped with wooden beams.

Cured logs of cedar were split into planks with stone hammers and wedges. The planks were from 1 to 3 feet in width, and could be up to 60 feet long. Planks were usually at least several inches thick. The size of the planks was determined by the type of structure to be built. Planks were then attached to the vertical posts using cords braided of roots or vines. The structure was sealed with a

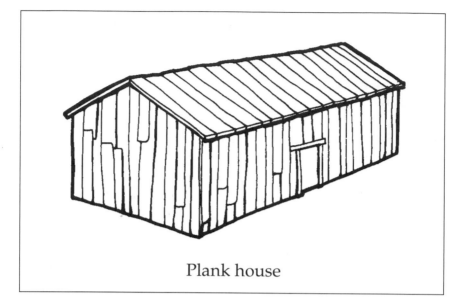

Plank house

mixture of pitch and charcoal or other substances which made it waterproof and windproof.

The roofs of plank houses could be either single or double pitch. A hole was made in the roof to allow smoke to exit and air to circulate. Doors were cut into either end.

Large longhouses with elaborate carvings on the posts and beams were common north of the Puget Sound and Columbia River areas. Several families could occupy each house. Common hearths were established in the center, with living areas to each side partitioned off by mats, skins, or other means, which allowed some privacy. The size and style of plank houses tend to become smaller and simpler the further south the tribal group.

Michael W. Simpson

See also: Architecture: Northwest Coast; Longhouse.

Pochteca

Tribe affected: Aztec

Significance: *In the 1364-1520's, the pochteca were a specialized group of long-distance traders commissioned by the Aztec ruler to obtain luxury items.*

The pochteca were an elite group of Aztec traders who traveled from the capital of Tenochtitlán in central Mexico to various places in Mesoamerica to obtain luxury goods and resources for the Aztec nobility. Jaguar pelts, chocolate, and feathers were listed by the Spanish chronicler Bernardino de Sahagun as being among the trade goods acquired by the pochteca. Although the pochteca were highly ranked in Aztec society, they hid their wealth and disguised themselves as poor traders. Transportation involved human porters carrying goods on tumplines, since there were no draft animals domesticated in Mesoamerica.

Often referred to as "trader-spies," the pochteca traded with rulers of other regions on behalf of the Aztec king and subsequently participated in military campaigns to conquer and incorporate new lands into the Aztec empire. On the philosophy that it is cheaper to exact tribute than to trade, the Aztecs conquered the Soconusco area of the Pacific coastal area of Chiapas, Mexico, to exact chocolate as tribute. Aztec trade enclaves may have existed on the gulfs of Mexico and Honduras, where Maya traders met with the Aztec pochteca. Archaeological evidence indicates extensive trade between the Aztec, Maya, and others in the Late Postclassic Period prior to the arrival of the Spanish in 1521.

Heather McKillop

See also: Aztec Empire; Trade.

Political Organization and Leadership

Tribes affected: Pantribal

Significance: *While Native American tribes and nations employed several modes of governance, counselor democracy was widespread; traditional modes of government survive today, alongside structures created and supported by the U.S. and Canadian governments.*

Across North America, indigenous nations and tribes evolved varied methods of ordering their political affairs. European colonists arriving in eastern North America encountered variations of a confederacy model, usually operating by methods of consensus that were unfamiliar to people who had been living in hierarchical societies governed by queens, princes, and kings. The best known of these consensual governments was the Iroquois Confederacy, which occupied a prominent position in the diplomacy of the early colonies. Although the consensus model seems to have been the one most often used across the continent, some native peoples maintained societies that were strikingly different. For example, the Northwest Coast peoples paid great attention to political hierarchy and economic status within their communities.

Eastern Confederacies. All along the Atlantic seaboard, Indian nations had formed confederacies by the time they encountered European immigrants, from the Seminoles (Michel-Guillaume-Jean de Crèvecoeur called them "a federated republic") to the Cherokees and Choctaws to the Iroquois and the Hurons, as well as the Pennacook federation of New England, among many others. The Illinois Confederacy, the "Three Fires" of the Chippewa, Ottawa, and Potawatomi, the Wapenaki Confederacy, the Powhatan Confederacies, and the tripartate Miami were other examples. These systems had evolved to coordinate governance across geographic distances that seemed huge to European eyes at the time and to permit maximum freedom to nations within confederations and to individuals within nations.

Iroquois Confederacy. The Iroquois system was the best known to the colonists, in large part because of the *Haudenosaunee*'s pivotal position in diplomacy not only between the English and French but also among other native confederacies. Called the Iroquois by the French and the Five (later Six) Nations by the English, the Haudenosaunee (the word is Iroquois for "people of the longhouse") controlled the only relatively level land pass between the English colonies along the coast and the French settlements in the Saint Lawrence Valley.

Cadwallader Colden, who, in the words of Robert Waite, was regarded as "the best-informed man in the New World on the affairs of the British-American colonies," provided the first systematic study of the Six Nations in 1727 and augmented it in 1747. In his *History of the Five Nations Depending on the Province of New York in America*, Colden, an adopted Mohawk, compared the Iroquois to the Romans because of their skills at oratory, warfare, and diplomacy, as well as the republican nature of their government: "When Life and Liberty came in competition, indeed, I think our Indians have outdone the Romans in this particular."

Describing the Iroquois form of government extensively, Colden wrote that it "has continued so long that the Christians know nothing of the original of it." "Each Nation is an Absolute Republick by its self, governed in all Publick affairs of War and Peace by the Sachems of Old Men, whose Authority and Power is gained by and consists wholly in the opinions of the rest of the Nation in their Wisdom and Integrity," Colden wrote; "They never execute their Resolutions by Compulsion or Force Upon any of their People." Colden wrote that "The Five Nations have such absolute Notions of Liberty that they allow no Kind of Superiority of one over another."

The Iroquois Confederacy was formed by the Huron prophet Deganawida (called "the Peacemaker" in oral discourse). Deganawida enlisted the aid of a speaker, Aiowantha (also called Hiawatha), to spread his vision of a united Haudenosaunee confederacy because he stuttered so badly he could hardly speak. The oral history attributes the Peacemaker's stuttering to a double row of teeth. The confederacy originally included the Mohawks, Oneidas, Onondagas, Cayugas, and Senecas. The sixth nation, the Tuscaroras, migrated into Iroquois country in the early eighteenth century.

Peace among the formerly antagonistic nations was procured and maintained through the Haudenosaunee's Great Law of Peace (*Kaianerekowa*), a complex system of checks and balances between nations and sexes. Rights, duties, and qualifications of sachems were explicitly outlined in the Iroquois Great Law. Clan mothers could remove (or impeach) a sachem who was found guilty of any of a number of abuses of office, from missing meetings to murder. A sachem guilty of murder not only lost his title but also deprived his entire family of its right to representation. The women relatives holding the rights to the office were "buried," and the title was transferred to a sister family.

The Great Law stipulated that sachems' skins must be seven spans thick to withstand the criticism of their constituents. The law pointed out that sachems should take pains not to become angry when people scrutinized their conduct in governmental affairs.

European and European American shapers of thought from Benjamin Franklin to Friedrich Engels expressed astonishment at how the Iroquois and other Native American groups maintained social cohesion and resolved interpersonal conflict without lawyers, jails, and edicts. Instead of formal instruments of authority, the Iroquois governed behavior by instilling a sense of pride and connectedness to the group through common rituals. Ostracism and shame were the punishments for transgressions until people had atoned for their actions and demonstrated that they had undergone a purification process.

Huron Confederacy. The system of the Hurons was remarkably similar to that of their neighbors, the Iroquois. According to Bruce G. Trigger's *Children of the Aataentsic: A History of the Huron People* (1976), the Hurons' polity, like that of the Iroquois, was rooted in family structure. Leaders of the various clans used public opinion and consensus to shape decisions. Issues "were usually decided upon by majority vote [and] discussed until a general consensus was reached." People would not be expected to be bound by a decision to which they had not given their conscious consent.

As with the Iroquois, the clans—Porcupine, Snake, Deer, Beaver, Hawk, Turtle, Bear, and Wolf—created familial affinity across the boundaries of the four confederated Huron nations. Members of each clan could trace their ancestry to a common origin through the female line. In each village, clan members elected a civil chief and a war chief. The titles were carried through the female family line but bestowed on men, again resembling the Iroquois approach. While the titles were hereditary in that sense, they did not pass from head to head of a particular family as in most European monarchies. When the time came to choose a leader, members of each clan segment in a particular village had a choice of several candidates, among whom, according to Trigger, personal qualities counted most heavily: "intelligence, oratorical ability, reputation for generosity and, above all, performance as a warrior."

The four Huron nations held a central council, which, according to Trigger, probably consisted of all the village chiefs, representing all the clans. The central council dealt with issues that affected all four nations, such as trade with Europeans and treaty negotiations.

Cherokee Consensus. The Cherokee, who called themselves *Ani-Yunwiya* ("the real people" or "the principal people"), were organized in settlements scattered in fertile bottomlands among the craggy peaks of the Great Smokey Mountains. The Cherokees took public opinion so seriously that they usually split their villages when they became too large to permit each adult a voice in council. In the early eighteenth century, the Cherokee Nation comprised sixty villages in five regions, with each village controlling its own affairs. Villages sent delegates to a national council only in times of national emergency. The villages averaged three hundred to four hundred persons each; at about five hundred people, a village usually split in two.

In Cherokee society, each adult was regarded as an equal in matters of politics. Leadership titles were few and informal. When

Europeans sought "kings" or "chiefs" with whom to negotiate treaties, they usually did not understand that whomever they were speaking with could not compel allegiance or obedience of others.

As among the Iroquois, each Cherokee was a member of a matrilineal clan: Wolf, Deer, Bird, Blue, Red Paint, Wild Potato, or Twisters. The clans formed an intervillage kinship system which linked them in peaceful coexistence. As in many other confederacies, a clan system among the Cherokees bound the individual villages. The clan system cemented the confederacy, giving it a strength and enduring quality that prevented a high degree of local autonomy from degenerating into anarchy.

Cree Governance. Among the Crees, a subarctic people who inhabited the southern reaches of Hudson Bay in present-day Ontario and Quebec, there was no central political organization, as among the Iroquois and Hurons to the south. Even the individual bands or hunting parties had little or no organized political structure. Such a lack of structure is sometimes called "atomistic" by scholars.

Instead of formal council, Cree bands informally selected a wise elderly man, usually the head of a family, as a source of advice. He exercised informal, limited influence. As with the sachems of the more organized farming and hunting peoples to the south, these informal leaders usually did not relish the exercise of power, probably because most of the people who sought their advice resented any attempt to dictate. According to John J. Honigmann, who studied the Cree social structure, "Too great evidence of power is resented and feared by those whom it affects."

Cree life was marked only rarely by multifamily celebrations or rituals. Social life and social control were usually functions of the extended family. Outside the family, a Cree might appear ambivalent or reticent, usually out of respect for others' autonomy. People who transgressed social norms of interpersonal behavior became targets of gossip or sorcery (a technique for social control that was used widely across the continent). Although their society was family based, the Crees recognized no clan or other kinship system between different bands. The society thus did not have the interconnections between settlements offered by the clans of the Iroquois, Hurons, and Cherokees.

Western Apache. Apache society was centered on groups of two to six matrilocal extended families, a unit sometimes called a *gota*. Members of the gota lived together, and members of the different households cooperated in the pursuit of game and the raising of crops. A gota was usually led by a headman who assumed his status over several years by general consensus of the extended families in the gota. The headman in some cases inherited the title of "true chief." He would not retain the position, however, unless he displayed leadership. If no qualified headman was raised through inheritance, a consensus would form in favor of another leader who would be informally "elected" by members of the gota. Headmen were invariably male, but women exercised influence as political advisers. Their kinship lineages maintained the Apaches' matrilineal society.

A headman could wield considerable influence but only if the people in the extended families he led were willing to follow his advice regarding how to hunt, the techniques of agriculture, and who should work with whom. He also coordinated labor for hunting and foraging, advised parties engaged in disputes, and was sought for advice regarding who should marry whom. As a chief aged, he was charged not only with maintaining exemplary behavior but also with identifying young men who might become leaders in the future. He was expected to tutor younger men in the responsibilities of leadership. A chief was also charged with aiding the poor by coordinating distribution of donations from more affluent members of the gota. If two or more gotas engaged in conflict, their headmen were charged with resolving the dispute.

Each Apache was a member not only of a gota but also of one of sixty-two matrilineal clans which overlapped the individual settlements. Members of a clan (and, in some cases, of others identified as being close to it) helped one another in survival tasks and usually did not intermarry. Unlike the Iroquois and Hurons, however, the Apaches did not maintain a formal political structure beyond the local level except for the interpersonal networks of clans.

Mandan and Cheyenne. Political organization among the Mandans (who occupied present-day North and South Dakota) was restricted to the village level, with no central governance. The Mandans' village governance system included elements of representative democracy but also recognized some degree of rank and economic status, which was often determined by a family's ownership of sacred medicine bundles that were vital to tribal rituals. The owners of such bundles often built their lodges closest to the ceremonial center of a given village. Most Mandan villages were quite similar, with closely packed family lodges clustered around the central plaza, which was usually at least 100 feet across. Men selected from lodges which held sacred bundles comprised a council. These men selected two from their number, one of whom displayed special talents at organizing war parties. The other leading chief's talent lay in his peaceful disposition and his ability to broker disputes, dispense wisdom, stage feasts and rituals, and greet diplomatic envoys.

The Cheyennes maintained a powerful central government which united the various Cheyenne bands as well as family-based affinities. At the head of this organization was the Council of Forty-four, on which civil chiefs served ten-year terms. The Cheyenne system closely resembled the Sioux "Seven Fires" confederacy, although the Sioux were not as tightly organized.

Six Cheyenne military societies served as police as well as organizers of war parties. These voluntary organizations were open to all men in the nation and were similar to the police societies of the Lakota. All these societies grew out of the horse culture of the Plains. As a civil function, the military societies often carried out the council's orders. As the periods of peace dwindled with the onset of the European American invasion, the police societies evolved into war societies which took over much of the authority of the Council of Forty-four. Cheyenne myth says that the Council of Forty-four was started by a woman, but its members were male. New chiefs were chosen by the council itself to replace those who left at the end of their terms.

Classes, Castes, and Slavery. The Nootka peoples of the Northwest Coast, who occupied the west coast of Vancouver Island in present-day British Columbia and the extreme northwest coast of Washington State, departed from the general reliance on a consensus model of government. This departure was not slight: Their system was entirely different. It was status-driven, caste-bound, and, compared to those of many native peoples, very aggressive, even among peoples who shared cultures very similar to their own. From the Chickliset in the north to the Makah in the south, the Nootkan peoples took sturdy whaling canoes to sea; in times of war, which occurred with a frequency and intensity that usually surpassed most native peoples in North America, the canoes could be used for raiding and for capturing slaves from neighboring native nations.

Nootkan peoples recognized three classes that seemed as imperishable as the red cedar from which they constructed their lodges: nobility, commoners, and slaves. The nobility comprised chiefs and their closest relatives; the eldest son was the family head. He, his family, and a few associates lived in the rear right-hand corner of the house, abutted by people of lower status. These people were said to be "under the arm" of the chief. The next highest ranking chief, usually a younger brother of the head chief, invariably occupied the rear lefthand corner of the house, with his family. He, too, had a number of people "under the arm." The other two corners were occupied by lesser chiefs' families. The space between the corners, along the walls, was used by commoners' families, and a few very junior-ranking members of the nobility. They were called "tenants"; the nobility in the corners reserved the right to ownership of the house.

Commoners could move from one house to another at will, and since they often performed arduous but necessary skilled labor (such as carpentry or whaling), chiefs competed to retain the best workers. The most successful chiefs were affectionate and generous toward the common families who chose to live in their lodges. Slaves had no designated lodgings or rights; they were captured in raids of other peoples along the coast and were sometimes traded for other slaves or for goods. A noble in one village could be captured and sold into slavery in another. The captive's relatives might then mount a counter-raid to free him.

The speakers and war chiefs of a village usually were reared from youth through inheritance among the children who had a small quantum of royal blood. They tended to be administrative officers who carried out the will of the chiefs. Although most war chiefs were selected by the high chiefs from their families, one of the few ways in which a Nootka commoner family could advance in the village class structure was to have its eldest son receive such an office. Once a common family had been elevated in this way, the title of war chief remained with it as a right of inheritance.

Unlike some of the more democratic native peoples elsewhere on the continent, the Nootka did not have an elaborate kinship system. The existence of clans tends to create affinity structures independent of class structures, and the Nootka defined themselves, above all, by rank. Notions of status also seemed to be the major method of controlling interpersonal conflict. Should a verbal disagreement explode into a fistfight, members of each participant's family would urge him to cease or risk bringing shame on them. The two combatants might then relapse into a vigorous verbal battle, throwing the worst imaginable insults at each other, as relatives continued to pacify them: "Don't think about him anymore. It's not right to fight. You have a good name. Don't bring it down. Don't think about it—just let it go." In some cases, people who engaged in fisticuffs might be upbraided before the community and abjectly humiliated at public occasions. Outside of this, the Nootkas, unlike the Cheyenne, Huron, Mandan, and Iroquois, had no formal methods of social control within their communities. The Nootkas' use of sorcery was infrequent and mild compared to that of peoples who were less class conscious.

Colonial Governance. From the beginnings of contact with Europeans, Native Americans faced the imposition of governmental systems by colonial authorities. During the years of subjugation, much native governance on reservations was conducted in a summary fashion by the United States military. In the later nineteenth century, the Bureau of Indian Affairs (BIA) was created to conduct reservation governance as a civilian agency. In 1934, with the passage of the Indian Reorganization Act (IRA), native reservation-based governments recognized by the Bureau of Indian Affairs were granted very limited autonomy through elective councils.

Even with limited self-government, Native Americans in the United States still operate within a legal system that in the 1830's began defining Native Americans as "wards of the state." This legal characterization continued to shape BIA policy throughout the twentieth century, as Native Americans asserted their rights to act on their own behalf. The definition of wardship often conflicts with the rights of citizens, extended to American Indians as a whole in 1924.

Today, many traditional forms of governance survive on native lands throughout North America. They often operate with very little outside publicity on reservations that also have BIA-recognized "elective" governments, which some Native Americans boycott as vestiges of colonialism.

Bruce E. Johansen

Sources for Further Study

Bowers, Alfred W. *Mandan Social and Ceremonial Organization*. Chicago: University of Chicago Press, 1950. Provides an overview of Mandan social structure and organization.

Cohen, Felix S. "Americanizing the White Man." *The American Scholar* 21, no. 2 (Spring, 1952): 177-191. An early article describing ways in which Native American concept of governance helped shape the thoughts of American society generally. For details regarding the use of Iroquoian and other Native American precedents in the evolution of democratic thought, see Donald A. Grinde and Bruce E. Johansen's *Exemplar of Liberty*

(Los Angeles: UCLA American Indian Studies Center, 1991).

Corkran, David H. *The Cherokee Frontier: Conflict and Survival, 1740-62*. Norman: University of Oklahoma Press, 1962. Traces the evolution of Cherokee social structure during the early contact period.

Drucker, Philip. *Cultures of the North Pacific Coast*. San Francisco: Chandler, 1965. Surveys of Northwest Coast tribes' lifeways, including political organization.

Fenton, Willam N. *The Great Law and the Longhouse: A Political History of the Iroquois Confederacy*. Norman: University of Oklahoma Press, 1998. An examination of the Iroquois political legacy.

Grinnell, George Bird. *The Cheyenne Indians: Their History and Ways of Life*. 2 vols. 1923. Reprint. Lincoln: University of Nebraska Press, 1972. A comprehensive guide to Cheyenne political society.

McKee, Jesse O., and Jon A. Schlenker. *The Choctaws: Cultural Evolution of a Native American Tribe*. Jackson: University Press of Mississippi, 1980. Describes the development of Choctaw society and political organization.

Reid, John Phillip. *A Better Kind of Hatchet: Law, Trade, and Diplomacy in the Cherokee Nation During the Early Years of European Contact*. University Park: Pennsylvania State University Press, 1976. Evaluates the effect of colonization on Cherokee social structure, including governance. See also Reid's *A Law of the Blood: The Primitive Law of the Cherokee Nation* (New York: New York University Press, 1970).

Trigger, Bruce G. *Children of the Aataentsic: A History of the Huron People to 1660*. Montreal: McGill-Queen's University Press, 1976. The authoritative work on Huron social structure, governance, and other aspects of Huron culture.

Wallace, Paul A. W. *The White Roots of Peace*. Philadelphia: University of Pennsylvania Press, 1946. Describes the origin epic of the Iroquois League.

Wilkins, David E. *American Indian Politics and the American Political System*. Lanham, Md.: Rowman & Littlefield, 2002. An extensive introduction to the history, organization, and role of tribal governments, the rights of Native Americans as individuals, and the relationship between tribal governments and the various branches of American government.

See also: Cacique; Clans; Ethnophilosophy and Worldview; Sachem; Social Control; Societies: Non-kin-based.

Potlatch

Tribes affected: Bella Coola, Chehalis, Chinook, Coos, Haida, Hupa, Karok, Klamath, Klikitat, Kwakiutl, Nootka, Quinault, Salish (Coast), Takelma, Tillamook, Tlingit, Tsimshian, Wivot, Yurok

Significance: *Widely practiced throughout the Northwest, the potlatch involved feasting and gift-giving, and it helped ensure or lift the status of the person giving it.*

The word "potlatch" is from the Chinook language, although it originated in the Nootka language as *patshatl*, which means "gift," or "giving." A potlatch is a ceremonial winter feast. The details of organizing and carrying out the event vary from one areal group to another. Preparation could take months or even years. Each guest invited was fed, housed, entertained, and often given many valuable gifts for the duration of the event, which could last from a few days to a few weeks, depending on the status of the hosts and size of their community.

Invitations were sent out in the form of elaborate beaten copper plates of various shapes representing deities, ancestors, or clan symbols. These "coppers" could be from 1 to 3 feet wide and up to 4 feet in height. They were very thin and intricately engraved with stylized designs. They were sometimes referred to as the "bones of the dead" because they might depict a deceased relative. On occasion they were broken up and given out to a number of members of a given family or clan and then presented and reassembled upon arrival at the host village.

Dancing, storytelling, group activities, and other (often elabo-rate) entertainment, including mourning the dead, commemora-tion of deceased relatives and friends, speeches, and the exchange of gratuities occurred. These would honor the host and ensure the host's importance. Initiations into secret societies, tattooing, pierc-ing of body parts for adornment, and other ceremonial and ritual activities also took place. All those in attendance would then be ob-ligated to the host in one way or another, thus assuring that the host would improve or maintain high social position and status.

Some potlatches were of the grand sort. At the end of these enormous festivities, the host would destroy (by burning) great quantities of goods in addition to those already given away. To-ward the southern reaches of the Northwest Coast culture area, the potlatches were less dramatic and consisted only of gift giving and an elaborate display of wealth by the host.

After colonization, missionaries eventually managed to have the potlatch prohibited (it was prohibited from 1884 to 1951), as it

A potlatch photographed in Alaska circa 1900. *(Museum of New Mexico)*

appeared to them to be unnecessarily destructive and to impoverish many lower-status members of the community. In spite of this incorrect perception, and the prohibition based on it, the practice continues to this day, although in a somewhat modified form, again depending on the nature of the local culture.

Michael W. Simpson

Source for Further Study

Simeone, William E. *Rifles, Blankets and Beads: Identity, History, and the Northern Athapaskan Potlatch*. Norman: University of Oklahoma Press, 2000.

See also: Dances and Dancing; Feasts; Gifts and Gift Giving; Totem Poles.

Pottery

Tribes affected: Pantribal

Significance: *A variety of pottery-making techniques were used to make vessels for cooking and carrying as well as items used for ceremonial purposes.*

Pottery is made of clay. Such wares as bowls, plates, storage containers, animal effigies, smoking pipes, and beads are made by using a wide variety of methods, materials, tools, finishing processes, and firing methods.

The earliest evidence of the crafting and use of pottery in the United States has been found in the Southeast culture area. Types of clay, methods of building, and firing procedures vary enormously from tribe to tribe. The making and use of pottery is nearly universal in temperate climates where it is needed for daily use. In wetter or colder climates, pottery may be absent or used only rarely. Other types of objects, such as baskets in the Northwest and animal skins or stone in the Arctic and elsewhere, were used for cooking and storing.

Evidence of Pottery Vessels

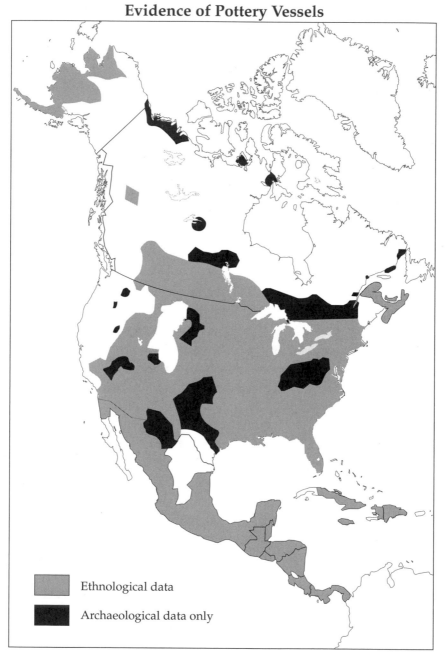

Ethnological data

Archaeological data only

Source: After Driver, Harold E., and William C. Massey, *Comparative Studies of North American Indians*, 1957.

Materials. Clay is composed of aluminum and silicon in the form of aluminum silicate or of calcium and carbon in the form of calcium carbonate. The presence of hydrated trace minerals in clay, such as magnesium, manganese and iron, gives the respective gray and white types of pure clay their various colors, most notably red, yellow, black, green, and blue.

Erosion, earthquakes, landslides, and water movement are some of the natural processes that both reveal and mix the elements into the various types of clay used in the making of pottery. Clay is usually found along streams, rivers, and lakes. Pure clay must be mixed with fine particles of sand, ground-up pottery, ashes, or other substances which will ensure slow even shrinkage of pots as they dry and are fired. The larger the pot to be built, the more of this "grog" the potter must use to ensure the integrity of the walls of the piece.

Pottery clay is gathered, cleaned, processed, and stored, either wet or dry, for future use. It is collected with respect for Mother Earth, with songs, prayers, and offerings of sacred plants; permission is asked and thanks given for its use. The clay is worked by hand to the proper consistency to remove air bubbles and foreign material that could cause cracks if not removed. It is then wedged or pounded with a wooden paddle into a uniform mass.

Process and Craft. Pottery is formed using many different methods and tools. It is made by pinching, from slabs, by coiling, or in wooden molds. Tools such as wooden sticks and paddles, bone implements, and stones were used to shape, incise designs, mold, or finish the clay. A variety of brushes and paints (vegetable- and mineral-based) were used to add color and symbolic meaning to the surfaces of pots.

Pottery is slowly dried, and in the drying process it may be incised with a variety of abstract designs, decorated, or painted, and then perhaps rubbed with a stone, bone, or other smooth implement ("burnished") to a glassy finish. Some potters paint a thin layer of clay of another color—called "slip"—over the pot to add depth and color to the design.

Firing Pottery. After the pottery is thoroughly dried, it is ready to be fired. Many methods and materials are used in the firing process. Some tribes use a shallow open pit, some a walled enclosure made of dung, wood, bark, or clay, and others more complex methods involving an earthen mound. Fuels include grass, hard and soft woods, barks, and animal dung. Firing times can be anywhere from several hours to three days.

The pottery which results can be red, black, yellow, or multicolored depending on whether the firing process involves oxidation or reduction. The longer and hotter the fire, the harder and longer-lasting the pottery. Temperatures can vary from 900 to 1300 degrees Fahrenheit at the peak of the firing. When the ashes cool and the pots are removed, they are gently cleaned with a piece of cloth or hide and rubbed with fat to make them shine. Some pottery was made impervious to water by a smoking process that impregnated the inner walls of the pot with oily carbon compounds derived from pine pitch, corn cobs, or other substances.

A photograph of the renowned Hopi potter Nampeyo displaying her work. *(Museum of New Mexico)*

Traditional pottery was porous "bisqueware" and therefore was not usually put into direct contact with either water or fire unless especially made for those purposes. Pots used for cooking were often filled with water and heated stones placed therein to bring the water to a boil.

Pots usually only lasted a few months if put to daily use. The broken and cracked pieces or shards were often placed in a dump a short distance outside of villages—leaving modern investigators a wealth of artifacts to puzzle over and analyze.

Cultural History. During the early colonial period, the use of pottery began to be displaced by the introduction of glass, iron, and copper wares. In many cases the traditional building and firing methods were nearly lost as new materials and technology took over where tradition left off. As tribes were exterminated, consolidated, or removed to reservations there was loss or fusion of the old ways.

Modern American Indian pottery retains many of the traditional qualities, and most of the classic beauty, of works produced in prehistoric times. Individual potters from a variety of tribes have become well-known artists in their own right, selling their work for hundreds or thousands of dollars per item.

Modern pottery is often fired twice, in gas-fired kilns, the second time at much higher temperatures, a process that makes it impervious and as hard as glass or stone. Earthenware, stoneware, and even porcelain are produced by native artisans across the land. Intricate and innovative methods of carving, painting, and glazing are used today to preserve ancient and traditional designs and forms, while new techniques and designs are used to create beautiful fine arts.

There are many books and films on the subject available today, but these will never replace the knowledge that still can be gained from elders, through the oral tradition, who know the craft and subtleties of the art and are willing to teach it to the next generation.

Michael W. Simpson

Sources for Further Study

Bushnell, G. S. H., and Adrian Digby. *Ancient American Pottery.* London: Faber & Faber, 1955.

Cooper, Emmanuel. *Ten Thousand Years of Pottery.* 4th ed. Philadelphia: University of Pennsylvania Press, 2000.

Peterson, Susan. *Pottery by American Indian Women: The Legacy of Generations.* New York: Abbeville Press, 1997.

Quimby, Ian M., ed. *Ceramics in America.* Charlottesville: University Press of Virginia, 1980.

Savage, George. *Pottery Through the Ages.* Harmondsworth, Middlesex, England: Penguin Books, 1959.

Simpson, Michael W. *Making Native American Pottery.* Happy Camp, Calif.: Naturegraph Press, 1991.

Spivey, Richard L. *The Legacy of Maria Poveka Martinez.* Santa Fe: Museum of New Mexico Press, 2003.

See also: Art and Artists: Contemporary; Arts and Crafts: Southeast; Food Preparation and Cooking; Paints and Painting.

Pow-wows and Celebrations

Tribes affected: Pantribal
Significance: *American Indians, historically as well as currently, have placed great emphasis on ceremony and celebration, which often have religious significance and almost always involve music and dancing.*

Ancient and traditional tribal ceremonies are still held on reservations and other places in many areas of North America. In some cases they remain a serious and integral part of contemporary life; in others, they represent rather a means of remaining in touch with ancient cultural traditions. In still other cases, they may be performed primarily for tourists. In addition to those gatherings and events unique to individual contemporary tribes, many intertribal gatherings are held each year. Pow-wows generally include food, music, and dancing, as well as events such as dance competitions, and are often open for all to attend.

Religious Beliefs. Since so much of tribal ceremony is related to religious beliefs, it is essential to consider the current state of American Indians' religious beliefs and practices. The original inhabitants of North America had as diverse a culture as that of the Europeans or Asians, but there were certain beliefs that were nearly universal. There was a strong tie to the earth. Few Indian tribes considered the possibility that people could "own" land; on the contrary, they belonged to the land. There was a reverence for all life. Spirits lived in trees, in animals, in the sky, and the waterways.

In modern times a great many Indians have adopted Christianity, but with the exception of totally urbanized Indians who have no connection with their origins, there is always a mixture of the new and the old. In some of the more traditional tribal cultures, for example, when a person dies, two funerals will be held: one Christian, one tribal. As a general rule, non-Indians are excluded from the tribal rituals.

Song and Dance. Tribal ceremonies are intimately tied to singing and dancing. Both of these tend to be highly ritualized, often repeating cycles of songs and dances in specific sequence; a hundred or more individual dances and chants may be tied to a specific ceremony. The forms of all these songs and dances, like the religious beliefs they represent, are many and varied among the various Indian cultures, but they are largely concerned with the earth and the spirits that represent and control aspects of the land, sky, and water.

There are ceremonies and accompanying songs for hunters to gain control of animal spirits. There are elaborate rituals, songs, and dances involved in initiation into puberty and into priestly societies, as well as relating to births and deaths. There are rituals to encourage rain in desert areas and to appease the water gods in times of flooding, all with their elaborate dance steps and chanting cycles.

A Native American in full ceremonial dress at a pow-wow. *(Unicorn Stock Photos)*

Potlatch and Pow-wow. Finally, some Indian ceremonies are not religious or are only tangentially religious in their intention. The Northwest potlatch, for example, is basically a party, sometimes planned years in advance, given with the intent of increasing the host's status among the tribe and surrounding tribes. A person of stature will call a potlatch, invite the people he wants (or needs) to impress, and give out a large number of gifts, thereby increasing his standing in the group.

"Pow-wow" is an English rendering of an old Algonquian word originally referring to the shamans widely termed "medicine men." It was later applied to the practice of religious ceremonies and then further broadened so that it means little more than a big gathering of people for a celebration. There are many such gatherings—to celebrate births, deaths, marriages, initiation ceremonies, changes of season, and many other aspects of life.

Generally, these gatherings are joyful, filled with singing, dancing, and feasting, and sometimes have religious significance. In many cases, Christianity has been worked into these ceremonies. Christmas, for example, is often celebrated with virtually the same ceremonies once used to celebrate the winter solstice.

Current Practice. The best place for non-Indians to see traditional Indian ceremonies may be the West, especially the Southwest. This is the area with the greatest number of Indian reservations, and the demonstration of tribal cultures has become a commercial enterprise. In the Northwest, especially in Alaska and in northwestern Canada, the old tribal traditions still exist, relatively untouched by white culture. However, these areas tend to be difficult to reach; sometimes there are no roads, and the only alternatives for travel are bush planes and dogsleds.

Marc Goldstein

Sources for Further Study

Bancroft-Hunt, Norman. *People of the Totem*. New York: G. P. Putnam's Sons, 1979.

Browner, Tara. *Heartbeat of the People: Music and Dance of the Northern Pow-wow*. Urbana: University of Illinois Press, 2002.

Hudson, Charles. *The Southeastern Indians*. Knoxville: University of Tennessee Press, 1976.

Reichard, Gladys A. *Navaho Religion: A Study of Symbolism*. 2 vols. Princeton, N.J.: Princeton University Press, 1950.

Spencer, Robert F., Jesse D. Jennings, et al. *The Native Americans*. New York: Harper & Row, 1977.

White, Julia C. *The Pow Wow Trail: Understanding and Enjoying the*

Native American Pow Wow. Summertown, Tenn.: The Book Publishing Company, 1996.

Wissler, Clark. *Indians of the United States*. Garden City, N.Y.: Doubleday, 1966.

See also: Dances and Dancing; Feasts; Music and Song; Pan-Indianism; Potlatch; Religion.

Praying Indians

Tribe affected: Northeast Algonquian (Massachusett)

Significance: *Seventeenth century Puritan missionaries urged Indian converts to Christianity to establish their own communities away from the influence of other, non-Christian Indians.*

John Eliot was a Puritan missionary involved with preaching to and converting Indians in the earliest British colonies in the "New World." Eliot himself was of a scholarly orientation, having learned the Algonquian dialect of the people he was working with to such an extent that he translated the entire Bible into their language.

Scholars debate the impact that Puritan missionaries had on the Algonquian tribes of the Northeast. Some suggest that the conversions were the creative and self-preserving response of a people who realized that their old lifestyle was gone forever, while others see it as the violent imposition of a foreign lifestyle on Native American tribes who were weakened by waves of disease that accompanied early European contact on the coasts of Canada and the United States.

However their conversions are now understood, as a number of Indians became converts, they were resettled in villages and towns to be separated from those of their tribes who did not convert to Christianity. The idea was to separate them from their cultural influences in order to train them more easily in the ways of

"Christianity and civilization." In the Puritan mindset, work and productivity were measures of spiritual maturity, and thus the "civilizing" influence was explicitly seen as part of the message of Christianity.

In her analysis of the "praying Indian town" phenomenon, Elise Brenner stated that these praying towns were, in actuality, strongly akin to reservations. Furthermore, the goal of settling otherwise nomadic peoples made them easier to control and inculturate. As Brenner states, "Christian Indians . . . were part of the European long-term plan of establishing total colonial authority in New England."

Eliot experimented with a number of different styles of governance in his attempt to transform the "praying Indians" into proper European converts. For example, he borrowed a "Mosaic" code of governance taken from his interpretation of the Book of Exodus, which imposed "leaders of ten," over whom were "leaders of fifty," who answered to "leaders of one hundred," with a court composed of "leaders of a thousand."

A full integration into European American society was never the goal of the praying town system. There was constant suspicion among the English settlers themselves, and funds were typically raised among Christians in England whose image of the work in the colonies was colored by the reports of missionary fundraisers. When it was seen that these praying Indians might be armed as a buffer between the European settlers and the hostile tribes further west, however, settler interest increased.

Recent scholarship has focused on the manner in which praying Indian towns were as much new expressions of Indian society and cultural values as they were a system imposed by European settlers. In fact, there was considerable self-governance and authority among the Indian converts, and many aspects of traditional society and creativity were maintained within the context of the newly proclaimed Christian faith. Indigenous expressions of Christianity, such as the continued use of native terminology to refer to God, were not unusual in these villages, although the use of native terms and concepts raised the suspicions of some missionaries who believed such "syncretism" to be unacceptable. Eliot himself was not above using whatever similarities he saw between native traditions and Christian conceptions.

When compared with more violent contacts between Europeans and Native Americans, the praying town phenomenon had certain humane features, and Eliot was certainly more informed of native language and culture than most settlers. Ultimately, however, the separation of Native Americans from their fellow tribal members must be seen as being part of the systematic destruction of native life that has occurred in American history.

Daniel L. Smith-Christopher

Sources for Further Study

Brenner, Elise. "To Pray or to Be Prey: Strategies for Cultural Autonomy of Massachusetts Praying Town Indians." *Ethnohistory* 27, no. 2 (1980): 135-152.

Cogley, Richard W. *John Eliot's Mission to the Indians Before King Philip's War*. Cambridge, Mass.: Harvard University Press, 1999.

Eliot, John. *A Late and Further Manifestation of the Progress of the Gospel Amongst Indians in New-England*. London: J. Allen, 1655.

Jennings, Francis. "Goals and Functions of Puritan Missions to the Indians." *Ethnohistory* 18, no. 3 (1971): 197-212.

Salisbury, Neal. "Red Puritans: The 'Praying Indians' of Massachusetts Bay and John Eliot." *William and Mary Quarterly* 31, no. 1 (1974): 27-54.

Vaughan, Alden T. *New England Frontier: Puritans and Indians, 1620-1675*. Boston: Little, Brown, 1965.

See also: Missions and Missionaries.

Projectile Points

Tribes affected: Pantribal
Significance: *Projectile points tipped spears, arrows, and other tools for thousands of years in prehistoric North America.*

Projectile points are thin, symmetrical artifacts with bases thinned for mounting on shafts. The name is somewhat misleading, since many of these items were never used on projectiles (such as javelins or arrows), but rather were the points for thrusting spears; some clearly were used as knives and similar tools. Most points were made of flaked stone, though some were made of ground stone (especially slate) or bone. The width of the base of a point indicates the type of weapon on which it may have been used, since its basal width must approximate the width of the shaft on which it was mounted, and thick shafts could not be used for arrows. A few types of points had cylindrical bases and presumably were mounted in sockets at the tips of their shafts. Recognizing that the characteristics of projectile points vary greatly over time and among tribes, archaeologists have expended considerable energy in studying them, and the dates of manufacture for point types in North American now are largely known.

Russell J. Barber

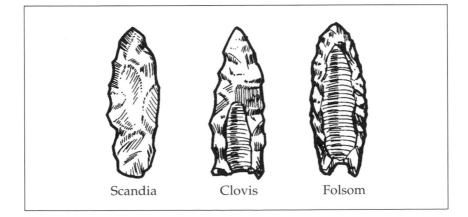

Scandia   Clovis   Folsom

Sources for Further Study

Justice, Noel D. *Stone Age Spear and Arrow Points of California and the Great Basin*. Bloomington: Indiana University Press, 2002.

_____. *Stone Age Spear and Arrow Points of the Midcontinental and Eastern United States: A Modern Survey and Reference*. Bloomington: Indiana University Press, 1995.

_____. *Stone Age Spear and Arrow Points of the Southwestern United States*. Bloomington: Indiana University Press, 2002.

Knecht, Heidi, ed. *Projectile Technology*. New York: Plenum Press, 1997.

Yeager, C. G. *Arrowheads and Stone Artifacts: A Practical Guide for the Amateur Archaeologist*. 2d ed. Boulder, Colo.: Pruett, 2000.

See also: Bows, Arrows, and Quivers; Knives; Lances and Spears; Weapons.

Puberty and Initiation Rites

Tribes affected: Pantribal

Significance: *Puberty and initiation rites represented the important transition from childhood to adulthood in the Indian life cycle.*

American Indian cultures contained special ceremonies and tribal guidelines marking one or more stages of the life cycle—birth, puberty, reproduction, and death. Puberty, especially for girls, held great importance as it represented the formal end of childhood and the availability to marry. (Some tribes, such as the Blackfoot and Arapaho, however, had no special ceremonies for puberty.)

Because of close living quarters, children grew up aware of sexual relations. Puberty often altered familial relations, as brothers and sisters were no longer permitted to be by themselves without supervision. In addition, postpuberty children would often sleep separated from their parents. These changes were celebrated, as puberty and initiation rites represented the movement of the tribes' children to adulthood. Common community events marking this life change included gift giving, feasts, and musical celebrations.

Becoming a Woman. Almost every tribe put strict limitations on the behavior of menstruating women. Because of a strong belief in the spiritual nature of blood, women were isolated during this time to avoid contamination of food, weapons, and other essential elements of Indian life. During her first menstruation, an Indian girl was isolated from the community and instructed on these taboos. A special tribal ceremony commemorating the girl's new adult status often accompanied this isolation.

The Navajo puberty ceremony for girls, Kinaaldá, was one of the most elaborate rituals in Indian culture. The ceremony, which took place as close to the first menstruation as possible, lasted four days and ended with a community celebration. A specific order of events was followed, including a symbolic molding of the body to resemble the Changing Woman (the first mother), which prepared the girl for motherhood. Another event involved three daily runs toward the east—at dawn, noon, and sunset—to strengthen the body. Each day, corn was ground in preparation for a community celebration on the final day. Immediately prior to this celebration, the young girl was bathed and dressed in new clothing to represent her new status. The Apache also conducted a puberty ceremony similar to the Kinaaldá.

Other tribes marked the first menstruation with a variety of ceremonies. Among the Hopi, when a girl "came of age" she moved to a bed distant from her parents and was instructed on the religious secrets of the culture. Sioux girls, upon their first menstruation, added an eagle plume to their hair; this symbolized their new status as adult women. A special ceremony was also held in the girl's honor. The father of a Cheyenne girl called out the news of his daughter's menstruation. She would then be painted red and sent to a special lodge for the duration of her menstruation. When the girl emerged from the lodge, she walked through smoke to purify her body.

Becoming a Man. Few tribes celebrated formal ceremonies for their male children. Young boys started their quest for adult status at a young age with increased responsibilities such as caring for warriors on the hunt and using larger bows. In many cases, taking care of the tribes' horses represented the first "adult" rite. When a boy's voice changed, parental authority passed from his mother to his father and he received advanced instruction on the arts of hunting and war. Some tribes had ceremonial dances, such as the Sioux Sun Dance, which acted as a test of endurance for young warriors. Physical toughening served as a measure of status in the Apache path to manhood.

Hunting also served as an initiation rite for boys, who were trained since early childhood for the hunt. The first large kill was a gift to the needy people of the group and represented a proud moment for the boy's family. Cheyenne boys received adult status for a successful hunt or war record.

Male puberty also included a strong spiritual element. Vision quests, common among the Plains Indians, often took place for the first time during puberty and represented not only a religious rite but also an initiation rite. Young boys first visited the sweatlodge to breathe the "breath of life" created when water was poured on hot stones. The youth was then left with no clothing or food in a secluded area for four days and nights. Facing the elements as well as hunger and loneliness, the youth's bravery and courage was tested while he waited for a vision (dream). This vision would then be interpreted by tribal elders and used to give the boy his adult name and, in some cases, his occupation. The Lakota vision quest, *Hanblapi*, was also undertaken by the tribes' girls.

Another major element in male puberty was the initiation into a sodality. Similar to a modern fraternity and often strongly tied to religion, a sodality represented a social as well as educational passage into adult life. Among the Pueblo and Hopi, youths between the ages of ten and twelve were initiated into a sodality called the kachina cult. Boys moved into a sacred building called a kiva, where they were freed from parental supervision and trained in the tribes' religious beliefs. The process almost always included physical beatings to impress the seriousness of tribal and religious responsibilities. Algonquians separated their boys from their families for nine months some time between the age of ten and fifteen for their introduction to religion.

Reservation Rites. After Indians were forced onto reservations, tribal rites and ceremonies were limited because of the U.S. government's restrictions on assembly (caused by fear that assembly would lead to war parties and rebellion). Events such as the Kinaaldá were scheduled once a year and lost many of the ancient taboos. In addition, the separation of brothers and sisters virtually ended once Indian children were enrolled in public schools. Reservation life did not completely remove the importance of puberty, however, and tribes, determined to carry on ancient rituals, found ways to maintain tradition in a modern world.

Jennifer Davis

Sources for Further Study

Driver, Harold E. *Indians of North America*. 1961. Reprint. Chicago: University of Chicago Press, 1969.

Frisbie, Charlotte Johnson. *Kinaalda: A Study of the Navaho Girl's Puberty Ceremony*. Middletown, Conn.: Wesleyan University Press, 1967.

Gill, Sam D. *Dictionary of Native American Mythology*. Santa Barbara, Calif.: ABC-Clio, 1992.

Lowie, Robert H. *Indians of the Plains*. New York: McGraw-Hill, 1954.

White, Jon Manchip. *Everyday Life of the North American Indian*. New York: Holmes and Meier, 1979.

See also: Children; Gender Relations and Roles; Menses and Menstruation; Names and Naming; Rites of Passage; Sweatlodges and Sweatbaths; Visions and Vision Quests.

Pueblo

Tribes affected: Pueblo people (prehistoric to modern)

Significance: *The Anasazi, the most creative and enduring of the prehistoric cultures of the Southwest, were the first to acquire the architectural and engineering skills needed to build aboveground pueblos, establishing a tradition that survives today.*

At the beginning of the Pueblo period, around 700 C.E., the Anasazi pit house evolved in two different directions: It came up above the ground to become a house, and it sank deeper into the ground to be formalized as a kiva. Building on mesa tops and in valleys at sites such as Chaco Canyon, Mesa Verde, and Kayenta, the Anasazi chose communal dwellings over individual houses. They constructed slightly curved rows of single-story contiguous rooms, using a method known as "jacal." Walls were built using posts set a few inches apart, with adobe packed into the spaces between. Then, around the base of each wall, stone slabs were set in place with adobe mortar. Roofs consisted of slender cross-poles interlaced with brush and twigs and topped with a layer of mud several inches thick. The rooms, each housing an entire family, faced to the inside of the curve, with several kivas in the center.

Gradually, the Anasazi dispensed with the wooden framework and developed a crude masonry technique using large, unshaped rocks laid in irregular rows and packed with adobe, which often made up more than half the wall. As they refined their masonry techniques, the Anasazi began to shape sandstone into building blocks by using stone tools that were not much harder than the sandstone itself.

As construction techniques improved, the size and complexity of the pueblos increased, finally resulting in the great cities of the Classic Pueblo period. The largest of these, Pueblo Bonito in Chaco Canyon, housed a probable population in excess of one thousand people in its more than eight hundred rooms, which rose to four and five stories and covered some 3 acres of ground. Pueblo Bonito was arranged in a horseshoe pattern around a central plaza, with

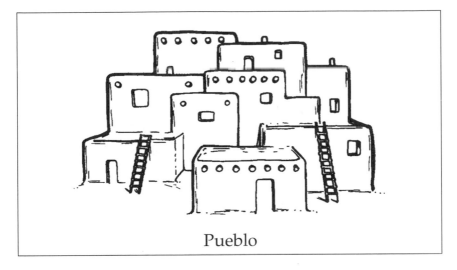

Pueblo

each row of rooms rising one story at a time toward the rear. A row of single-story rooms across the front enclosed the plaza, which contained the ceremonial kivas. As they had done since Developmental Pueblo times, the women of the pueblo used the rooftops for cooking and other household chores.

Under Anasazi influence, the Mogollon and Hohokam peoples began to build surface pueblos, as did the later Sinagua and Salado. As the Anasazi moved away from the northern plateaus around 1300 C.E., they migrated to three main areas: the Rio Grande Valley and Zuñi in New Mexico, and the Hopi Mesas in Arizona. The cultures that developed in these areas in the fourteenth and fifteenth centuries are ancestral to the Pueblo cultures that exist there now. Although construction of these pueblos varied with time and place, in general the Anasazi traditions of communal living have prevailed, with pueblos consisting of large numbers of rooms, built of masonry or adobe, arranged around a central plaza containing several ceremonial kivas.

LouAnn Faris Culley

See also: Adobe; Anasazi Civilization; Architecture: Southwest; Cliff Dwellings; Kivas; Pit House.

Quetzalcóatl

Tribes affected: Aztec, Maya

Significance: *Quetzalcóatl, one of the three great Aztec gods, was a benevolent deity who presided over learning and the priesthood.*

Quetzalcóatl, commonly referred to as the Feathered or Plumed Serpent, was one of the three Aztec "great gods." These gods ranked in importance immediately under the four creative deities and above the various gods of fertility, nature, the planets, and constellations. The other two great gods were Huitzilopochtli, Hummingbird Wizard or Hummingbird of the South, war and sun god, the chief god of Tenochtitlán (present-day Mexico City), and Tezcatlipoca, Smoking Mirror, chief god of the pantheon, often described in solar terms, the chief god of Texcoco.

Quetzalcóatl, the third great god, was the god of learning and the priesthood and the chief god of Cholula (where the ruins of a temple dedicated to him may still be seen). Aztec myth held that Quetzalcóatl had once been a man, presiding over a golden age in the state of Anahuac. He is generally depicted in sculpture, fresco, and carvings as a man of tall stature with a light complexion, long, dark hair and a substantial beard. Quetzalcóatl somehow angered one of the principal gods and was exiled. He left his followers at the Gulf of Mexico, departing in a wizard skiff made of serpent skins, promising to return. Given Quetzalcóatl's physical characteristics and his gallant promise to return as recorded in Aztec folk myth, the Spaniards cannot have understood their phenomenal luck in chancing to approach the Mexican coast from the same Gulf of Mexico waters whence Quetzalcóatl left.

In an interesting expression of crosstribal influence, Laguna Pueblo novelist Leslie Marmon Silko uses the Aztec Quetzalcóatl in *Almanac of the Dead* (1991) as one of the recurring symbols of the text (a stone serpent that appears overnight) and in the retelling of the Aztec cosmogony myth (similar to the Osiris limb-gathering creation myth).

Richard Sax

See also: Aztec Empire.

Quillwork

Tribes affected: Pantribal throughout the porcupine's natural habitat

Significance: *Quillwork is a form of decoration that was used across the northeastern United States and Canada and as far west as the western slopes of the Rockies and through the central Plains south and east to the coast—the area where porcupines are native; it is still used today by artists from these areas.*

Porcupine quills provided many tribes with material that could be dyed a variety of bright colors. Several methods were used, and the quillwork of the Plains may be differentiated from that of the eastern nations. In both cases the quills were taken from the porcupine by rolling it in a soft robe. The quills would stick and could be removed individually; the barbs were cut off and the quills were cleaned. Quills are tubular in shape but could be flattened by pulling them between the teeth. Plant and animal dyes were used to dye them bright colors. Popular colors were bright pink, bright yellow, purple, green, and red. Some northern nations used quills in their natural color, off-white with dark brown ends.

After dyeing, they were ready to be plaited together, often in rows creating both geometric designs and pictorial representations. Plains nations preferred geometric designs, whereas those of the Eastern Woodlands tended to be floral in pattern. Good quillwork was tiny, tight, and colorful, and it created beautiful decorations on any article of clothing. Several techniques were used. The quills could be wrapped around a narrow strip of stiff rawhide or one that had been cut into symbolic shapes, such as medicine wheels. These small strips of wrapped rawhide could also be sewn onto any article of clothing, often in adjoining rows as decoration. Another technique was to quill directly onto the garment, weaving the quills together; they were then secured by sinew threads. This was a more common technique for larger pictures or whole areas of clothing that were quilled.

Quality quillwork was greatly valued, and girls were taught the art carefully by loving and talented relatives. A talented quillworker was revered for her artistry, and her creations were highly valued by those lucky enough to wear items of her handiwork. Quilled moccasins, shirts, bandoliers, gloves, hats, jackets, breechcloths, leggings, dresses, and robes were all valued exchange items in giveaways and other acts of generosity, necessary in demonstrating a family's goodness. Quillwork was a lightweight decoration that was both durable and flexible. It could get wet and retain its shape, so it was an exceptionally practical form of ornamentation.

Quillwork was later replaced by beadwork as Europeans poured into the continent, disrupting and influencing the native peoples. Like any new item, beads were desired. Beadmaking with European glass beads replaced native beadmaking from seashells. Because the European beads from Czechoslovakia and eastern Europe were colorful and small, they could be used to replicate quillwork decorations. The colors, however, were different. No longer were the bright pinks, yellows, and purples of quillwork common; now, reds, blues, yellows, and greens became more popular. The best quillworkers continued as long as they could find quills. Their work can be seen in many museums, still beautifully durable.

Nancy H. Omaha Boy

Sources for Further Study

Dubin, Lois Sherr. *North American Indian Jewelry and Adornment: From Prehistory to the Present*. New York: Henry N. Abrams, 1999.

Halvorson, Mark J. *Sacred Beauty: Quillwork of Plains Women*. Bismarck: State Historical Society of North Dakota, North Dakota Heritage Center, 1998.

See also: Arts and Crafts: Subarctic; Beads and Beadwork; Dress and Adornment.

Ranching

Tribes affected: Pantribal

Significance: *Many Native American tribes adopted the cattle and sheep ranching practices of European Americans, which gave them a steady food supply and a means of livelihood.*

North American Indians' experience with ranching may be dated back to the appearance of the Spanish in the Southwest during the sixteenth century. Although at first the Indians captured stock for food and consumed the stolen animals quickly, eventually they began to breed animals acquired as gifts or through further raiding.

When the Spanish established settlements in the Southwest, their *rancherías* of cattle and sheep became targets for stock raids to supplement the desert fare of local Indians. Cattle were as yet not tended but were butchered and prepared for food as was native wild game, such as buffalo, the only "cattle" the Indians had known.

The Navajo learned the value of ranching early, and sheep herds became a focal point of their lifestyle. The sheep provided them with a manageable food source in the arid Southwest, and the wool provided material for superior clothing and blankets. The nomadic lifestyle of sheepherders suited the Navajo people, who had earlier been raiders of the Pueblo tribes.

Eastern Indians subdued by European invasion attempted to assimilate themselves into the dominant society by taking up farming and the management of livestock. The Cherokee, in particular, did very well until they were forced westward by the pressure of white settlers.

Western Indians who found their reservation lands unsuitable for farming often attempted ranching to survive. Sometimes these ventures were successful, but often grazing lands were instead leased to European Americans to provide some income for the tribe or individual.

Modern American Indians continue to engage in ranching as a means of livelihood. The Navajo, for example, raise sheep, horses, and cattle, and their colorful rugs woven from animal fibers command high prices. In Arizona, the San Carlos Apaches operate five cattle associations on their reservation. As an additional source of revenue, the tribe owns two herds, one of which is designated as the "old folks herd" and benefits elderly Apaches.

Patricia Masserman

See also: Agriculture; Subsistence.

Religion

Tribes affected: Pantribal

Significance: *American Indian religions are varied, but they generally contain concepts that stress harmony and the interrelatedness of all life and existence; a wide range of activities may be considered religious, because American Indian religions are not based on the division into sacred and secular realms that is characteristic of many modern religions.*

Until relatively recently, descriptions of American Indian religions have been written from the perspective of Europeans and their American descendants, ranging from the earliest explorers and missionaries to modern anthropologists. Discussions tended to be framed by a number of questions that reflected the European tradition, including whether American Indians had religion at all, what type of religion they had, and what they held sacred. Another problematic aspect to the study of Indian religions is that there is no way to determine what American Indian religions were truly like before contact with Europeans; there is no way to recover the stories, rituals, norms of behavior, and organizational norms as they existed before they were influenced—sometimes subtly, sometimes radically—by Europeans.

Pre-Contact. The first written details of American Indian religion were recorded by French and Spanish Catholics or English

Protestants. For them "religion" meant the Christian religion, and specifically their own version of it. One either had this religion or did not. Clearly the American Indians did not. Thus they were called pagans and were criticized for their superstitions; sometimes they were feared as agents of the devil. For these European Christians, religion dealt with God, the supernatural, an invisible world, and sacred books, rites, and people. Religion was thought to be able to move beyond ethnic or national borders without losing its validity.

They found little of this type of religion among American Indians. One reason was that there was not one single American Indian religion. There were many American Indian religions. In a sense, each tribe *was* its own religion; some tribes had no word or idea equivalent to the Western notion of "religion." The concept as presented by Europeans was foreign to their way of life; the typical religious institutions, stories, and rituals of Christianity did not stand out as religiously distinct from nonreligious ones. Europeans looked for religious stories and activity which resembled their own. An Indian's entire life was religious: Constructing a canoe among the Nootka was a religious act, a treaty discussion among the Iroquois was religious, farming among the Hopi was a religious act, the rabbit drive among the Rappahannock was a religious act. These acts were not considered religious from the perspective of Europeans and thus they saw no religion in them. On the other hand, they heard stories which sounded like some of their own religious stories and saw rituals that seemed somewhat like theirs. These they described as the Indian religion.

The French missionaries were most acute among the Europeans in showing respect for what they considered the religion of the Indians. The Great Spirit became God. The vision quest was viewed as the search for one's call by God. The French saw in their versions of American Indian religions hints of the ancient Roman and Greek religions to which they wished to bring, as a complement, Catholicism.

The American Indians, however, saw little of religious import in the European way of life. The things that gave the Indians' lives direction and purpose seemed lacking in the Europeans' way of life. Europeans did not honor and respect equally the material and immaterial world, and they did not seek to keep a balance between their inner and outer life. They viewed the afterlife as a horrible place for those who disobeyed religious law, and they were unable to speak, chant, sing, dance, and celebrate their life without written words. The Europeans, from the Indian perspective, lacked coherence and direction to their life. At the same time there were many attractive aspects to European life. Surrounded by the European way of life, of which its religion was a part, the Indian religions were overwhelmed and changed but not destroyed.

Post-Contact. From the moment of first contact, Indian religions changed. All religions change when they encounter powerful new cultural traditions. When these religions have a written history, scholars can trace how they change. Since Indian religions are not based on a written tradition, however, there is no clear idea of how much they have subtly changed in accepting European Christian ideas, items of worship, rituals, and images.

It has been suggested that many Christian Indians kept their tribal religions alive while adopting and practicing Christianity without realizing that they were also maintaining their traditional religions—in other words they adopted the Christian view of what was "religious" and did not consider that the tribal traditions they were maintaining were in fact religious ones. Christianity never considered, for example, making a canoe to be religious; therefore, European Christianity had nothing "religious" to say about it. Many aspects of American Indian religions were retained because the nature of Indian religion itself is dynamic. An oral tradition is able to adapt and change in a way that a literate tradition is not. Because Indian religions kept their inherent vitality and practical qualities, Indians were many times able to accept Christianity and keep their own religion.

Animistic Approach. When cultural anthropologists have studied the religions of various cultures, they have frequently employed the views and descriptions of a field of study known as comparative religion. One example is the classification of types of religious systems, one of which is called animism. Another is the concept that religion involves the realm of the sacred, which is contrasted with the secular or profane realm of everyday life.

Animism is a theory of religious origins which claims that early humans believed that everything that exists has its own spirit or living power which governs its existence. Thus the first humans heard the wind howl and thought that it must possess a life like the lives of animals that howl. They found themselves surrounded by spirits: rain spirits, tree spirits, pond spirits, sun and moon spirits. As small children talk to trees and flowers—and wait for an answer—so these first, primitive people did the same. The conversation among the spirits, human and otherwise, became the first prayers, rituals, rules, and institutions known as religion.

A theory of origins is nothing unless it also describes what comes afterward. What eventually came after the "primitive," according to this theory, was the modern Western world of writing, mathematics, and science. In this classification system, since American Indians did not write and had not developed the other "advanced" aspects of European societies, they were primitive peoples. Therefore, it was assumed, they probably had a spirit religion, or animistic religion. It did not take long for a significant body of literature to develop which described the animistic world of Indian religion. The Lakota *wakan* and the Algonquian *manitou* were understood to belong to the world of the spirits. The Pawnee Indians of the Plains were seen to have a hierarchy of star spirits, all subservient to the great spirit in the sky, Tirawa. The Plains Indians' Sun Dance was seen as a dance to win support from the Great Spirit. Buffalo Spirit, Caribou Spirit, and Corn Spirit were seen to direct the coming or growth of these animals or plants. There are guardian spirits won in fasting visions by youths of the Plateau and the Northeast Woodlands. The hunting tribes were described as depending on their hunters' ability to be possessed by one or several of these spirits in order to be able to have the power of that spirit. The tribe itself was seen to have a deep relation with its guardian spirit, or totem, which appeared in the form of an animal. Many books written about Indian religion have used the theory of animism to describe that religion.

The Sacred. Throughout most of the twentieth century, the sacred and its various manifestations were understood to be central to religious life by most scholars of religion. Although they disagreed about details, they agreed that the sacred was separate from the profane or ordinary, was a manifestation of eternal realities, was known in ways different from those by which ordinary reality was known, and existed before and after those who experienced it. From this perspective, Indian life was surrounded by the sacred. It was manifested in all nature, in special people such as the shamans and medicine men and women, in rituals in which sacred objects and sacred sounds enabled people to be in contact with the power of the surrounding spirits, and in sacred poles which held up the sky.

Their sacred stories or myths enabled them to reach back to the beginning of time and to re-create time and life itself. They could reach back to the creation of a sacred reality that gave direction and purpose to all life; this reality was the people themselves. A number of scholars exploring American Indian religion from the perspective of religion's sacred realm have found it an attractive alternative to the way modern Western religion divides the sacred and secular into two realms, thereby helping make possible the repetitive boredom of industrialized societies.

Influence of Lifestyles. Indian religion has been described in terms of hunting and agricultural lifestyles. The religion of the Paleolithic hunting culture of Eurasia is seen reflected in such common American Indian beliefs and practices as Thunderbird, Mother Earth, the bear ritual, hunting taboos, and certain shamanic rituals. This religion was gradually replaced (7000-5000 B.C.E.) by religions reflective of specialized regional farming cultures in which maize and tobacco became central parts of religious rituals.

The religion of the hunter centers on the hunt: going into the field and tracking, then killing, the animal. This religion sees a symbiosis between the hunter and the hunted. They share the same life energies or spirit. The intricate rearrangement of bones after a kill found among some tribes reflected this sharing. The placing of a small piece of salmon underneath the floor of a snowhouse by the Netsilik Inuit was a sign of respect for the salmon's "soul." Chants to a dead bird or animal were common. Another common feature among hunting religions is the belief that animal species have a "master spirit" that, under, certain conditions, allows them into the hunter's world. The Caribou Man among the Naskapi Indians of Labrador, for example, is said to live in a world of caribou hair as white as snow and deep as mountains. These mountains are the immense house of the Caribou Man. He is surrounded by thousands of larger-than-life spiritual caribou, who pass in and out of his caribou paradise along paths which he controls for his purposes. The animals' spirits circulate, waiting to be sent back to the hunter's world in new fleshly bodies. If the bones and the animal are treated properly, the enfleshed animal will return.

The religion of the farmer focused on earth, seasons, life, and death. While in many parts of the world farming religions seem to have led to an increase in animal, human, and plant sacrifice, this does not seem to have been the case in North America. Sacrifice did occur, however: White dogs were sacrificed by the natives of Northeast Woodlands; self-mutilation occurred in the Sun Dance of the Lakota and in the Mandan Okeepa (Okipa) ceremony; the Pawnee sacrificed a young captive girl to Morning Star. This latter example is expressive of the major life-death-life theme found in farming religions, for the young girl was a personification of the vegetation whose necessary death promotes the growth of plants. Farmers' cultures are more settled, and their religions reflect the complexity of living all year long in the same place. The intricate religious hierarchy of the Pueblo Indians reflects this complexity.

Religion Today. Passage of the American Indian Religious Freedom Act in 1978 in the United States and the recognition of aboriginal rights in the Canadian constitution have had far-reaching consequences. The search for identity now occurring among American Indians is also a search for religion. This search proceeds in two directions: one which seeks to find an Indian religion that can be shared among all tribes—a pan-Indian religion—and another which attempts to affirm the religious distinctiveness and variety found in each tribe before the first encounters with the Europeans. Current writings take strong stands in support of either of these positions.

Indian religion has always been a vital part of Indian life, and it continues to be. Since the beginning, missionaries and scholars alike have tried to impose their questions and answers on Indian ways of life, which always contained more than they saw. Therefore, Indians have always had to struggle to retain Indian spirituality, Indian sacrality, Indian Christianity, and Indian lifestyles.

Indian religions began as oral traditions. They were sung, danced, spoken, and lived. The written investigations of non-Indians, while valuable in recording a tradition, abstracted that tradition from the people who enlivened it. This orality is still present, contextualizing the everyday religious life of American Indians.

Harmony. Harmony is found in a deep sense of connectedness with the entire universe. Harmony and balance are to be expected and considered normal. One's life (individual and social) is to sustain this harmony among creatures and within space and time. There is harmony among all creatures, living and dead. Names such as Grandmother Spider, Corn Mother, and Coyote the Trickster help indicate this. The entire universe is like an intricate network of family members, each dependent upon each.

There are stories that connect the past and present in such a way that the listener becomes aware of how alive this present world is to its past. When one hears the Inuit story of Sedna the unwilling bride, one becomes aware of how the game animals of the sea grew from the joints of her fingers. When one hears the Pueblo stories of Corn Woman, one sees them reflected in the four colors of corn.

The best-known stories of the various Tricksters such as Coyote, Raven, Mink, and Blue Jay help one realize that each of these reorders the universe through its actions and thus returns the surrounding world to the harmony necessary for it to continue. These are not stories that attempt only to connect one to an ancient past; they are stories that enliven the present.

The world is always more than meets the senses. What one experiences is a world which is connected: a harmony of the inner world of one's dreams and visions and the outer world of one's senses. The vision quest of the young teen seeks not so much a spirit as a harmony between the inner self and the surrounding world marked by taking a new name which reflects that harmony. When one is sick, harmony has been destroyed, either because some object has entered into the sick person or because one's inner world has been stolen. The task of the "medicine" man or woman is to bring into balance the inner and outer worlds so that health or wholeness returns.

This same harmony is achieved through prayers, offerings, and ritual actions. Prayers may be short or long but are always seen as creative. In a literate culture the "pen is mightier than the sword"; in an oral culture the spoken word is the creative and ordering word. Offerings are found in many forms, but the pipe ceremony was, and is, one of the most common.

Center of the Circle. Space, time, and inner and outer worlds are all connected in the circle. Circles are sacred for Indians because they reflect and imitate shapes in nature. To be in harmony means to live as part of the circle. When a person stands and thinks of the six directions at equal points around him or her, the person is at the center of a three-dimensional circle.

It is in this knowledge of one's place in the circle that one realizes one's home. The horizon one sees from one's place in the circle reflects that landscape which is home. Land itself is important and central because it is coextensive with one's sense of harmony and thus identity. "Here" includes the waters, the earth, the shape of the horizon, the variations in the weather. That is why so many Indian tribes designate the four points of the compass as important. Directions enable one to know where one lives. In ways of life that focus on the land, on telling the story, and on the harmony between the inner world of dreams and visions and the outer world of hunting or planting, anything can be religious. In the world of today's American Indians, awareness of one's place within the harmony and interdependence of life leads to new questions and new answers about Indian religion and life.

Nathan R. Kollar

Sources for Further Study

Deloria, Vine, Jr. *God Is Red: A Native View of Religion*. Rev. ed. Golden, Colo.: Fulcrum, 2003. A plea by an American Indian for recognition of the uniqueness and pervasiveness of Indian life and religion.

Fogelson, Raymond D. "North American Religion: History of Study." In *The Encyclopedia of Religion*, edited by Mircea Eliade. New York: Macmillan, 1986. A summary review of the foundational materials necessary to describe Indian religion.

Gill, Sam D. *Native American Traditions: Sources and Interpretations*. Belmont, Calif.: Wadsworth, 1983. Advocates recognizing the tribal diversity of American Indian religion while striving to discover what is unique to those tribes.

Hultkrantz, Ake. *Belief and Worship in Native North America*. Edited by Christopher Vecsey. Syracuse, N.Y.: Syracuse University Press, 1981. Describes American Indian religion through discussion of supernatural spirits, sacred events, and hunter-agricultural lifestyle influences.

Paper, Jordan. "Methodological Controversies in the Study of Native American Religions." *Studies in Religion/Sciences Religieuses* 22, no. 3 (1993): 365-377. Reviews the state of contemporary studies of Indian religion with an argument for what is pan-tribal.

Silko, Leslie Marmon. *Ceremony*. New York: Viking Press, 1977. A popular and easy-to-read description of important Indian rituals.

Vecsey, Christopher. *Imagine Ourselves Richly: Mythic Narratives of North American Indians*. New York: Crossroads, 1988. A review and thoughtful commentary on stories that exemplify the oral traditions of American Indians.

See also: Death and Mortuary Customs; Ethnophilosophy and Worldview; Longhouse Religion; Native American Church; Peyote and Peyote Religion; Religious Specialists; Sacred, the; Sacred Narratives; Visions and Vision Quests.

Religious Specialists

Tribes affected: Pantribal
Significance: *Religious specialists such as shamans, priests, elders, and, at times of cultural upheaval, prophets, have all been crucial in guiding and maintaining tribal cultures.*

Observers of American Indian religions from Western traditions have often focused on aspects of supernaturalism in Indian religions, but that is only one way of approaching it. Another viewpoint emphasizes religion as maintaining harmony and reflecting the interdependence of all life. Both views can provide insights into the roles of religious specialists in Indian cultures.

Specialists and Otherworldly Religions. The supernatural is the realm beyond the natural world of the senses. The natural and supernatural worlds are linked by spirits that move back and forth between the two worlds. These spirits have power to change things in the natural world, and their presence may be sensed through the power inherent in special (sacred) things, people, times, places, words, and actions.

Religious specialists can interact with the spirit world through the use of sacred symbols in a manner that respects both the natural and supernatural worlds. The religious specialist's title differs from tribe to tribe. The following discussion will use terms (such as shaman and priest) devised by academic theorists to describe American Indian religions as they existed before contact with European Christian religions and, in the case of prophets, as they changed after contact.

Shamans. Mircea Eliade's 1964 description of the shaman has left its imprint on all descriptions of religious specialization. He described religious specialists who, through the use of trances, leave their bodies to go to a supernatural world to bring back techniques for dealing with the problems of the everyday world. Shamans may be selected a number of ways. Their own ecstatic experience may mark them as shamans; they may inherit the role from a parent or other ancestry. They may also be chosen by the people themselves. Once they are chosen, they are taught how to interact with the spirit world through dreams, visions, or trances and through traditional techniques learned from other shamans.

In general, a shaman undergoes an ecstatic experience in order to gain a spiritual status so as to practice divination and healing. In North America, however, ecstatic techniques are seldom used outside the Subarctic and Pacific Northwest as a consistent technique for dealing with the spirit world. Nevertheless, a set of common traits can be offered which more or less are found in certain people in each tribe. It should be noted that shaman is not a word often used by American Indians to describe these people.

Certain individuals profess to have a supernatural power that they use in this natural world. Sometimes this power is obtained in an initiatory vision. Such initiatory visions are especially found among the Inuit, where the shamans describe themselves as going to a supernatural world and, through great trial, gaining certain knowledge and techniques which are beneficial to their people. Part of this knowledge and technique is reflected in the use of esoteric language and rituals that are used to manipulate the spirit world and its powers. This power, as expressed in esoteric formulas, charms, songs, and certain objects, is often translated into English as "medicine." "Medicine" therefore is the power of the supernatural world as found in these words, chants, rituals, and objects. Many of these objects are beautiful and could be considered works of art; others are rather common looking. The Crow medicine bundle might contain feathers, bird and animal skins, animal and human bones, teeth, herbs, pigments, and minerals. Outside the tribal religious context, these things appear valueless. Yet within its religious context, such a bundle contains the history, power, and authority of an ancient people.

This power and knowledge are used by the shaman to predict the future and decide a course of action for individuals or the entire tribe. A shaman is thought to be able to control the weather, game animals, the course of war, and the search for lost objects. Among the Inuit, for example, Sedna, who lives under the sea, is the mistress of animals. The shaman helps control the hunt by going to Sedna and caring for her. The shaman many times has to clean her hair, which has become filthy because of the people's breaking of taboos, so that she will allow the animals to be captured.

The ability to tell the future is demonstrated by Plains shamans in the Shaking Tent Ceremony. In this ceremony the shaman enters a tent and reads the messages communicated by the spirits through the shaking of the tent. Among the Algonquian peoples, divination many times occurs by scorching an animal's shoulder blade and reading the resultant cracks and spots to determine the future.

There are other individuals who use supernatural powers to deal with sickness and wounds. Within a supernaturalist perspective, sickness results either from some object entering the body or from one's spirit leaving the body. The shaman has techniques to deal with either of these causes of illness. The object in one's body may be there either because a person put it there or because an illness, with a spirit life of its own, enters the body. The common ritual for withdrawing the evil object is to suck it out, with a tube, a horn, or one's mouth. Sometimes the extracted object is shown to everyone; sometimes it is not. Contending with the spirit life that somehow is not in the body is a more complex affair. The shaman many times must go into a trance, enter the spirit world, and fight for the person's life spirit to deal with this type of illness. These trances involve dramatic rituals that usually fill spectators and patient alike with a sense of awe and mystery.

Shamans are essential to all tribes; some are recognized and honored for their role, while others are feared and avoided for the power they possess. The *ichta* among the Tlingit (in British Columbia and the Yukon) is an example of a shaman who lives at the edge of society. He is dirty, his hair is unkempt, and his dress is rags. He has a number of masks, however, each of which represents and attracts a particular spirit. His power depends upon his ability to control these spirits. By going into a trance and dancing like an animal, he achieves his objectives.

A shaman's power can be used for good or for evil; it is beyond the ordinary or natural means of control. In many traditional North American cultures, the shamanic role is usually open to men and women. Males generally predominate except in California, where there are more female shamans. While the shamanic roles are, for the most part, played by individuals, there are some shamanic societies. The midewiwin of the central Algonquian is an example of a shamanic society. Depending on the tribe, these societies act as carriers of knowledge, as sharers of power, and as necessary helpers in achieving certain ceremonial objectives.

A quick survey of the various American Indian cultural areas reveals that among the Inuit the shaman is closest to the now-classic model of Eliade (Eliade based his model on the study of Siberian tribes). They work individually or in groups through the use of ecstasy and dramatic performances to cure, control the weather, and procure game. Among the Northwest Coast Indians, techniques of ecstasy are less common. There is a shamanic festival during the winter months among some Northwest Coast Indians in which dramatic canoe journeys are taken into the spirit world to struggle with the spirits to win back the souls of the sufferers gathered at the ceremony.

The Basin, Plateau, and Northern California areas find the sucking techniques of great importance to the shaman. The costumes assume more importance there than in other shamanic areas. Although visions and trances are expected of many individuals among the Plains and Prairie Indians, shamans stand out in how their spiritual power shows itself in their celebration of public ritual, tipi decoration, and the medicine bundles. The Southwest has a complex culture with a mix of various spiritual specialists, including priests.

Priests. Another type of religious specialist is the priest. The priest stands as a constant intermediary between the natural and supernatural worlds. In societies that emphasize hunting as a means of subsistence, there is a sense in which every hunter may be considered a priest. Through ritual action, the hunter balances the needs of both worlds so that the natural world sustains its ability to provide the tribe with food and security. Hunting is a sacred responsibility wherein killing animals is a religious act that makes the hunter into a priest. The hunter must be careful of taboos and must show proper respect for the spirits. The Blackfoot hunter, for example, gained his role in the tribe through a vision quest. In his vision or dream he found his role as hunter and his connection with the spirit world; the weapons became part of the spirit world revealed to him in the dream.

In an agricultural society priests play a unique role. The Pueblo Indians of the American Southwest, for example, are an agricultural society with a significant priestly class of religious specialists. Pueblo life is one of rich ceremony which is woven into every part of the day and is manifested in all tribal members' relationships with others. Each Pueblo town has an independent society of priests in charge of the rituals.

A general rule, with many exceptions, is that shamans dominate hunter societies and priests dominate agricultural societies. There is another type of religious specialist who has helped American Indians to respond to the challenge of change in their way of life—the prophet.

Prophets. In 1925, sociologist Max Weber provided a topology used by many in discussing religious specialization. He wrote of three types of religious leaders: magicians, prophets, and priests.

The description of the shaman used here includes many of the characteristics of what Weber would call the magician. Priests influence the spirit world by worship and petition; shamans influence it by the power of their spells and personal skills; priests are supported by the entire tribe and exercise their functions regularly; shamans work on an individual basis and do what is needed when it is needed; priests are powerful because of the class to which they belong and the techniques they learn; shamans' power comes from their personal experience. Both priest and shaman are part of the everyday life of the tribe. In times of crisis there arises another specialist whom Weber calls the prophet.

Prophets are agents of change who take personal responsibility for breaking with the established way of doing things. Prophets claim to know what to do because of their visions. Much like shamans, prophets find their role in life through their visions; unlike shamans they receive no remuneration for what they do. The fulfillment of the prophet's vision is its own reward.

There have been many prophets since first contact: San Juan Tewa of the Pueblo people (1680), Neolin of the Delaware (1750's), Handsome Lake of the Seneca (1799), Tenskwatawa of the Shawnee (1811), Smohalla of the Wanapum (1855), Wodziwob of the Northern Paiute (1860's), John Slocum of the Puget Sound Salish (1880's). From these prophets and many more there came a common message: The ways of white culture were evil, a return to the ancient ways as described by the prophet was necessary for the salvation of the tribe, and strict codes of morality must be enforced. The message was ritualized in many different ways. The prophets and the religions which flowed from them have been a significant force in revitalizing the religions of American Indians.

Beyond the Supernatural: Harmony. A description of Indian religions from a supernaturalist perspective, while valuable and founded on large amounts of written material gathered by non-Indian researchers, is dualistic. It has a bias in that it tends to focus on what is, or was, important to the European Christian: God, spirits, the other world, the power to change things, and a deeply felt conversion experience. The supernaturalist description many times leaves one with the impression that Indian religions are dualistic, with the spirits "out there" in the supernatural world and the shaman, prophet, priest here in the natural world. This is a religious model very much dependent upon European Christianity. Indian religion can be better described not in a dualistic sense but by using a holistic model of harmony and interdependence. An essential characteristic of Indian religions has been their oral character. Any non-Indian religion had to adapt itself to this orality to make any deep and significant headway into the Indian way of life. An oral culture recognizes the need of interdependence and harmony among the generations for its continuance; the need to live in the circle of life for the continuance of life itself. This is best shown in the central role of the elders.

Elders and Other Specialists. One's age is very important in Indian culture. Most tribes have some form of initiation of the young, for example, which often corresponds to the beginning of religious awareness and the acceptance of religious responsibilities. There are many rites of passage which give social form to the necessity of bringing the young more deeply into what is required for community survival.

Many tribes have formal religious societies into which individuals are initiated. These societies are sources of religious authority in the tribe. Members of the Crow Tobacco Society, the Winnebago Midewiwin, and the Tewa "Made People" bear enormous responsibility for religious actions.

Elders are especially important because with them resides religious wisdom, religious memory, and religious experience. In an oral culture the elders bring the "how, what, and why" of the past into the present in order to forge the future. Without the elders there is no religion and no purpose and direction to life; in a sense, without their guidance there can be no tribe.

An oral culture also places great emphasis on storytellers. These religious specialists tell the stories which provide explanations for the why and how of present living. There are the stories told by the elders, but in many tribes there are also individuals who specialize in storytelling. Among the Zuñi an individual is appointed as Kyaklo, responsible for telling the creation story cycle. Once every four or eight years Kyaklo comes to a Zuñi village to tell the story. No Zuñi ever hears the entire story in one telling, yet the story is told. In an oral culture telling the story or stories is essential to religious life. Although these stories may deal with everyday life and the reasons for its existence, they are religious since they provide a purposeful direction and unity to individual and social living.

The same is true of the Indian sense of place and home. Land itself is important and central because it is coextensive with one's sense of harmony and thus identity. "Here" includes the waters, the earth, the shape of the horizon, and the variations in the weather. That is why so many Indian tribes give a religious meaning to the four points of the compass. Directions enable one to know where one lives. The stories reinforce the sense of place. Those who tell the stories, build the homes, and provide for "home" are religious specialists. In the Tlingit religion, for example, the house is a ceremonial and spatial representation of the special landscape. The house is a holy place dwelt in by the most recent expression of the ancestor, the *yitsati*. The house is the male domain. The wife does not know the meanings of the carvings inside the house. Childbirth happens outside the house. The keeper of the house (yitsati) is a priest whose only task is to perform the rituals associated with the house.

Nathan R. Kollar

Sources for Further Study

Eliade, Mircea. *Shamanism: Archaic Techniques of Ecstasy.* Rev. ed. Princeton, N.J.: Princeton University Press, 1964. This is the classic work on shamanism.

Gill, Sam D. *Native American Religions: An Introduction.* Belmont, Calif.: Wadsworth, 1982. Gill is an exponent of how investigators have read into the written materials their own desires about Indian religion. He should be read to balance the exaggerated romantic claims for a historical pan-Indian religion.

Hultkrantz, Ake. "Spirit Lodge: A North American Shamanistic Seance." In *Studies in Shamanism*, edited by Carl-Martin Edsman. Stockholm: Almquist & Wiksell, 1962. Various definitions of shamanism are reviewed which lead one to conclude, if one uses ecstasy as a normative, that the term "shaman" can be used only in a broad sense when dealing with North America.

Paper, Jordan. "Methodological Controversies in the Study of Native American Religions." *Studies in Religion/Sciences Religieuses* 22, no. 3 (1993): 365-377. Argues that because of the dynamic character of Indian religion the individual religions adapted and shared what was necessary for survival. Thus there are common religious elements today among the various tribal religions.

Weber, Max. *Economy and Society: An Outline of Interpretative Sociology*. Translated by Ephraim Fischoff et al., edited by Günther Roth and Claus Wittich. Berkeley: University of California Press, 1978. Weber provided religious studies with practical categories for discerning religious leadership.

See also: Death and Mortuary Customs; Ethnophilosophy and Worldview; Longhouse Religion; Medicine and Modes of Curing: Pre-contact; Native American Church; Peyote and Peyote Religion; Religion; Sacred, the; Sacred Narratives; Visions and Vision Quests.

Relocation

Tribes affected: Pantribal

Significance: *Though the relocation program launched by the U.S. government in the 1950's did not achieve its goal of assimilation, it did contribute to the rapid urbanization of Native Americans.*

The 1930's saw a departure in federal Indian policy from the usual goal of assimilating Indians into the mainstream of American society; instead, the "Indian New Deal" stressed the idea of tribal self-determination. After World War II, however, Congress and the Bureau of Indian Affairs (BIA) began to press for a return to assimila-

Relocation Routes, 1830's

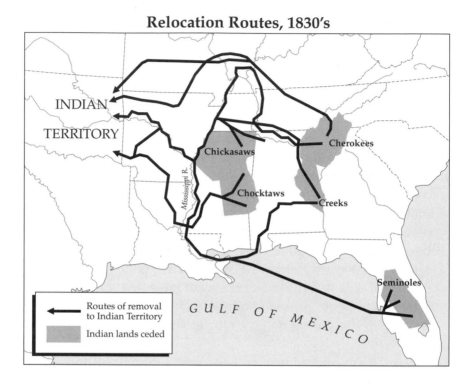

tion. In the early 1950's several assimilationist policies emerged: termination, which sought to "free" Native Americans by dissolving their tribes; the assumption by the states of more legal jurisdiction over Indian communities; and relocation, which sought to move Indians to large cities. Although at the time termination gained the most attention, relocation proved more persistent and had the more lasting effect.

Planning and Implementation. The BIA began its relocation efforts on a small scale in 1948, with efforts to place Navajos, whose reservation was believed to be overcrowded, in western cities. In 1952 the program was expanded into the national Voluntary Relocation Program. Offices were established on most reservations and in Oklahoma. BIA agents working on a quota system employed a hard-sell approach as they pressured Indians to relocate. Los Angeles, Chicago, and Denver were first designated to receive the new urban dwellers; seven other western and midwestern cities were later added to the list. Indians were sometimes sent to more distant cities on purpose in the hope that distance would lessen tribal ties.

Indians volunteering for the program were given a month to prepare for the transition. When the time came, they were given one-way bus or train tickets, fifty dollars each to cover moving expenses, and modest sums for subsistence. Once arrived in their new home cities, they received help from the local relocation office in finding housing and employment and a month's financial assistance (forty dollars per week for an individual or couple).

Urban Problems. The experience of many participants in the program often ended in frustration. Most reservation Indians were poorly prepared for life in urban America. Coming from cultures that were communal and cooperative, many found it hard to adjust to the impersonal and competitive character of metropolitan life. The BIA often provided little job training and inadequate counseling. Many Indians found that they could obtain only menial or temporary jobs. Too often, those relocating found themselves becoming slum dwellers cut off from family and friends. Alcoholism became a particular problem. The death in 1955 of war hero Ira Hayes, a Pima whose life was shattered by despair and alcoholism after he was relocated to Chicago, brought attention to the problems often faced by the new urban Indians. By 1959, a third of those participating in the program had returned to the reservation.

The BIA attempted to respond to mounting criticism of the program. Relocation officials began to moderate their sales pitches in the later 1950's, and more attention was given to preparing participants prior to departure. The program continued to attract criticism, however, and many Native Americans closely associated it with the widely hated policy of termination. After the latter policy was ended in 1962, relocation continued. During the administration of President John F. Kennedy, the program's name and focus changed to employment assistance. More attention was paid to job training, and more of an effort was made to place Indians in cities closer to their reservations.

Impact of Relocation. As a program to foster the assimilation of Indians into American society, relocation largely failed to achieve its aim. Yet, in other ways, some of them paradoxical, the program had important influences on Native American life.

The most evident effect of the program was to foster one of the most important Indian demographic trends of the second half of the twentieth century: urbanization. Despite the difficulties they encountered, Indians continued to move to urban areas. In 1940 only about 7 percent of Indians lived in cities; by 1980 almost half did, and by 2002 nearly two-thirds, or 66 percent, lived in urban areas (although still the lowest percentage of any racial group in the United States). There is some irony in the fact that the majority of Indians who moved to cities did so on their own and not as pro-

Relocated family outside of their home in South Dakota. *(National Archives)*

gram participants, largely because of suspicion of the BIA and the tendency to associate relocation with termination. The relocation program, however, did contribute to this informal migration. More than thirty-five thousand Indians relocated under the program, and the cities to which they moved (the ones with relocation offices) became the main centers of Native American urbanization.

Regardless of whether they were program participants, urban Indians continued to have more than their share of social problems. They also tended to be less tolerant of substandard conditions and more critical of government policies than reservation Indians. It is not surprising that many of the leaders of the more radical Indian movements of the 1960's and 1970's had urban backgrounds.

Moreover, urbanization contributed to the growth of Pan-Indianism. By bringing together Indians of many different tribal backgrounds, the relocation program encouraged interaction among them and the discovery that they shared many problems. It may be the greatest irony of relocation that this assimilationist program fostered instead a greater sense of Indian separateness and encouraged a more activist and confrontational attitude toward the federal government.

William C. Lowe

Sources for Further Study

Burt, Larry W. *Tribalism in Crisis: Federal Indian Policy, 1953-61.* Albuquerque: University of New Mexico Press, 1982.

Fixico, Donald Lee. *The Urban Experience in America.* Albuquerque: University of New Mexico Press, 2000.

Lobo, Susan, and Kurt Peters, eds. *American Indians and the Urban Experience.* Walnut Creek, Calif.: AltaMira Press, 2001.

Olson, James S., and Raymond Wilson. *Native Americans in the Twentieth Century.* Provo, Utah: Brigham Young University Press, 1984.

Philp, Kenneth R. *Termination Revisited: American Indians on the Trail to Self-Determination, 1933-1953.* Lincoln: University of Nebraska Press, 1999.

Prucha, Francis Paul. *The Great Father: The United States Government and the American Indians.* 2 vols. Lincoln: University of Nebraska Press, 1984.

See also: Alcoholism; Demography; Employment and Unemployment; Pan-Indianism; Urban Indians.

Repatriation

Tribes affected: Pantribal
Significance: *Repatriation is the process by which tribes are regaining their ancestors' human remains and sacred objects that are housed in non-Indian museums and other institutions.*

In ordinary usage, repatriation generally refers to the return of individuals, either of their own volition or by coercion (deportation), to their countries of origin. Within the context of modern Indian-white relations, however, the term denotes that process through which cultural, religious, and funerary objects and human remains are restored to their original tribal communities.

During the nineteenth and twentieth centuries, vast numbers of material goods were transferred from Indian to non-Indian hands. Historian Douglas Cole's description of the draining of Northwest Coast Indian communities of their cultural patrimony suggests the immense proportions of this removal:

> During the half-century or so after 1875, a staggering quantity of material, both secular and sacred . . . left the hands of their native creators and users for the private and public collections of the European world. The scramble was on. . . . By the time it ended there was more Kwakiutl material in Milwaukee than in Mamalillikulla, more Salish pieces in Cambridge than in Comox. The City of Washington contained more Northwest Coast material than the state of Washington and New York City probably housed more British Columbia material than British Columbia itself.

The situation was equally dire, if not worse, with regards to skeletal remains and funerary objects. Ethnohistorian John Wunder reported that in as many as two million Native American remains were disturbed in the twentieth century alone: "Grave robbers [were] encouraged and employed by museums, universities, government agencies, and private tourist businesses."

In 2000, attorneys Jack F. Trope and Walter R. Echo-Hawk identified the unilateral transfer of Indian property into non-Indian hands as one of the defining patterns of Indian-white relations in the United States. Lacking political influence and voice, tribes were powerless throughout most of their history of dealings with non-Indian Americans to challenge the social and economic structures and assumptions that generated this pattern. However, with the advent of the Civil Rights movement in the 1960's, the passage of the Indian Self-Determination and Education Assistance Act in 1975, the American Indian Religious Freedom Act in 1978, and continuing debates over the nature and operation of Indian sovereignty, the sociocultural and legal groundwork was established for tribes to litigate for the return of their deceased ancestors and burial objects for reinterment. During the 1980's, attorneys from the Native American Rights Association (NARA) and other organizations filed a series of suits in state courts to retrieve skeletal remains and funerary objects housed in the collections of state museums and historical societies. They also engaged in intense lobbying in several states, winning passage of repatriation acts in the Kansas, Nebraska, Arizona, and California legislatures.

With the discovery by a group of Northern Cheyennes in 1986 that the Smithsonian Institution housed nearly nineteen thousand Indian remains, these advocates shifted their attention from a state to a federal level, pursuing passage of a law that would protect native grave sites from future intrusions and would aid in the return of those remains and funerary objects held by nontribal institutions. Their efforts culminated in congressional passage of the National Museum of the American Indian Act (Public Law 101-185) on November 28, 1989. This law provided funds for the creation of a new Smithsonian museum (the National Museum of the American Indian (NMAI)) dedicated exclusively to the histories and cultures of the native peoples of the Americas. More important, it also instructed the museum to inventory the human remains and funerary objects in its possession, determine their tribal provenance, and establish a procedure that would allow tribes to petition for their return and traditional disposition, usually ceremonial reburial. The law also directed the NMAI to pursue its missions of repatriation, preservation, and education in consultation with tribal lay and spiritual leaders.

Nearly one year following its passage of the NMAI Act, Congress approved the Native American Grave Protection and Repatriation Act (Public Law 101-601). Generally referred to by the acronym NAGPRA, this law strengthened the protection of Native American burial sites set forth in earlier bills. It also ordered all federal and federally funded institutions to make available inventories of their Indian artifacts and human remains to their tribes of origin and to establish policies and procedures for the repatriation of these holdings. Noncompliance on the part of these organizations carried with it the loss of federal monies.

The philosophy and goals of repatriation remain sources of contestation, especially between tribes and archaeologists. Anthropologist Larry J. Zimmerman summarized the range of positions and responses found in each these two groups. According to Zimmerman, many Indians consider the "excavation, study, and curation of human remains [as] sacrilegious or, at the very least, disrespectful to the dead and spiritually dangerous." Many, he continues, see the issue as

> a form of scientific colonialism by the dominant society. Some demand no archaeological excavation or study and the complete return of all remains in existing collections. Others are more willing to compromise, realizing that potentially valuable information is provided by the remains.

With regard to archaeologists, Zimmerman has observed that their responses vary: Some wish to see passage of resolutions against reburial, whereas others hope for compromise legislation.

Whatever course the debate over repatriation might take, it seems clear that most of the decisions surrounding the contested rights and responsibilities at issue will be debated in the country's courts and legislatures. At the center of this evolution will be the increasing sentiment among many tribes that decision-making power over the disposition and treatment of their ancestors' remains, funerary objects, and cultural and religious artifacts is an essential part of their struggle for sovereignty.

Harvey Markowitz

Sources for Further Study

Cole, Douglas. *Captured Heritage: The Scramble for Northwest Coast Artifacts*. Norman : University of Oklahoma Press, 1995.

Mihesuah, Devon A., ed. *Repatriation Reader: Who Owns American Indian Remains*. Lincoln: University of Nebraska Press, 2000.

Trope, Jack F., and Walter R. Echo-Hawk. "The Native American Graves Protection Act: Background and Legislative History." In *Repatriation Reader: Who Owns American Indian Remains*, edited by Devon A. Mihesuah. Lincoln: University of Nebraska Press, 2000.

Zimmerman, Larry. "Reburial Issue." In *Archaeology of Prehistoric Native America: An Encyclopedia*, edited by Guy Gibbon. New York: Garland, 1998.

See also: Pan-Indianism.

Resource Use: Pre-contact

Tribes affected: Pantribal
Significance: *Native Americans traded food and other utilitarian resources along established routes.*

All Native Americans utilized surface and subsurface resources, which, in raw or finished form, were often traded with contiguous groups or to more distant areas along established trade routes. The natural differential occurrence of resources (and related manipulative skills) was the primary basis for some exogamous marriage patterns, the maintenance of complex group trading relationships, the development of inherited trading partners, and the existence of trade languages. Trade was conducted directly or by stages between groups from different culture areas, in some instances covering distances of many hundreds of miles. Trading by maritime groups and peoples inhabiting major riverine systems was facilitated by watercraft, and it was frequently a way for individuals to achieve socioeconomic status.

The control, esoteric knowledge, and skill of manipulating certain resources was sometimes based on a person's particular supernatural power, which was often maintained within a family by inheritance. Great respect for natural resources tended to characterize the worldview of Native Americans. Individual or collective ritual was observed before collecting and utilizing many food resources, and one's activities were controlled by behavioral and dietary taboos.

The primary concerns of all Native Americans, when exploiting and gathering natural resources, particularly foods, were the logistical strategies of converging at sites of productive occurrence when the resource was available, and of transporting such needed resources to inhabitation and storage areas. Consequently, hunters and gatherers subscribed to an annual subsistence round, one which required a high degree of mobility and knowledge of the terrain and its so-called carrying capacity, particularly of animal protein. Hunting and gathering cultures stored approximately three times the amount of food resources normally needed in case of prolonged winters or the destruction of stored foods by weather or animals. It was not unusual, during times of starvation, for people to partially exploit the stored nuts, seeds, and certain tubers of rodents and muskrats.

Dried high-protein foods, such as bison, salmon, and even pemmican, were traded to peoples devoid of such resources. The various highly prized by-products of land mammals and birds were traded in raw form or after skillful conversion by artisans. An example is laminated bows made of mountain sheep horn traded on the Plains. Traded food products became a necessary part of the utilitarian predation technology, but there was also a vast inventory of non-utilitarian trade resources, particularly various mollusk and dentalium shell beads.

Lithic (stone) materials, such as obsidian, slate, and chert for making projectile points and knives, were traded usually as "blanks"—the user would finish the tool as desired. Clays and orchers, and even native copper, were valuable natural resources, traveling considerable distances. In such cases, the item became more valuable the farther it was traded from the place of exploitation or mining. Resource areas, whether clamming beaches, hunting areas, nut or cambium groves, lithic sites, root fields, berry patches, or animal jumps, were the property of a particular group, but permission for exploitation (right of usufruct) was usually extended to non-kin members if requested.

The incursion of European American peoples and the early introduction of their trade items had, in some instances, a devastating effect upon the indigenous utilization and distribution of traditional resources, particularly the socioeconomic behaviors that had maintained land-use patterns. Tribalization and the insidious development of restricted reservations, invariably on nonproductive lands, essentially destroyed Native American access to and preservation of natural resources and effectively terminated a traditional way of life and sociopolitical and economic autonomy. For example, the destruction of bison and the reduction of salmon runs forced a drastic change in many people's subsistence base, bringing a rapid deterioration of health and creating a sense of relative deprivation.

As time passed, various governmental legislation further reduced the Native American land base and subsequent control of resources. In 1955, with the U.S. government's need for uranium, coal, oil, and certain metal ores facing off against pending native lawsuits for loss of traditional lands and resources, government legislation was passed to terminate reservations and Indian status. It is only relatively recently that some Native American tribes have been able to gain partial control of some of their resources, particularly in the development of tourism by those tribes situated on navigable bodies of water. Some Native American tribes receive annual per capita payments from resources, such as oil, gas, and timber, extracted from aboriginal areas.

John Alan Ross

See also: Metalwork; Resources; Subsistence; Technology; Tools; Trade.

Resources

Tribes affected: Pantribal
Significance: *Reservations and tribal governments confront a difficult task in deciding on the most effective ways to develop a reservation's natural resources.*

Natural resources such as coal, timber, natural gas, uranium, and oil have important places in many tribes' economic development plans. Reservations comprise some of the poorest regions in the United States, so the type of development and the extent of tribal control over these assets is crucial.

General History. Tribal economic dependence on the sale of natural resources gained importance in the late nineteenth century as tribal leaders and individuals began to sell reservation land and individual allotted lands. Though tribes retained possessory rights to timber and subsurface minerals, the absence of market demand and of legislation that granted tribes authority to sell timber or minerals apart from the land hindered development. Resources were simply ceded during land sales of this era, depriving tribes of benefits from these commodities.

In 1891, Congress enacted leasing legislation that provided a mechanism for tribes to lease land, coal, oil, and natural gas without selling their real estate. Tribes could control outside access to energy minerals by approving or disapproving of leases. At the time, few leases were made because of low demand for tribal resources.

Congress revised reservation leasing in the 1938 Omnibus Tribal Leasing Act, which required competitive bidding and the posting of bonds by successful bidders. The legislation favored outside developers, not the tribal landowners, because it emphasized quick monetary returns for the tribe in the leasing process rather than ensuring technical expertise on a tribe's behalf.

These reservation leasing guidelines were quickly outdated, but they remained operative for the next four decades. During that time, outsiders leased tribal minerals at less than market value and continued to enjoy the privilege thanks to continuous production clauses. Some outside interests even built power plants on reservations.

Energy Minerals. As a result of the 1970's energy crisis, tribal leaders demanded greater roles in making energy mineral decisions and in writing regulations governing reservation mineral development. Reservations possessed 3 percent of the nation's oil and natural gas reserves and 13 percent of the coal reserves.

Rising demand for reservation energy resources created a false impression that tribes possessing coal, oil, and natural gas were wealthy. In 1976, the comptroller general reported that tribal resources were underdeveloped and that information on the extent of tribal energy resources was lacking, depriving tribes of revenue. At the same time, the United States failed to monitor lessor reclamation compliance, production figures, and royalty collection from reservation energy contracts. As a result, some tribes were reluctant to enter into energy development simply because too many questions remained unanswered. The Council of Energy Resource Tribes was created, its primary task to provide tribal leaders with energy mineral information. Tribal leaders became increasingly convinced of the need for local tribal control over energy mineral resources.

As a result of Native American assertions regarding control over resource development on tribal land, the Bureau of Indian Affairs in 1977 began requiring reservation energy mineral leasing contractors to comply with the provisions of the 1977 Surface Mining Control and Reclamation Act. In 1982, as a result of tribal initiative, Congress passed the Indian Minerals Development Act, allowing tribes to become energy producers.

Greater tribal control did not end energy mineral development problems. Monitoring and compliance issues continued to hinder tribal efforts to secure fair market value for their resources and to assure that tribal lands were not ruined in the process of mineral extraction.

Timber. In 1910, Congress passed legislation authorizing the logging of reservation forests. To fund a professional forestry program, administrative charges were deducted from tribal timber contracts. In 1972, the administrative fee program was modified and passage of the 1975 Indian Self-Determination and Education Assistance Act gave tribal leaders increased tribal control over reservation timber.

Reservation leaders began planning to increase timber revenues by developing value-added wood product industries. The creation of the Intertribal Timber Council in 1979 provided tribes with technical assistance to develop wood product industries. In 1990, Congress passed the National Indian Forest Resources Management Act, which increased tribal decision-making powers over reservation timber and provided the potential for greater monetary support for tribal conservation efforts.

Despite positive directions in reservation natural resource development, tribes do not possess adequate energy minerals and forested lands to control markets. As a result, tribes remain market dependent. At best, natural resource revenues provided sporadic, small per-capita payments to tribal members during the duration of a timber cutting contract or an energy mineral lease. Natural resources have not provided long-term reservation employment opportunities because of the vagaries of the energy and lumber markets.

Richmond Clow

Sources for Further Study

Ambler, Marjane. *Breaking the Iron Bonds: Indian Control of Energy Development*. Lawrence: University Press of Kansas, 1990.

Fixico, Donald L. *The Invasion of Indian Country in the Twentieth Century: American Capitalism and Tribal Natural Resources*. Niwot: University Press of Colorado, 1998.

Reno, Philip. *Mother Earth, Father Sky, and Economic Development: Navajo Resources and Their Use*. Albuquerque: University of New Mexico Press, 1981.

U.S. Congress. Senate. Select Committee on Indian Affairs. Special Committee on Investigations. *Final Report and Legislative Recommendations: A Report of the Special Committee on Investigations of the Select Committee on Indian Affairs*. Washington, D.C.: U.S. Government Printing Office, 1989.

See also: Land Claims; Resource Use: Pre-contact.

Rite of Consolation

Tribes affected: Iroquois Confederacy, including Cayuga, Mohawk, Onondaga, Oneida, Seneca

Significance: *This religious, social, and political funeral ceremony functions to ease grief and restore leadership.*

The Rite of Consolation is a ceremonial event that takes place on the death of one of the principal chiefs of the Iroquois Confederacy. The members of the confederacy, in the persons of the assigned leaders, assemble. The bereaved nation is host and is visited by those called the "clearminded," who come to offer consolation, advice, and support. The rite consists of a prescribed series of songs and orations. Taken together, these compose a long elegy; the songs and speeches—traditionally keyed to belts of wampum—offer spiritual insight into the meaning of life and rationalize death within a philosophical system.

The rite offers more, however, than comfort for the loss of an individual. It reminds the participants of the founders and history of the league, in particular the heroic Hiawatha and his antagonist, Atotarho, making it an educational and patriotic event. Furthermore, the rite provides for the choice and installation of a successor to the late chief. The new leader is given the name of his predecessor, and in this way the names of the original leaders are preserved. The rite thus offers a symbolic death and rebirth, both of the individual leader and of the healed and restored community.

Helen Jaskoski

See also: Death and Mortuary Customs; Political Organization and Leadership.

Rites of Passage

Tribes affected: Pantribal
Significance: *Rite of passage ceremonies mark status-changing events in the life cycle, such as birth, naming, puberty, initiation, marriage, and death.*

Rites of passage are ceremonies associated with the transformation from one stage of life to another. The four primary events of birth, naming, puberty, and death are celebrated as spiritual occasions. The secondary events of marriage and initiation into societies are considered social by some tribes and spiritual by others.

Three stages can be identified in any rite of passage. In the separation phase one loses the old status; in the marginal phase one has essentially no identity; and in the re-entry phase one takes on a new identity within the community, gaining new rights and obligations. An element of danger exists in the transition. The time between two states has a mysterious quality, during which the individual requires protection from potential harm. This marginal phase is a symbolic death of the old status.

Childbirth. Among traditional people, childbirth was a time of crisis for mother and child, since the mortality rate for both was highest then. Childbirth was also regarded as a time of danger for males in the community. The miraculous new life within the mother's body held the sacred power of the Creator. It could endanger those not as powerful. This belief, along with the practical concerns of comfort and privacy, plus the need for concentrated attention during birthing, led to the segregation of women in labor. The period of labor represented the "between" phase, requiring protection for both mother and infant through petitions to the spirits for guidance.

A woman in labor was usually assisted in the birthing hut by other women, but a Southwest Caddo woman went alone to a nearby river when labor began. She built her own shelter, delivered her baby, and, even in winter, bathed herself and the child in the river. She returned to the village right away. Among the Nez Perce of Idaho, mother and infant were secluded for as long as three months after delivery, and in the Great Basin tribes the father also stayed in bed and ate special foods.

Naming. Anyone without a name was considered powerless, because the spirits would not recognize them. Not all babies received names; some tribes waited until a particular trait suggested a name. A name could be revealed through a parent's dream, or given in a formal ceremony after months or years of waiting. A person could have several names throughout life: as an infant, a young child, at puberty, and upon a worthy achievement.

Omaha newborns were thought to be just other beings in nature. An infant was presented to the powers of nature with prayers for safety on its journey through life. With its first steps, the baby became a member of the tribe and was given a new pair of moccasins containing a little hole. In case the spirits called, the child could respond, "I can't travel now; my moccasins are worn out."

Marriage. Some tribes had no marriage ceremony. A couple would announce their plans, but the tribe might not consider them truly married until a child was born. In more formal marriages, the groom brought gifts for the bride's parents, such as horses in the

Plains, and cedar blankets or carved boxes in the Northwest. Marriage was accomplished through an exchange of gifts between both families among the California Pomo.

A Cherokee bride and groom feasted separately with their relatives, then met later in the community ceremony. The groom's mother gave him a leg of venison and a blanket; the bride's mother gave her an ear of corn and a blanket. The couple exchanged the food and wrapped themselves in their blankets. A similar ritual completed an Ojibwa marriage; in addition, the couple had the hems of their coats sewed together.

Hopi marriage customs required the girl to grind corn for several days at home, then go to her groom's home and grind corn for three more days. The groom's aunts called her lazy and jokingly taunted her for stealing their favorite nephew. On the wedding day, the two were joined for life when the couple's mothers washed the bride and groom's heads in one basin and twisted their hair together. Later, they went to the edge of the mesa to pray to the rising sun. After the wedding breakfast, the groom went with townsmen into the kiva (ceremonial chamber) to weave the bride's wedding garments while she spent the long days grinding more corn. The two white robes and the long white belt would be used eventually to wrap her body for her journey into the spirit world.

Death, Burial, and Mourning. The greatest of mysteries surrounds this final rite of passage, and the most varied ceremonies mark the transition. Among the Apache and Navajo, where death is deeply feared, burial is simple and swift, and mourning is brief. The deceased is bathed, dressed in fine clothing and jewelry, and then placed in a crevice and covered with stones. If the person died at home, the house and possessions were burned and the family moved to a new house.

In the Great Basin, burial sites were caves, and on the Plains, scaffolds and trees were used. Cremation was common in California; wooden cabins, boxes, or canoes on posts were burial places in the Northwest. The Eastern Ojibwa wrapped their dead in birchbark and placed them in a grave lined with cedar boughs. A small house was built over the grave, a fire was lit, and food was left for the spirit's journey.

The Iroquois Rite of Consolation, a ceremony for a deceased sachem (chief), recounted deeds of ancestors, acknowledged the departed one's greatness, and comforted the bereaved, symbolically reinforcing the past, present, and future of the Iroquois League.

The Huron of the East held a Feast of the Dead every ten to twelve years. The souls were released in an extended mourning ceremony as relatives removed bodies from temporary burial sites, cleaned the bones and put them into bundles. Mourners carried their bundles to a communal burial site, and at dawn, with a great wailing, they deposited their bundles into the pit. This mingling of ancestral bones symbolized an obligation to tribal unity.

An extraordinary burial custom existed among the Natchez of the Southeast, where the highest class members were required to marry commoners. When the highborn one died, the commoner spouse and children were sacrificed to accompany the deceased on the journey.

Gale M. Thompson

Sources for Further Study

Allen, Paula Gunn. *The Sacred Hoop: Recovering the Feminine in American Indian Traditions*. Reprint. Boston: Beacon Press, 1992.

Garbarino, Merwyn S. *Native American Heritage*. Boston: Little, Brown, 1976.

Johnston, Basil. *Ojibwa Ceremonies*. Illustrated by David Beyer. Toronto: McClelland and Stewart, 1982.

Niethammer, Carolyn. *Daughters of the Earth: The Lives and Legends of American Indian Women*. New York: Collier Books, 1977.

Turner, Victor W. *The Ritual Process: Structure and Anti-Structure*. Chicago: Aldine, 1969.

See also: Children; Death and Mortuary Customs; Feast of the Dead; Marriage and Divorce; Menses and Menstruation; Names and Naming; Puberty and Initiation Rites; Rite of Consolation; Women.

Sachem

Tribes affected: Massachusett, Mohegan, Narragansett, Nauset, Niantic, Nipmuc, Pawtucket, Pequot, Pocomtuck, Quinnipiac, Wampanoag

Significance: *The general term "sachem" was used to designate band leaders and tribal chiefs among the Algonquian-speaking peoples of southern New England.*

Along the coastal region of southern New England in the early contact period, the word *sachem* was used for political leaders. In northern New England, the corresponding term was *sagamore*. The sachem was most commonly the head or leader of a single village (or band). Some sachems, however, had a more extensive but ill-defined influence over an entire tribe or alliance of villages. Examples of sachems with this wider influence were Massasoit and his

A sketch depicting the sachem Atotarho (right), a founding member of the Iroquois confederacy. *(Library of Congress)*

son Metacomet (King Philip) of the Wampanoag, and Miantonomo of the Narragansett. Whether a sachem's authority was confined to a single village or was much wider, his power was limited by tribal traditions and exercised through persuasion. Important decisions were made in consultation with a council of important men (called *pneises* among the Massachusett and Wampanoag). Sachems were chosen from among men born into a chiefly lineage or family, the office descending most commonly from father to son. Occasionally women served as sachems (called "squaw sachems" by the English). Weetamoo of the Pocasset was an example. The sachem assigned agricultural fields, sentenced criminals, and was responsible for diplomacy and external trade. A sachem dwelt in an unusually large wigwam and was supported by the work of his wives, by the yield from special fields cultivated for him, and by gifts or tribute. This food and other goods were given back through feasts and reciprocal gifts.

Bert M. Mutersbaugh

See also: Political Organization and Leadership.

Sacred, the

Tribes affected: Pantribal
Significance: *Every American Indian tribe holds a concept of the sacred at the core of its belief system; although known by different names, this concept is related to spiritual power.*

In American Indian tribal languages, there is no word for "religion." Religion is not a separate category with specific times and places for expression. Rather, the spiritual is embedded in everything that exists and is therefore part of every activity. Sacred ways were, and are, the technology of tribal peoples. Through a system of shared beliefs, symbols, and practices, this technology of the sacred provides the structure which determines the customs and guides the daily life of a people.

Aside from formal ceremony, everyday tasks such as hunting, gathering, preparing food, making art and music, and fashioning tools and clothing are performed within the context of sacred knowledge and often involve ritual action. When these common activities are combined with the use of symbols, colors, or numbers and various songs, chants, or prayers, the invisible is brought into visibility and is to some degree a manifestation of the sacred.

The sacred is equivalent to spiritual power, and according to tribal peoples, it can be manifested in seemingly inanimate objects such as a star, a lake, or a stone. These things are not worshiped for themselves but are honored because they express the intangible, yet very real power of the sacred. In this way, they become something else, while paradoxically remaining in their original forms. They are held in awe and respect by all, but only people who have power, or "medicine," can perceive their sacred quality and appropriately use sacred objects.

The acquisition of power is arduous and sometimes dangerous. Technicians of the sacred have gained their wisdom by experimenting with the forces of nature. After extensive guidance from an elder, and then ritual "purification" in preparation to receive it, they must undertake the solitary journey to seek their power. Once received, the power must be honored and rightly used. Spiritual power is respected, even feared, by the untrained. For example, some tribal people express concern about repercussions if they do not act correctly in the presence of a medicine bundle.

Spiritual leaders carry responsibility for sacred ways, not for themselves, but on behalf of the people. Humility and integrity are desirable characteristics for those granted power, because the use of sacred power for personal gain has serious consequences. Power can turn against the one who misuses it, and the result can be illness, loss of power, or even death. To keep the sacred ways alive, they must be shared by the people. In the context of sacred ceremony, both the people and the traditions are revitalized.

Names of the Sacred. The source of sacred power is known by various names such as *Manitou (Manido, Manito)* to the Ojibwa,

Wakan (Wakanda) to the Sioux, and *Orenda* to the Iroquois, with each tribe having its own way of interpreting, contacting, and making use of this power. Manifestations of power can be found most often in nature, and these spiritual forces can be addressed through offerings, prayer, and a sacrifice, a term which means "to make sacred" or to empower with ritual. After the time of European contact, comparisons made to Christianity led to misinterpretations of some of the original meanings of the terms wakan, manitou, and orenda. For example, Kitchi Manitou, Great Spirit, became commonly accepted as the equivalent of God. Many tribes also use the term Creator when referring to this source of sacred power.

Manitou. As chief of the manitous, Kitchi (also spelled "Gitche" and "Gitshe") Manitou is not a personality but the expression of all good. Beneficent, yet invisible and nonmaterial, Kitchi Manitou is the Uncreated God, the source of all. Other manitous, eternal spirits brought into being at the creation, are prototypes of rocks, plants, animals, birds, and elemental forces. Sun, moon, winds, thunder, lightning, and even the seasons are manitous.

In Ojibwa belief, everything was animate, and manitous had power to cause great problems. Fortunately, in such a potentially hostile environment, the help of compassionate spirits could be obtained though humble petition. For the Ojibwa, the seeking of a vision was the preferred method for finding one's manitou or guardian spirit. The seeker went out in solitude, prayed, offered tobacco, and sacrificed by fasting for several days until contact had been made, often in a dream. It was believed that the more humble or pitiable the seeker, the more likely the spirits were to grant a vision.

Once a relationship was made, it was usually kept secret so that the sacred power received would not be diminished. The person could call upon the guardian spirit for help in many circumstances. Among the manitous were cedar and birch trees, deer, bear, moose, otter, sturgeon, hummingbird, and eagle. Spirit helpers responded to prescribed rules within the tradition, and members of the Midewiwin, the Grand Medicine Society, could assist in making contact with the appropriate manitous for any situation.

Wakan. As a general term, "wakan" means sacred or holy, imbued with the life-giving force of spiritual power. A thing or person is wakan to the extent that the principles of that sacred quality are expressed. Although originally wakan had many meanings and several manifestations, perhaps the order of spiritual powers of the Sioux would be most comparable to the hierarchy of Christian deities, with Wakan (Great Mystery) akin to the Godhead and Wakan-Tanka (Great Spirit) similar to God. Wanbli Galeshka (Spotted Eagle), who carries prayers to Great Spirit, could be compared to Jesus Christ.

A holy person, wichasha wakan, has the power to make others wakan. Their powers have been acquired through dreams and vision experiences, often over many years, and they are qualified to lead others in seeking spiritual vision. Holy people are sometimes incorrectly called "medicine people." In some traditions the terms "medicine" and "spiritual power" are synonymous; however, among the Sioux, a medicine person is one who has knowledge of curative herbs. When using herbs, a medicine person is said to be "doctoring." It is possible for a holy person to be a medicine person as well.

A wakan woman brought the calf pipe to the Sioux. White Buffalo-Calf Maiden, known also as Calf Pipe Woman, presented the pipe bundle to the people, calling it lela wakan, very sacred, and telling them, "When you pray with this pipe, you pray for and with everything." The sacred pipe, sometimes incorrectly called peace pipe, was given so the people might have knowledge. This wakan woman also taught that the wingeds, the two-leggeds, and the four-leggeds, and those born to them, were all wakan. As gifts from Wakan-Tanka (Father or Grandfather) they deserved respect. She explained that the earth (Mother or Grandmother) was wakan and that every step taken upon her should be a prayer. Through the sacred pipe, the people were connected to all that is sacred and told to walk the path of life—the sacred red road—and to honor everything and everyone as wakan.

Orenda. The Iroquois term "orenda" identifies a power that can be likened to electricity in that it is invisible, flowing energy. As limitless power orenda is not a spirit or entity but is present in earth, sky, nature—all that exists. Inherent in this power, and derived from it, are the dualisms of visible and invisible, material and spiritual, life and beyond life. The Master of Life, who willed the world into being, had an evil brother who constantly battled against him. Although the Iroquois had no hierarchy of spirit beings to direct orenda, all supernatural power came from this impersonal energy, which was accessed through dreams. A deep reverence was held for one's own orenda. Beyond this power the Iroquois believed in animal spirits, such as eagle and bear, and many unranked supernaturals, including the Earth Mother, Sun, and the Master of Life.

Adults and young people sought to communicate with the supernatural individually through vision experiences or collectively through tribal ceremonies. The Iroquois had no category of spiritual guides to the people; such duties were performed as needed by those designated to maintain the traditions. These males and females were called Keepers of the Faith. Others had acquired the ability to cure illnesses. Members of the False Face Society, a well-known Iroquois curing society, would arrive at a patient's house wearing wooden masks carved to represent spiritual beings. Amid grunts, shouts, and scraping of their turtle-shell rattles, they entered the house and scattered ashes on the patient to drive away the illness. They were given gifts and special food in exchange for the curing ritual.

A practical application of the concept of the sacred exists within the Iroquois' agricultural tradition in the special designation given to the main foods of the Iroquois—corn, beans, and squash. They were known as "the three sisters," and the people called them "our life" or "our supporters." It was believed that each kind of food was originally brought about by supernatural causes, and it was the custom to offer the first harvest obtained to the particular spirit who controlled it. Festivals were held to honor strawberries, maple sap, green corn, and ripe corn.

Feminine Aspects of the Sacred. For many Pueblo tribes, the source of the sacred, the spirit within everything, is seen as predominantly female. Many tribal people consider the power to make life to be the source of all power. Old Spider Woman, Corn Woman, Earth Woman, and Thought Woman—all are aspects of this female Creator, for out of thought all things are born. In her various aspects, woman makes all things sacred. Creative power, made visible in the mystery of birth, gives predominance in many tribes to the role of mother. Nor is woman's power only life-giving; she also destroys. Born of Earth Mother, all life returns to her in death to complete the sacred cycle.

Gale M. Thompson

Sources for Further Study

Allen, Paula Gunn. *The Sacred Hoop*. Boston: Beacon Press, 1986. Reprint. Boston: Beacon Press, 1992. Essays written from the perspective of a Laguna-Sioux Indian woman. Shows importance of Native American female deities to creation myths. Poetry, chants, and stories emphasize the significance of oral tradition. Detailed notes, extensive categorized bibliography, index.

Beck, Peggy V., Anna Lee Walters, and Nia Francisco. *The Sacred: Ways of Knowledge, Sources of Life*. Redesigned ed. Tsaile, Ariz.: Navajo Community College Press, 1992. A comprehensive study of sacred ways. Incorporates numerous quotations from well-known texts and from interviews with members of various tribes. Includes definitions within text. Suggests additional readings for each chapter. Photographs, illustrations, drawings, maps, and charts. Extensive bibliography, listing of films and filmstrips, index.

Black Elk. *The Sacred Pipe*. Edited by Joseph Epes Brown. Norman: University of Oklahoma Press, 1953. Narrative of teachings from Black Elk, holy man of the Oglala Sioux, from 1947 to 1950.

Features story of the sacred pipe. Details the seven rites of the Sioux, including sweatlodge, vision quest, and Sun Dance. Photographs, illustrations, index.

Brown, Joseph Epes. *The Spiritual Legacy of the American Indian.* New York: Crossroad, 1982. A collection of essays on the diversity of Native American spiritual heritages within the context of world religious traditions. Quotations, songs, chants, and myths. Chapter notes; map of North American culture areas.

Eliade, Mircea. *The Sacred and the Profane.* Translated by Willard R. Trask. New York: Harcourt, Brace, 1959. Defines the opposition between two modalities of experience: sacred and profane, or real and unreal. Discusses sacred space and time; examines concept of nature as sacred. Compares Christianity, Buddhism, Hinduism, and Native American religions. Bibliography, index.

Highwater, Jamake. *The Primal Mind.* New York: Harper & Row, 1981. A contrast of lifestyles and worldviews of American Indians with ideas and values of Western culture. Highwater redefines "primitive" mind and suggests the possibility of a potent blending of primal and Western thought. Bibliography, name and source index, subject index.

Landes, Ruth. *Ojibwa Religion and the Midéwiwin.* Madison: University of Wisconsin Press, 1968. An anthropological account of Ojibwa life in the 1930's. Enhanced by narratives from two Ojibwa informants, a shaman and a visionary. Rituals, songs, and prayers of the Midewiwin. Photographs and illustrations. Glossary, bibliography, index. Appendices include dreams, birchbark, scrolls, rock paintings.

See also: Bundles, Sacred; Calumets and Pipe Bags; Ethnophilosophy and Worldview; Religion; Religious Specialists; Sacred Narratives.

Sacred Narratives

Tribes affected: Pantribal
Significance: *Sacred narratives, important to tribal identity and reflecting tribal philosophy, tell of such things as the origin of the world, of the people themselves, and of certain ceremonies.*

The most ancient and sacred narratives are those that recount the origins of the earth and the development of its life forms. Many of these events also incorporate understanding of historical events such as migrations, establishment of clans, or the transition from hunting-gathering to an agricultural economy. Two major creation story themes are the earth-diver story and the emergence myth; these stories explain how the present world of human beings and society came into being, and both are widely distributed over North America.

Earth-Diver Stories. Earth-diver stories tell of the creation or re-creation of the world. An Ojibwa (Chippewa) story provides an example. The great trickster/hero Wenebojo (or Manibozho) has, by failing to curb his instincts, caused a flood to cover the world; it has left him standing on top of a tree. Wenebojo sends down small animals to bring up a bit of earth, but the first ones fail. Finally, Muskrat floats up dead but with a grain of sand in each paw and in his mouth; Wenebojo breathes life back into Muskrat and then, flinging the grains of sand over the water, creates an island that will become the present world. The previous world was considered to be a different place, one which is now inaccessible to ordinary people. The story has been interpreted on various levels: a psychological/moral interpretation sees Wenebojo as Everyman, who must dive within himself to form his character; a symbolical/historical exegesis notes that the story offers a symbolic union between Wenebojo and the earth, establishing the people belonging to Wenebojo as the appropriate dwellers in this particular place.

Emergence Stories. Also distributed throughout the continent but most concentrated in the Southwest are emergence narratives of creation. These stories recount the travels of the people as they begin in lower worlds under the earth and move upward through succeeding levels until finally, with the help of powerful beings such as Hummingbird, they are able to squeeze through a narrow passageway such as a reed or hollow log into the present world. The number of underground worlds varies from story to story, as do the identities of the sacred helpers and the natures of the underground worlds.

These are stories of evolution and progression, modeled on the processes of fetal development and birth, which also depict moral and social evolution. Typically, the people begin in a sorry state, sometimes blind or maimed, copulating and killing indiscriminately, and they learn human and humane behavior as part of their progress to the present world. Emergence stories establish the relationship of the people to their territory through the metaphor of being born from the earth; they also include migration stories and establish the origins of clans and tribal laws. Choctaw origin stories show many of these features: the Choctaw origin story tells of a migration from the southwest, from the great cultures of central Mexico, and of an emergence from a sacred burial mound at the center of their homeland along the Mississippi.

Other Creation Stories. Emergence and earth-diver stories are well known and have been published in many versions and texts. Many other stories, equally profound, are less noted. For example, the creation myth of the Achumawi, a small nation living near Mount Shasta in northern California, is a story rich in insight, humor, and mystical understanding. The world emerges from a haze of mist and hills through the thinking and acting of mysterious beings Annikadel, Aether Man, Sun Woman and Moon Man, Coyote, Frog Woman and others. In many stories the first creator is a mysterious or remarkable being such as Annikadel, but in other cases the creator is a familiar creature, such as Grandmother Spider, who, in the Southwest, spins the world from her body and creates things by thinking of them and naming them.

Trickster Stories. The figure of Coyote the Trickster has entered the folklore of the mainstream culture. Originally, Coyote, like the other trickster figures, was a being of supernatural power who determined through his various adventures the shape and function of the present world. Paul Radin's publication of *The Trickster* (1956) and subsequent commentary by scholars such as Karl Kerenyi and Carl Gustav Jung made this figure one of the most familiar to non-Indians. The Winnebago trickster story is an extended meditation on the relationship between nature and society as it examines the possibilities and consequences of the behavior of purely "natural" man unmediated by any social structures. It has also been read as an allegory of development from immaturity and infantilism to something approaching adulthood, and it includes an account of trickster's part in creating the world. The Winnebago trickster is a warrior; other beings that play the part of trickster in different tribes include, besides Coyote, Blue Jay, Raven, and Hare.

Origins of Ceremonies. A great many sacred stories relate the origins of a religious ceremony. These stories often follow a pattern of infraction/punishment-exile/test/guidance/return. The protagonist breaks some rule or law, is punished by exile or even death, receives the guidance of supernatural beings in passing various tests, and eventually returns to the community with a ceremony or song that was learned on the journey and that will help the community heal and sustain itself. A highly elaborated example of one of these ceremonial origin myths is the story of the stricken brothers that underlies the Nightway, the most complex of the Navajo chantways. The journey theme of ceremonial origin myths has inspired contemporary writers such as Leslie Marmon Silko, whose novel *Ceremony* (1977) is structured as such a story.

Helen Jaskoski

Sources for Further Study
Bierhorst, John, ed. *The Red Swan: Myths and Tales of the American Indians*. New York: Farrar, Straus & Giroux, 1976.

Bright, William. *Coyote Stories*. Chicago: University of Chicago Press, 1978.

Diné bahane: The Navajo Creation Story. Translated by Paul G. Zolbrod. Albuquerque: University of New Mexico Press, 1984.

Hale, Horatio. *The Iroquois Book of Rites*. 1883. Reprint. Edited by William N. Fenton. Toronto: University of Toronto Press, 1963.

Jones, William, ed. *Ojibwa Texts*. Edited by Truman Michelson. Publications of the American Ethnological Society 7, no. 2 (1919).

Matthews, Washington, ed. *The Night Chant*. 1902. Reprint. New York: AMS Press, 1978.

Radin, Paul, ed. *The Trickster: A Study in American Indian Mythology*. London: Routledge & Kegan Paul, 1956. Reprint. New York: Schocken Books, 1972.

Thompson, Stith, ed. *Tales of the North American Indians*. 1929. Reprint. Bloomington: Indiana University Press, 1968.

See also: Ethnophilosophy and Worldview; Manibozho; Oral Literatures; Religion; Religious Specialists; Tricksters.

Salmon

Tribes affected: Northwest Coast tribes

Significance: *The abundance of salmon in predictable spawning runs made them a critical food resource on the Northwest Coast.*

Salmon frequent the oceans off both coasts of North America, but Pacific salmon have had the greatest significance to American Indians. Pacific salmon (*Oncorhyncus*) are of five species: pink, chum, coho, sockeye, and chinook. All are anadromous, living primarily in the ocean and returning to fresh water to spawn. During those spawning runs, huge numbers of salmon surge upstream and can be caught with ease, usually with nets, weirs, or traps, but sometimes with spears, clubs, or even the hands.

Salmon transformed the Northwest Coast Indian way of life. All salmon spawn primarily in the fall, though chinook spawn

Salmon drying in an Alaskan Aleut village during the late nineteenth century. *(National Archives)*

almost year-round. Indians began coming to falls and rapids to capture salmon at least by 4000 B.C.E. By 1000 B.C.E. huge quantities of salmon were being caught, then dried and smoked for use throughout the year. Carrying the store of salmon through seasonal movements was no longer practical. Villages became fixed at or near good fishing spots, sometimes with a single year-round village, sometimes with separate winter and summer villages. Prosperity derived from salmon translated into great wealth, impressive arts, and material comfort. Chiefs controlled rights to particular salmon-fishing areas, consolidating their political power.

Traditionally, all aspects of salmon usage were surrounded with rituals and taboos. Overfishing and obstruction of waterways by dams have jeopardized the future of both commercial and traditional salmon fishing by Indians.

Russell J. Barber

See also: Fish and Fishing; Pemmican; Weirs and Traps.

Salt

Tribes affected: All agricultural tribes

Significance: *Salt, a necessary nutrient, was used as a condiment by agriculturalists; the salt trade was particularly significant in eastern North America.*

Human beings require salt in their diets, and hunting-gathering people usually consume adequate amounts of salt through the meat they eat. Agriculturalists, however, typically consume less meat and are forced to use salt as a condiment.

Salt was produced and traded extensively in prehistoric eastern North America after about 800 C.E. At Avery Island, Louisiana, for example, a salt dome was mined more or less constantly from around 800 to the mid-1600's. The salt removed was placed in pottery jars and traded to agriculturalist tribes around the South and perhaps as far north as Illinois. Certain tribes, such as the Tunica, became prosperous through the salt trade.

Salt also was produced by evaporation of briny water. This was particularly important in the Ohio Valley after about 1000 C.E. There, salty water was placed in distinctive broad, shallow ceramic vessels. After the water had evaporated completely, the salt crystals left behind were scraped from the bottom of these "salt pans." Salt for the tribes of the Southwest mostly was produced by evaporation on the coast and traded inland.

Wherever salt was used in native North America, there were taboos associated with it. Among the Pueblo peoples, for example, men had to abstain from consuming salt before participating in religious ceremonies in the kivas. Salt also typically was forbidden during rites of passage among many tribes.

Russell J. Barber

See also: Agriculture; Food Preparation and Cooking; Subsistence; Trade.

Sand Painting

Tribes affected: Apache, Arapaho, Blackfoot, Cheyenne, Gabriel-ino, Luiseño, Navajo, Pueblo, Tohono O'odham

Significance: *Sand paintings are pictures made of finely ground sand derived from stone or other colored material; such paintings are at the center of the Navajo ceremonial system.*

Traditionally an impermanent art form between painting and mosaic, sand painting (or dry painting, as it is also known) has been used by American Indians of the Southwest and Plains for ceremonial and religious purposes. Little is known about sand painting done by tribes other than the Navajo, either because they did not do sand painting to a great extent, the paintings vanished from use, or they were never recorded. Navajo sand painting was borrowed from the Pueblos and altered to conform to the Navajo worldview. There are possibly as many as six hundred different sand paintings referring to different aspects or events in Navajo mythology, with every chant or ceremony having its own paintings.

The paintings, representing the Navajo cosmological myths and events, are circular, semicircular, or rectangular in shape and are made in three major patterns composed with either a linear or radial emphasis or a dominant center motif. The design is surrounded on three sides by a guardian spirit, with the opening to the east. Designs are symmetrical overall but contain asymmetrical details. Motifs include plants, animals, astral bodies, and supernatural entities called "Yei." Abstracted figures are shown frontally or in profile with full face. Traditional sand paintings are softly colored in tones of brown, red, blue, black, and gold on a tan background.

In sand painting, the act of creating the painting is an essential element in the ritual use of the painting. The paintings are made by singers, also called chanters, with the help of many apprentice assistants, and are made from memory in a prescribed order. Left unfinished or incomplete, the paintings remain secular in nature. The paintings must be made completely and accurately in order to attract supernatural beings called "Holy People" to the paintings, making them sacred and efficacious to the ritual purpose. The final step occurs when the singer sprinkles the complete painting with sacred corn pollen. Immediately after ritual use, the paintings are destroyed to guard against misuse of the sacred power.

Because of the highly sacred nature of sand painting, the Navajo long did not allow them to be observed or made by laymen or unbelievers. When the Navajo began to allow them to be reproduced in permanent form around 1900, it was only because there was a growing concern for preserving this aspect of Navajo life. By leaving them incomplete or inaccurate, they believed the sacred content would be protected because the Holy People would be prevented from infusing them with their power.

Today, sand paintings are made and marketed by both Indians and non-Indians. The Indian Arts and Crafts Board has established

Two Navajo sandpainters in Ganado, Arizona. *(Museum of New Mexico)*

criteria for authentic Navajo sand paintings in an attempt to designate as authentic only those sand paintings made by American Indians.

Diane C. Van Noord

Sources for Further Study

Berlo, Janet Catherine. *Native North American Art*. New York: Oxford University Press, 1998.

Congdon-Martin, Douglas. *Navajo Art of Sandpainting*. 2d ed. Atglen, Pa.: Schiffer Publishing, 1999.

Parezo, Nancy J. *Navajo Sandpainting: From Religious Act to Commercial Art*. Albuquerque: University of New Mexico Press, 1991.

See also: Arts and Crafts: Southwest; Chantways; Hand Tremblers; Symbolism in Art.

Scalps and Scalping

Tribes affected: Pantribal
Significance: *Scalping appears to have been a widespread custom of warfare that antedated European contact; it is often connected with spirit-keeping traditions.*

Scalping was a widely diffused warfare custom among many Indian tribes in the United States, Canada, and South America. Strong evidence suggests that scalping was an aboriginal custom predating the arrival of Europeans, although Europeans, particularly the French and English, did eventually encourage scalp taking and paid bounties to Indian allies for enemy scalps. Scalping seems to have become more widespread after the arrival of Europeans.

The earliest European records carry accounts of scalping from widely different areas of the Americas. These European accounts express surprise at the practice of scalping, and they attempt to document and explain the ritualized customs connected with scalp-

An eighteenth century English engraving of a warrior holding a scalp. *(Library of Congress)*

ing. Indian languages from many culture areas also contain extensive and precise language referring to the scalp, the act of scalping, and the victim of scalping. Also widely diffused among tribes is the common hairdressing practice of wearing a small braid or lock of hair on the crown of the head. This scalplock was often adorned with paint or ornaments which marked achievements or honors. Hair, because it continues to grow throughout a person's lifetime, was commonly believed to be visual evidence that an individual's soul or spirit was a living thing. It was a commonly held belief among many tribes that the scalplock was synonymous with a person's identity or soul and so represented the metaphysical part of the individual's being. Therefore, it was a grave insult to touch the scalplock casually.

The physical act of scalping consisted of grabbing the braid of the scalplock with one hand and cutting a circle about two to three inches in diameter around the base of it with a knife; a quick jerk tore the scalp from the skull. Scalps were taken from dead and wounded enemies, but the act of scalping was not fatal. If a living person was scalped, the skin grew over the wound but hair did not. Among many tribes those who survived a scalping were feared, because the physical emanation of the soul had been taken.

There were many elaborate customs connected with the taking and care of scalps, and these extended broadly across culture groups. A common practice was to stretch the scalp on a small hoop and then attach this to a long pole or to a bridle or an item of clothing. Most tribes who practiced scalping had a victory dance (often referred to as a "scalp dance") in which the scalps were displayed and the scalp takers were honored for their bravery. Many tribes considered the scalp a living spirit of the enemy and therefore practiced spirit-keeping rituals. The spirit-keeping rituals varied from tribe to tribe, but essentially the scalplock was cared for because it represented the soul of the individual, a respected enemy. The scalplock was sometimes painted, washed, wrapped in a bundle, or buried on the battlefield. There is also evidence that among some tribes scalps were taken to desecrate a hated enemy because they would forever wander on this earth if they died an unwhole person.

Carole A. Barrett

See also: Grooming; Tomahawks; Torture; Warfare and Conflict.

Sculpture

Tribes affected: Pantribal

Significance: *Sculpture, whether in wood, pottery, stone, or—in more recent times—various metals, has been an important part of American Indian cultural expression.*

Native American sculpture represents a deep belief in rhythm, balance, and symmetry. For example, arrow and tool points from some twelve thousand years ago demonstrate admirable craftsmanship and a blending of form and function. Modern Native American sculptors embrace tradition, spiritual legends, and naturalistic symbols, combining these ideas with their own emotion to join feeling and design.

In the Hohokam culture (dating between 700 and 900 C.E.), carved bone objects were used for body ornamentations such as hairpins and armbands; designs included geometrics, birds, and animals. Clay figures decorated jars, and petroglyphs were distributed throughout the Southwest. The subject matter of the petroglyphs is fairly consistent: curvilinear patterns, geometric designs, and numerous life forms. Humans often appear sitting or standing, playing the flute, throwing a spear, or dancing in groups.

Skills in sculpture were passed down through the generations. As new materials became available and new techniques developed, each generation contributed interpretations and innovations. Regardless of their background, most contemporary Indian sculptors take pride in their ancestry and turn to traditional culture for inspiration. One problem that arises from this approach is the issue of using sacred objects in designs. Sculptors must decide where to draw the line between artistic freedom and the violation of their tribe's spiritual essence.

A variety of sculpture exists in contemporary Native American art. Designs in alabaster, brass, bronze castings, porcelain, clay, black soapstone, limestone, and cottonwood (often used for kachinas and Shalakos) are only some of the materials being used. Subject matter is equally varied. Native American cultures share the idea that humans should live in harmony with nature. Motifs of almost every natural element—the sun, plants, animals—appear from ancient times to the present, and depictions of everyday life as well as more ceremonial matters are common.

Kimberly Manning

Source for Further Study
Berlo, Janet Catherine. *Native North American Art*. New York: Oxford University Press, 1998.

See also: Art and Artists: Contemporary; Arts and Crafts: Arctic; Arts and Crafts: Southwest; Effigy Mounds; Metalwork; Petroglyphs; Pottery; Symbolism in Art; Totem Poles.

Secotan

Tribe affected: Algonquian
Significance: *Secotan is perhaps the most familiar of all American Indian villages.*

The village of Secotan (or Secoton) was immortalized by the English watercolorist and first governor of the English colony on the island of Roanoke, John White, who visited this Indian town on July 15 and 16, 1585, as part of Grenville's exploration of the Pamlico Sound. Many of White's now famous watercolors of native life in the region of Roanoke Island are depictions of scenes from Secotan. Through the years, his painting of the village probably has been the most frequently reproduced depiction of any native subject.

The painting indicates that this Algonquian village consisted of eleven houses, several fields, charnel house, dance ground, paths, and communal fires and cooking areas. It was an open village, not enclosed by a stockade wall. Corn, tobacco, and sunflower were growing unmolested by wildlife, as the fields were watched over by a person on a stand. Secotan was the westernmost town of the

Wingandacoa, or Secotan, whose leader was Wingina and whose territory was bounded by the Pamlico River and Albermarle Sound. The Secotan had been at war with their southern neighbors, the Pomouike of the Neuse River, just prior to the visitation by the Grenville party.

Unfortunately, more is known about the spatial arrangement of activities inside the village, because of White's painting, than is known about where the village was located. Several Englishmen mention the village during the era of the Roanoke voyages, giving a fairly good idea of its general position south of Roanoke Island and saying that it was the most southerly of their explorations.

The town itself was situated on the Pamlico River. A sketch map executed by an unknown artist in White's party placed Secotan on the north shore. The White map of Raleigh's Virginia shows Secotan to be on the south side of the first large river south of Lake Mattamuskeet. David Quinn's exhaustive study of the documents pertinent to the Roanoke voyages of 1584-1590 reconstructs Grenville's journey to have taken the group up the Pamlico River past the Pungo River then right up Bath Creek, where they visited Cotan, back across the Pamlico and up Durham Creek to Secotan, which he would place at present-day Bonnerton, North Carolina. The possibility of "Cotan" and "Secotan" being the same village has been advanced in the past and should not be dismissed.

Several archaeological projects have attempted to locate the famous village along either shore of the Pamlico River, with almost every new researcher proposing a new location. Attempts were made in 1954, 1955, 1965, 1968, and 1980, although only in the latter two projects was the area targeted by Quinn searched. As a result of these projects, all candidates for the historic village have been eliminated with the exception of one on the north shore of the Pamlico River.

Cheryl Claassen

See also: Architecture: Northeast.

Secret Societies

Tribes affected: Widespread but not pantribal
Significance: *Secret societies performed important political and religious functions within a tribe.*

No secret societies existed in the Plateau or Great Basin. They seem to be associated with cultures with true political organization and relatively complex socioeconomic institutions. Though kinship was on occasion a reason for one's membership, acceptance was based on invitation, apprenticeship, and initiation rites. During initiation, the novitiate might be abducted by men disguised as spirit monsters and taken to a secluded area, where he would undergo a metamorphosis and acquire a tutelary spirit. Rarely did an individual belong to more than one secret society.

Membership was usually voluntary, and sometimes a fee would be paid, as with the Ojibwa. Members instructed the neophyte in the religious meanings of their rituals, and membership was believed to ensure a long and successful life for members. Recruitment in some societies was based on replacing a deceased member. Among some Plains secret societies, membership was achieved by exceptional acts of bravery or military accomplishments.

Some groups, like the Kwakiutl, would wear elaborate costumes with concealed animal bladders filled with blood, which was released at the appropriate time during initiations. Members used masks representing various spirits or animals, some elaborately carved, painted, and even articulated—the outer mask would open to reveal an inside mask, indicating the individual's spiritual transformation. With many secret society members, once they assumed the garb of a particular animal or bird, they were then empowered with that animal's unique characteristics of sound and motion.

Secret society rituals were invariably staged within sacred dwellings or chambers, which sometimes served as dormitories, where members kept their religious paraphernalia. Performances were heightened through the use of hidden speaking tubes in the wall, or through the use of tunnels with trap doors for a sudden appearance of an actor, or by the presence of suspended articulated animals or birds worked by hidden cords. The most dramatic ceremony was when a person would be possessed by a cannibal spirit and commit mock anthropophagy by eating a small, smoked bear corpse representing a human. Hallucinogens were sometimes used for spirit flight and prophetic predictions.

Secret societies were internally graded or ranked, and served specific functions for the group, such as influencing central political control, training shamans, curing disease, particularly in ceremonies, and instructing in mythology and religion. Matters of weather and the occurrence of economically important animals were the ritual concern of certain secret societies. Affiliation further served to integrate members and afford them status with their peers.

Some secret societies originated after European American incursion, probably as a response to deculturative effects, but they were not true nativitistic movements.

John Alan Ross

See also: Military Societies; Social Control; Societies: Non-kin-based.

Serpent Mounds

Cultures affected: Adena, Hopewell
Significance: *Earthen mounds, whether effigy mounds, burial mounds, or temple mounds, are especially prevalent in North America from western New York State through the Great Lakes region and down the Ohio and Mississippi river valleys to the Southeast.*

It was estimated early in the twentieth century that there were ten thousand mounds in the Ohio Valley alone, but many have been lost to farming, construction, fortune hunters, and even a few archaeologists. The mounds appear in a number of different configurations: Some are conical or sectioned triangles; others are effigies of birds, reptiles, beasts, and people. Perhaps the best known and certainly the largest effigy mound in North America is the Great Serpent Mound on Brush Creek in Adams County, Ohio.

Scholarly conjecture about the identity of the Mound Builders of ancient America has held since early in the twentieth century that the Great Serpent Mound was produced during the Adena cultural tradition, roughly between 1000 B.C.E. and 700 C.E. (The name "Adena" comes from the name of the estate of Thomas Worthington where, in 1901, William Mills excavated a mound and found many significant artifacts.) The Great Serpent is 1,254 feet long, 20 feet in average width, and 4 to 5 feet in average height. The earthen serpent has a writhing, circuitous shape with seven coils in its long body and a triple-coiled tail. Its jaws are wide open, holding an oval figure that might be a frog, an egg, or a moon or sun symbol.

A serpent symbol is prevalent in many cultures, but since there is no oral or written tradition to describe either the Mound Builders or their purposes in fabricating the mounds, it remains problematic to establish with any certainty the cultural use of the serpent mounds. The enlarged head creates a natural oval embankment that could be variously used as a fireplace or altar or as a place of community meeting, ritual, or worship.

The Great Serpent Mound has been preserved for posterity. In 1883, F. W. Putnam of the Peabody Museum, Boston, viewed the Great Serpent Mound when it still belonged to John Lovett, a farmer. When Lovett decided to sell his land in 1886, Putnam started a campaign to raise money to buy the land in order to preserve the mound. In 1887, on behalf of many (mostly Boston-area) contributors, the Peabody Museum purchased the Lovett farm, including the Great Serpent Mound. In 1888, complete with a turnstile and horse trough, the area opened as Serpent Mound Park. In 1900, the Peabody Museum deeded the land to the Ohio Archaeological and Historical Society; it remains today as a state park.

Richard Sax

See also: Effigy Mounds; Mounds and Moundbuilders; Ohio Mound Builders.

Shaker Church

Tribes affected: Originally Skokomish; later most Northwest Coast tribes

Significance: *The Shaker Church of the Northwest Coast area, originating in the late nineteenth century, stresses healing and refraining from behaviors such as gambling and alcohol use.*

The Shaker Church is a native religious movement of the Pacific Northwest and western Canada that originated among the various tribes of the area surrounding Puget Sound in Washington State. This movement should be carefully differentiated from the more widely known historical movement, the "Shakers," founded under the leadership of former Quaker Mother Ann Lee. This latter Shaker movement has very few adherents today (it tends to be associated with furniture styles and American folklore), while the Indian Shaker Church is still widespread among native tribes of the Pacific Northwest. The two movements have no historic or ideological connection, and the "shaking" itself is a different phenomenon in each group.

The Shaker Church began as a result of the visions of John Slocum but was supplemented by the activities of his wife, Mary Slocum, who contributed the ritual movements that gave the church its "shaker" name.

Research by H. G. Barnett recorded a number of versions of the events leading to the founding of the Shaker Church, but a general description can be made. In 1881, John Slocum, a Skokomish (Coast Salish) Indian living at Mud Bay, Washington, appeared to die after spending many years involved in gambling and alcoholism. Many descriptions report that he said that he ascended into heaven, spoke with God, and was instructed to begin a new renewal movement to save the Indian people. The message appeared to involve a preparation for the second coming of Jesus Christ and demanded of his listeners that they stop gambling and give up alcohol. It was also suggested that the dead relatives of the Indian people would soon be restored. He was sent back to his body, where he began to awaken in the presence of family and friends who had gathered to mourn his death. His resurrection amazed his family and was the initial motivation for the starting of the movement. It is often said that Slocum immediately asked for a church building to be constructed, where he began to preach and teach the message that he believed he had been given.

After a period of time, Slocum himself returned to his previous lifestyle and went through another episode of near-death. During his long illness (or, in some versions, a second death), his wife Mary went to a riverbank to get some water; while there she was overcome by bodily shaking. When she returned to John's side, it was seen that her shaking was associated with John's recovery, and the shaking became a part of the movement at that time. This shaking was associated with healing power, and healing became one of the central activities of the adherents of the Shaker movement.

The movement spread rapidly among Northwest tribes, and adherents faced opposition and harassment by missionaries from other Christian denominations. There were also internal difficulties. The movement has experienced some divisions, based on both personalities and doctrine. In 1946, for example, a branch that asserted belief in the Bible broke away and called themselves "Full Gospel" to differentiate themselves from the Shaker Church, known among believers as the "1910 Shakers." The latter group maintains that the Bible is not central to its religious practice.

The movement asserts itself as a uniquely Indian movement, and whites are typically not invited to participate. Clearly part of Slocum's original vision was the restoration of Indian rights in the face of increasing white control of land. In 1855, tribes in the Puget Sound area had ceded all claims to their traditional lands and accepted reservations in return. The slow decline of many of the Northwest tribes resulted.

Today, the central tenets of the Shaker Church are the importance of the events of John Slocum's life and the significance of his message, and God's gift to the Shaker people of the shaking and its healing powers. The latter is particularly important, as Shaker

Church members value healing as historically one of the most important activities of the movement. The movement can be considered a Christian sect and may be seen as related to other native renewal movements such as the Ghost Dance religion and the Longhouse religion. As with those other movements, modern practitioners are chary of open discussions of the exact nature of the rites, rituals, and beliefs of the movement, particularly with non-Indians.

Sources for Further Study
Barnett, Homer G. *Indian Shakers: A Messianic Cult of the Pacific Northwest*. Carbondale: Southern Illinois University Press, 1957.
Ruby, Robert H., and John A. Brown. *John Slocum and the Indian Shaker Church*. Foreword by Richard A. Gould. Norman: University of Oklahoma Press, 1996.

See also: Longhouse Religion; Native American Church; Religion; Visions and Vision Quests.

Shaking Tent Ceremony

Tribes affected: Cree, Menominee, Montagnais, Ojibwa, other northeastern Canadian tribes
Significance: *The Shaking Tent Ceremony, a shamanistic tradition, was particularly important in Cree culture.*

The Shaking Tent Ceremony is practiced mainly by the Cree Nation in Canada. Although Cree religious life today is dominated by the influence of Christian missionaries, some aspects of traditional belief remain. Cree religion includes varying forms of belief in a central "great spirit" (Kitchi Manitu) and varying versions of a belief in a malevolent, evil spirit (Matci Manitu) who must occasionally be placated in order to prevent illness and other problems of social life. There are shamans who are practiced in various forms of witchcraft. One of the most prevalent features of Cree religious/ social life is the "Shaking Tent."

The actual tent is a structure reserved for this ceremony and storytelling. The ceremony is dependent on the context of shamanism as a major religious expression of the Cree Nation. A shaman figure would sit within a special tent erected solely for the ceremony, and the presence of various spirits would be perceived in the shaking of the poles and sides of the tent. Those who sought the help of the shaman in the shaking tent would typically be involved in an attempt to communicate with spirits, cure illness, or find the whereabouts of missing persons. A number of preparations were necessary to the ceremony, including fasting, praying, and a sweatlodge ceremony. Sometimes the shaman would participate in spectacular feats, such as escaping from fetters while hung upside down within the tent—attributed to the power of the spirits and the power of the shaman himself. The ceremony would involve hearing voices and discerning the spirits from the movement of the tent. The shaman would typically chant songs, sometimes revealed to him in dreams for his use in the ceremonies. The ceremonies were generally performed alone.

Although mainly a Cree phenomenon, the Shaking Tent ceremony spread among the Cree, Menominee, Montagnais, Ojibwa, Ottawa, and Saulteaux nations of northeastern Canada.

In European tradition, certain of the shamans gained fame or notoriety. Etienne Pigarouich, for example, was a seventeenth-century Montagnais who converted to Catholicism in 1639 but often reconverted—to the considerable consternation of the local Jesuits, who recorded many stories about him. There are many recorded instances of Jesuit challenges to the reality of the Shaking Tent powers.

Today, the Shaking Tent is still a feature of larger Cree social gatherings but often as a source of amusement rather than an occasion for awe at the power of spirits.

Daniel L. Smith-Christopher

See also: Religion; Religious Specialists.

Shalako

Tribe affected: Zuñi
Significance: *Shalako was a winter ceremony to mark the return of the supernaturals to the village, symbolizing the close relationship between the Zuñi and the spirit world.*

In the Pueblo ceremonial calendar, summer ceremonies stress agricultural abundance and rain, while in the winter, curing, warfare, and hunting ceremonies occur. The shalako ceremony takes place at the end of the ritual year, in late November or early December, before the winter solstice ceremonies. Shalako marks the annual return of supernatural beings to the village and reinforces the harmony of the Zuñi people with the spirit world. During Shalako, Zuñis have the opportunity to bargain with the supernaturals, calling upon them to cure illness or remove evil.

During the ceremony, the Shalakos (six masked kachina figures) enter the village in a procession symbolizing the migration of the Zuñi to "The Middle Place," or the world in which the people live. The Shalakos visit homes, where they are fed and spend the night, and where they hold a dialogue with the house owner, recounting the stories of creation and the migration of the Zuñi people. In the morning, the Shalakos return to their home in the west.

Lynne Getz

See also: Kachinas.

Shells and Shellwork

Tribes affected: Pantribal
Significance: *Shells have a long history of use for ornamentation by native peoples of the Americas; the presence of marine shells inland implies social interaction between groups.*

The oldest shell objects in North America may be the local freshwater gastropod shell beads recovered at the Ervin site in Tennessee, which are approximately seven thousand years old. Marine shells were modified as beads, cups, pendants, earspools, gorgets, hoes, and axes all across the eastern United States, where they largely appear as grave goods. Thirty-five species of marine shells (mostly gastropods) were utilized as beads during the Archaic period in western New York, for example. Most noteworthy are the gorgets and engraved shell cups of the Mississippian period, particularly those from the site of Spiro, and wampum used by Northeast tribes in historic times.

In the western United States, shell beads appeared about four thousand years ago. Shell button blankets were important cere-

During the early twentieth century this Tolowa woman wears an apron decorated with shells. *(Library of Congress)*

monial items in the Northwest. Shell jewelry and inlaid shell in the Southwest commonly consisted of the species *Oliva, Olivella, Glycymeris,* and *Conus.* Bracelets were the most popular jewelry form, followed by necklaces. Techniques for shellworking included incising, carving, abrading, mosaic, inlay, drilling, and etching. Etching was performed with a brew made from fruit of the saguaro cactus. The shell was covered with pitch to preserve a final shape, then acid was applied to the exposed shell. Etched shell was often painted.

Among the Maya, shell symbolized death, south, zero, completion, and fertility. In North American beliefs, gastropod shells served as hiding places for the soul and deities. Shell could hold the soul and help purify decaying flesh. In some regions shell bead usage resembled the usage of money, and in many regions below the Arctic, shell beads were among the most valuable items a person could own. Dentalium among the Northwest Coast tribes was so central to the social organization that young men were instructed to dream of dentalium and to think of it when walking.

In some cases the species of a shell is sufficient to indicate its origin. Shells excavated in southwestern sites came from the Gulf of California or the Pacific coast. Those from the Gulf of California were brought up the Gila River into Hohokam territory, then traded northward. West Coast shell followed several routes into the northern and southern Southwest. The route of the few shells which came from the Gulf of Mexico is not clear. There are dentalium shells from the West Indies present in Archaic sites in Alabama, and fossil dentalium shells were quarried and used in South Dakota. Pacific dentalium comes from local habitats. For the eastern United States, however, there are few species with limited habitats. There has been some success with chemically sourcing the Atlantic whelks of the *Busycon* genus, which has indicated origins for shells found in Kentucky, Missouri, and South Dakota as including both temperate and tropical waters. Other evidence suggests Tampa Bay and the coast of Veracruz as shell sources.

Cheryl Claassen

Source for Further Study

Dubin, Lois Sherr. *North American Indian Jewelry and Adornment: From Prehistory to the Present.* New York: Henry N. Abrams, 1999.

See also: Dress and Adornment; Money; Mosaic and Inlay; Ornaments; Wampum.

Shields

Tribes affected: Plains and Southwestern tribes

Significance: *From prehistoric times to the late nineteenth century American Indian warriors, principally those in the Southwest and Plains areas, carried thick rawhide shields into combat. Though the shield afforded some physical protection, its real protective powers were thought to emanate from the images painted on it. The shield was the most important object a warrior owned.*

History. Graphic evidence of the use of shields is found in prehistoric rock art on canyon or cave walls and boulders from southern Alberta and deep into the Southwest. The rawhide shields depicted in the rock art are large, thirty to forty inches in diameter, and are referred to as "walking shields." They covered large areas of the carrier's torso and were in use prior to the arrival of the horse among the North American tribes. After the horse came among the Southwestern and Plains people, the rawhide shields carried by warriors were considerably smaller, about 17 to 20 inches (approximately half a meter) in diameter. These shields were protective devices used by warriors, and they were believed to safeguard both the physical and spiritual well-being of the owner.

Construction. Shields were made from the thick hump or neck hide of a buffalo bull and construction of the smaller war shields is well-documented. In some tribes, such as the Apache, there was a select group of men who were considered to have the ability to

An Apache chief, San Juan, holding a shield and spear.
(National Archives)

manufacture strong and powerful shields. However, in most tribes each warrior made his own shield, and it became one of his most important possessions throughout his lifetime. A man prepared carefully for making his shield and he often called upon his close female relatives and his fellow society members to assist him. While engaged in constructing a shield it was common for a man to dress in his society regalia, pray, and sing sacred songs. The actual manufacture of a shield involved stretching a green buffalo hide about twice the size of the finished product across a pit filled with hot stones and covered with a thin layer of sand. Within an hour the hide shrank to half its original size, and then the warrior worked to make it flat and smooth.

Power and Use. The most important aspect of the shield was the unique design painted on it. This derived from the owner's personal vision, and the selection of color and design elements was very important. Drawings on shields are highly symbolic. Once the image was painted onto the shield the article was said to be invested with the power of the vision, and it was believed this would provide protection to the owner. Commonly men attached objects to their shields such as golden eagle feathers, small medicine bundles, strips of cloth, or tiny brass hawk bells. Each item had symbolic meaning to the owner and was thought to enhance the power of the shield. If the owner had a vision of a bear and he painted that image on his shield he was said to have the help and power of the bear each time he engaged in warfare. Most shields could provide protection against arrows, lances, and bullets from muzzle-loaded rifles; however they were not good protection against higher-powered munitions. Nonetheless, warriors carried them into battle, because they believed the real protection came from the spirit invested in the shield, not simply from the physical object. If a man was wounded or killed in battle while carrying his shield the people believed he had made some human error, but the power of the shield was still very strong. A warrior who carried a fine shield into battle often became the target for a coup, because it was evident that such a man had much power and it would be a great honor to touch him in battle.

Ownership of a shield often meant an individual had to observe certain taboos, and men came to understand these prohibitions through their visions. Sitting Bull received direction that he was not to eat food handled by women other than his wives or mother. Other owners of shields could not eat buffalo heart or food touched by metal, for instance. A warrior's face paint and the way he painted his war horse usually reflected the image and the colors on his shield. Men who owned shields believed they provided protection, and in return they observed any restrictions that came with ownership.

Warriors had to be sure their shields never touched the ground, and when the men were in camp they attached their shield to a sturdy tripod which they placed outside on a sunny day and turned to the west. It was believed the shield could absorb power from the sun as well as provide protection to the warrior's family. Because the images on the shield were sacred and powerful, the owners often made a buckskin cover to hide the face of the shield. The covers often had symbolic designs painted on them, but these differed from the sacred images on the shield itself.

Because the most sacred and potent possession a warrior possessed was his shield, it was placed with him at the time of his burial. It was believed that the shield would provide final protection to him as he journeyed into the next world.

Carole A. Barrett

Sources for Further Study

Dyck, Paul. "The Plains Shield." *American Indian Art Magazine* 1, no. 1 (1975): 34-41.

Irwin, Lee. *The Dream Seekers: Native American Visionary Traditions of the Northern Plains.* Norman: University of Oklahoma Press, 1994.

McCoy, Ronald. *Circles of Power.* Flagstaff: Museum of Northern Arizona, 1984.

Mails, Thomas E. *Mystic Warriors of the Plains.* New York: Doubleday and Company, 1972.

Powell, Father Peter J. "Beauty for New Life: An Introduction to Cheyenne and Lakota Sacred Art." In Evan M. Mauer, *The Native American Heritage.* Chicago: The Art Institute of Chicago, 1977.

Wright, Barton. *Pueblo Shields.* Flagstaff, Ariz.: Northland Press, 1976.

See also: Guardian Spirits; Sacred, the; Symbolism in Art; Visions and Vision Quests; Warfare and Conflict.

Sign Language

Tribes affected: Pantribal

Significance: *In North America, sign language facilitated communication and economic transactions among groups which spoke different languages, and it served additional purposes in some cultural settings.*

Sign language is a nonverbal communication utilizing movements of the hands or body to convey meaning. In many areas of the world, such as Africa or Australia, sign languages were used by hunters to communicate hunting strategies silently to one another.

In northeastern Mexico, Texas, and western Louisiana, sign language almost certainly predated European contact, since there are several early historical accounts of its use. A late seventeenth century journal entry of explorer Pierre le Moyne, Sieur d'Iberville records the use of sign language among the Bayogoula and other unnamed groups along the lower Mississippi River. Additional accounts of communication by signs were written by early traders.

It seems likely that the sign language used in these areas diffused northward into the Plains. In the nineteenth and twentieth centuries, the use of sign language continued to spread through the Plains and across the northern Plateau, as described in articles in D. Jean Umiker-Sebeok and Thomas A. Sebeok's *Aboriginal Sign Languages of the Americas and Australia* (1978). Among the Plains peoples, the Kiowa generally were deemed to be early users of sign language. The Kiowa occupied different locations at different time periods, but in the nineteenth century they were hunting bison in the southwestern Plains. Therefore aboriginal accounts uphold the thesis that sign language diffused from south to north and may have originated in the Gulf Coast region.

The Plains sign language is better documented than that of other areas, and the meanings of many signs were recorded; in the Southeast, on the other hand, the signs were lost at an earlier date. In addition, for the Plains area, information concerning the social context of sign language was recorded. For example, many nineteenth century reports indicate that signs were used primarily by Plains Indian men, although some women also knew the signs. Many Plains groups used signs in a variety of social contexts, such as during storytelling or intimate conversation among family members, in addition to recognizing its value for conversing with outsiders who did not speak the same language.

Susan J. Wurtzburg

See also: Language Families; Oratory; Trade.

Silverworking

Tribes affected: Navajo, Hopi, Zuñi
Significance: *Silverworking among the tribes of the Southwest is a highly developed art and a major source of income.*

The art of working with silver has been practiced by a variety of Native American peoples. In what is now Peru, Chimu and Sican silversmiths were master artisans long before the arrival of the Europeans. The Inca, who became politically dominant in Peru, learned silverworking techniques from the craftsmen of these other nations.

The Native American groups of North America generally learned work with silver from the Europeans. By the beginning of the nineteenth century, most of the nations of the Northeast Woodlands had taken up the techniques of silversmithing introduced by the European colonists. They worked mainly with coins, hammering these to flat sheets. Brooches were the most common pieces of silver jewelry, but the artists of the Northeast also made earrings, rings, combs, headbands, and other pieces.

The Navajo, Hopi, and Zuñi peoples of the North American Southwest developed the most sophisticated and best-known traditions in the art of working with silver. These three groups are responsible for about three-quarters of the Native American silver jewelry in North America. As in the Northeast, it is a relatively new art, introduced to by the Spanish, who dug silver mines in Mexico. The Navajo are believed to have been the first in this region to take up working with the metal. During the 1850's, the Navajo artisan Atsidi Sani is believed to have learned his craft from a metalworker from Mexico and to have passed his knowledge on to his four sons and then to other Navajo. Native silversmiths began

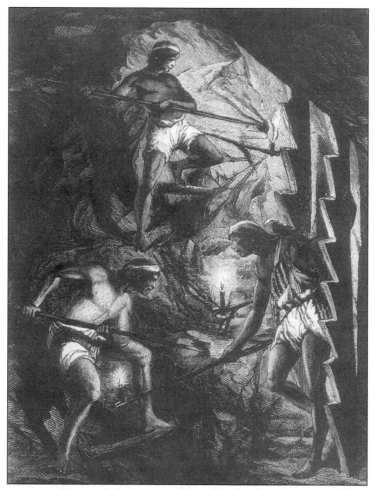

A late nineteenth century engraving of Indians working in a silver mine in Chihuahua, Mexico. *(The Institute of Texan Cultures, San Antonio, Texas)*

to make rapid progress in the late 1870's, after the Navajos went back to their reservation following several years of captivity by the U.S. Army at Fort Summer. By the time Atsidi Sani died, in 1918, silversmithing had become an established art form in the Southwest. The smith known as Atsidi Chon is said to have taught the craft to a Zuñi named Lanyade. In turn, Lanyade is believed to have taught a Hopi named Sikyatala.

The Navajo style involves placing fairly large turquoise stones in a relatively large quantity of silver. Today, the squash blossom necklace with a crescent pennant, the concha belt, and the *ketoh* bowguard may be the best-known pieces of Navajo silverwork. The Hopi tend to use little turquoise, relying primarily on silver overlay for decoration. The Zuñi frequently place small, elaborate settings of turquoise, jet, and coral in their silver.

Native American silverworking techniques and materials have become more sophisticated over the years. Before 1940, the artists used sandpaper or abrasive powders to polish their work. After that date, mechanical buffing wheels came into wide usage. In the nineteenth century, coins provided the silver, with Mexican coins preferred to the coins of the United States due to the higher silver content of the former. During the twentieth century, sheet metal became the commonly used material.

Carl L. Bankston III

Sources for Further Study

Cirillo, Dexter. *Southwest Indian Jewelry.* New York: Abbeville Press, 1992.

Dubin, Lois Sherr. *North American Indian Jewelry and Adornment: From Prehistory to the Present.* New York: Harry N. Adams, 1999.

Jacka, Lois Essary. *Navajo Jewelry: A Legacy of Silver and Stone.* Flagstaff, Ariz.: Northland, 1995.

See also: Arts and Crafts: Southwest; Gold and Goldworking; Metalwork; Ornaments; Turquoise.

Slavery

Tribes affected: Widespread but not pantribal
Significance: *Before European settlement, slavery helped determine status within many Indian societies; after European settlement, Indian slavery became an important economic institution and significantly influenced Indian-white relations.*

Slavery, a social institution which existed in most human societies before the twentieth century, was practiced by many native North American cultures.

Aboriginal Slavery. All forms of slavery exist to bring honor and power to the master. Before contact with Europeans, American Indian societies did not envision status and power in economic terms, and slavery was not primarily a system of labor. Aboriginal Indian bondage brought power and honor to the master through his absolute domination of a living being.

Most Indian slaves were acquired as war captives, and their enslavement was viewed as a substitute for death in battle. As a replacement for actual death, Indian slavery became a living "social death." The war captive forever lost his status as an independent person and became an appendage of his master's will. The loss of status was marked by rituals of dishonor. The heads of slaves were often shorn as a symbol of dishonor. Among the Tlingit of the Northwest Coast, female slaves were not allowed to adorn themselves with facial decorations. Slaves were often renamed to dishonor them and to sever connections with their lineage and past. The Nootka gave their female slaves insulting names. The Cherokee and Iroquois word for "slave" was also used to refer to dogs, cats, or other nonhuman living things that were owned. The master's absolute power reached its highest level in the Pacific Northwest, where Indians often killed their slaves while mourning dead family members or celebrating important ceremonial occasions.

Slave Trade. European settlement changed Indian slavery into an economic institution. The Europeans needed laborers to develop their colonies and often purchased Indian slaves. An elaborate Indian slave trade system eventually spanned the North American continent.

Each of the European nations which colonized North America participated in this system. In the 1640's, the Dutch colonists of present-day New York purchased slaves from the Indians and sold them to European colonies in the West Indies. Beginning in the late seventeenth century, French traders from Canada purchased slaves through Illinois middlemen. By the 1720's, French traders from Louisiana were conducting a thriving trade for Indian slaves with the Pawnee and Osage. Some slaves worked on French plantations in Louisiana; others were resold to the French West Indies. Russian settlers in Alaska began using Aleut and Eskimo slaves in the 1790's. Slavery caused a rapid decline in the native population, prompting the Russians to purchase slaves from the Fraser Valley and the region surrounding Puget Sound.

The Spanish and English conducted the largest trade in Indian slaves. In the 1530's, Spanish traders from Mexico began purchasing Indian slaves in the American Southwest. Although the Spanish government outlawed Indian slavery in the sixteenth century, the laws were often violated. By the mid-seventeenth century, the Spanish trade had expanded to the American Great Plains. During the eighteenth century, Taos in present-day New Mexico became an important trading center for Indian slaves. As late as the 1850's, the Taos-based slave trade remained active as the Utes sold their captives to Mexico. The Apaches, Comanches, and Pueblos were most often the victims of the Spanish slave trade.

The first Indians enslaved by the English were war captives, seized by Virginians in battle in 1622. Subsequently, every English colony used Indian slaves. By the 1670's, the English slave trade reached far into the interior of North America through Indian intermediaries. At a time when English settlement extended only 100 miles beyond the Atlantic Coast, the English slave trade reached beyond the Mississippi River. English colonists purchased slaves originally captured in Illinois, Missouri, and Oklahoma. Most of the English slave trade funneled through the Carolina colony. From Charleston, Indian slaves were sold to New England, New York, and the West Indies. Some slaves were kept in the Carolina colony, and in 1708 Indian slaves constituted nearly 15 percent of the Carolina population.

The trade in Indian slaves significantly influenced diplomatic relations among Indian nations. Because most Indian societies obtained their slaves from war captives, the economic demand for Indian slaves caused some tribes to wage war solely for the purpose of acquiring slaves. European colonies and Indian nations formed several military alliances to obtain slaves through warfare. English, Spanish, and French colonists often sold their own Indian war captives to the West Indies.

Decline of Indian Slavery. During the eighteenth century, Indian slavery declined as whites came to prefer African slaves. Indian slaves were increasingly hard to obtain because of the rapid decline of the native population from new diseases borne by white settlers. Whites also found it difficult to prevent Indian slaves from escaping in their own native land, and Africans provided more efficient labor because of their familiarity with large farms in Africa. The enslavement of Indians often created tension with nearby Indian societies and led to diplomatic difficulties for European colonies. Nevertheless, the use of Indian slaves by whites was surprisingly long-lived. There were still some Indian slaves in Louisiana and Rhode Island during the 1770's, in Massachusetts during the 1790's, and in the American Southwest during the 1850's.

Black Slavery Among the Indians. During the early nineteenth century, the international market for cotton caused the rapid expansion of white settlement into lands inhabited by southeastern Indian nations. Responding to this development, the Cherokee, Chickasaw, Choctaw, and Creek nations also turned to commercial farming and began to use black slave labor. Even after their forced migration to the Indian Territory in present-day Oklahoma during the 1830's, these Indian nations continued to use black slaves. By 1860, black slaves made up 14 percent of the population in the Indian Territory. During the Civil War, many Indian slaveholders supported the Confederacy against the Union. After the Union victory, the U.S. government required the abolition of slavery among the southeastern Indians, which was accomplished by treaty in 1866.

Harold D. Tallant

Sources for Further Study

Bailey, L. R. *Indian Slave Trade in the Southwest*. Los Angeles: Westernlore Press, 1966.

Gallay, Alan. *The Indian Slave Trade: The Rise of the English Empire in the American South, 1670-1717*. New Haven: Yale University Press, 2002.

Patterson, Orlando. *Slavery and Social Death: A Comparative Study*. Cambridge, Mass.: Harvard University Press, 1982.

Perdue, Theda. *Slavery and the Evolution of Cherokee Society, 1540-1866*. Knoxville: University of Tennessee Press, 1979.

Schneider, Dorothy, and Carl J. Schneider. *Slavery in America: From Colonial Times to the Civil War*. New York: Facts on File, 2000.

Starna, William A., and Ralph Watkins. "Northern Iroquoian Slavery." *Ethnohistory* 38, no. 1 (Winter, 1991): 34-57.

Washburn, Wilcomb E., ed. *History of Indian-White Relations*. Vol. 4 in *Handbook of North American Indians*, edited by William Sturtevant. Washington, D.C.: Smithsonian Institution Press, 1988.

Wiegers, Robert P. "A Proposal for Indian Slave Trading in the Mississippi Valley and Its Impact on the Osage." *Plains Anthropologist* 33 (May, 1988): 187-202.

See also: Adoption; Captivity and Captivity Narratives; Warfare and Conflict.

Snake Dance

Tribe affected: Hopi

Significance: *The Snake Dance promotes harmony between the Hopis and the universe and facilitates a bountiful supply of food, rain, and good hunting.*

The Hopi tribe believes itself to be an integral and interrelated part of nature and the universe. All parts must be kept in harmony, balance, and equilibrium. If the tribe upsets this balance, then it will suffer catastrophe. The Snake Dance is one of several Hopi ceremonial dances that facilitate this harmony and balance. It also enhances correct succession of the four seasons, an abundant supply of food and rain, and a profitable season of hunting.

The Snake Dance is performed in late August each year. A solar observance that begins about four in the afternoon, it is held in different villages during odd- and even-numbered years. The dance is an open ceremonial; visitors may attend and observe.

The dance is preceded by extensive preparation. Males of the snake and antelope fraternities leave their kivas in paint and costume. They go into the desert in each of the four directions for four days to gather snakes. The snakes are placed in a cottonwood tower, or *kisi*, in the center of the village plaza. A wooden plank covering a hole in the ground sits in front of the kisi and symbolizes the entrance to the underworld, or *sipapu*. Antelope priests line one side of the plaza to await the arrival of the snake priests. Upon arriving, the snake priests jump on the sipapu and so announce to the underworld gods the commencement of the snake dance.

Dance rattles made from gourds are vibrated to imitate the rattlesnake, and a chorus sings. At the end of the song the snake priests, who have lined up along the side of the plaza opposite the antelope priests, break up and regroup in threes. As they pass by the kisi, one is handed a snake by a priest hidden in it and places the snake in his mouth. The second member places his arm over the shoulder of the snake bearer and controls the snake if necessary. The third member walks behind.

Each snake priest dances a circle four times. He then drops the snake to the ground, and the third member picks it up. Depending on how many snakes have been caught and how many priests participate in the dance, a priest may repeat the dance several times with different snakes. When all the snakes have been danced with, they are dropped onto a circular design made of corn meal drawn on the ground. The snake priests then grab several snakes and run from the village into the desert to release them. The antelope priests jump on the plank so that the underworld knows the ceremony has ended, and the village then celebrates for four days.

Laurence Miller

See also: Dances and Dancing; Pow-wows and Celebrations.

Social Control

Tribes affected: Pantribal
Significance: *Social control among Indian tribes was maintained by mock battles, ridicule, gossip, public beatings, and execution, among a variety of other means.*

All Native American tribes had definite rules of behavior and strict concepts of what constituted permissible and antisocial behavior, as defined by the group's established norms. These norms, or mores, were traditionally accepted rules based on a peoples' religion and were long established through oral history as a "given way" for individual and group behavior, if the group was to survive. Admittedly, as in warfare and certain types of intergroup theft, ingroup behavior could differ from how one interacted with nontribal or non-aligned people. In fact, one could acquire certain status by violating the property of an antagonistic individual of an enemy group, or even taking the life of an enemy.

As with most unicentric political and legal systems, social control resided within the kin group and in daily face-to-face association with other village or band members. It was generally assumed that an extended family would resolve its conflicts privately. For example, among the Illinois, a man could punish his wife's adultery with mutilation or death. Once a conflict escalated and became public, however, the village or a council would intercede in an effort to restore harmony by resolving the family's problem. Social stability was favored; in-group antisocial behavior was deemed dysfunctional, interrupting basic survival tasks or leading to ongoing conflict.

Despite the usual involvement of the group with adjudication, there existed what is termed "self-help," or right of direct reprisal, often in the cases of murder, wife-stealing, or theft. For example, among the Inuit, when an individual was found guilty of a serious crime, a man was publicly executed by stabbing; a woman was publicly strangled.

Certain crimes of a public nature, ones detrimental to a group's welfare and tribal authority, often were reviewed by a council, chiefs, or, in some instances, by elders who gave advice and assistance in resolving moral transgressions and secular crimes. These leaders and advisers seldom had absolute power or the force to implement any decisions, but relied upon their office and prestige for settling transgressions and grievances, serving as mediators without coercive prerogatives. Consequently, legal decisions usually reflected the group's consensus of opinion. Among most Plains tribes, however, particularly during communal bison hunting, military societies were a real force who possessed undisputed authority to maintain uniform communal action, disciplining men whose individual actions jeopardized the hunt. The guilty man's weapons, property, and horse could be confiscated.

Witchcraft was a major crime, resulting usually in the accused's death. Accused sorcerers likewise could be assassinated without repercussions by the accused person's kin group. One accused of murder may provide the family of the deceased with wampum, or be expiated by other forms of compensation, depending upon the tribe. The bereaved family may refuse compensation, however, and could retaliate in kind without condemnation. An incorrigible thief could be killed with no fear of retaliation, for vengeance was rare and usually the offended family accepted compensation.

Among some Northwest Coast tribes, local feuds or accusations were settled by payment of traditional forms of wealth or by staging mock battles to resolve conflicts, sometimes "capturing" and holding as hostage high-ranking individuals. Many bands and tribes feared actions and retaliations that could lead to feuds, which usually meant counteraction and breaches, and could lead to excommunication or segmentation of a kin group if an equitable settlement was not reached.

The methods of social control differed cross-culturally, but the most effective means were through threat of sorcery or witchcraft, ridicule, consensus of opinion, mock battles between groups, gossip, excommunication, execution, public beatings or whippings, and even threats of serious illness or spiritual death. The Inuit employed song duels to ridicule their adversaries and engaged in public fistfights and wrestling, but withdrawal also remained an effective means of conflict resolution. Delinquent adolescent Native American children could be ostracized, mocked, or simply ignored.

Traditional native legal systems began to disintegrate in many northerly groups with the advent of the fur trade. Throughout North America, traditional native legal systems changed drastically through tribes' confinement to a reservation system, European American-induced religious and sociopolitical factionalism and the accompanying breakdown of clan and general kinship structure, replacement of traditional leaders by the Bureau of Indian Affairs, and general dominance by a multicentric European legal system.

John Alan Ross

See also: Clans; Humor; Kinship and Social Organization; Political Organization and Leadership; Witchcraft and Sorcery.

Societies: Non-kin-based

Tribes affected: Pantribal

Significance: *Non-kin-based societies provided American Indians with a sense of prestige, position, identity, and fraternity; ceremonies presented and supervised by the societies renewed tribal unity and traditions.*

Traditional American Indian societies had a wide variety of societies whose memberships were not limited to relatives or fellow clansmen. Non-kin-based societies served many functions for their membership and the tribe as a whole. These social organizations provided members with friendship, prestige and a sense of identity outside the family unit. Many societies supervised and/or performed public ceremonies that entertained, recounted tribal legends, celebrated traditions, and increased tribal unity.

Many societies existed for more than one purpose and did not fit into a single category. The lines defining different societal classifications, membership qualifications, and responsibilities were often intertwined. Membership qualifications were as varied as the number of societies. Memberships were based on personal achievement or ability, common beliefs, age, occupation, inheritance, or even a physical feature. Though a few societies accepted women, most memberships were restricted to adult males.

Medicine Societies. Medicine societies were the most widespread of Indian societies. Medicine society membership included shamans and curers considered to have special curative powers and/or contacts with the spiritual world. These societies usually met secretly and exchanged information regarding the curative powers of various rituals and plants. These clandestine meetings ensured that an element of secrecy and mysticism would cling to the society's curative powers. Each society possessed its own songs, dances, rites, and medicines particular to its area of expertise. Many medicine societies were formed to cure specific illnesses. Others contained experts in a particular treatment. The northeastern Little Water Society used water to cure the sick. The Plains Blood Doctors practiced bloodletting.

Membership requirements differed. Some candidates applied to a shaman for instruction. Others were recruited. Several societies accepted members who had been afflicted by and cured of a malady the society treated. Other members joined as a result of a dream directing them to become a member. Members sometimes belonged to more than one medicine society. Most members of the northeastern Shake the Pumpkin Society belonged to other medicine societies. This practice increased the expertise and prestige of the principal society.

As a group, medicine societies presented ceremonies believed to strengthen their medicine and cure the ill. During these celebrations, society members often demonstrated their remarkable powers. Members of the powerful Hopi Bear Shamans appeared to eat a human liver without harming the victim. Members of the Iruska Fire in Me Society, which treated burns, displayed their powers by walking on hot coals.

Medicine societies sometimes existed for reasons other than curing ill members of the tribe. Many medicine societies were in charge of annual celebrations and religious rituals. Curer societies of the Pueblo Indians were also responsible for the general welfare of the tribe. Pueblo curers were in charge of providing sufficient rainfall and ensuring fruitful harvests and healthy domestic animals. The Hopi Powamu Society possessed powers to make maize and beans grow. The headmen of the three Cochita Pueblo Indian medicine societies, the Flint, Giant and Shikami, chose important officials for the tribe, including the War Captains. The prestigious Kwakiutl Cannibal Society and the Hopi Agaves Society were in charge of initiating young males into the tribe.

Warrior Societies. Warrior and hunting societies were most prevalent in the western half of the United States. In many tribes, a man was not considered an adult until he was initiated into one of these societies. Most tribes had more than one warrior society. A single-warrior society usually boasted the bravest fighters, and rivalry among the societies was common.

Membership requirements varied from tribe to tribe and society to society. Warrior society membership was usually voluntary. Every adult male in the Southwestern Hopi tribe became a member of the Hopi Warrior Society. Some societies had to be applied to; others required an invitation. Some societies required the accomplishment of a special feat or act of bravery for membership. Laguna Pueblo warriors had to return with an enemy scalp to become a member of the Scalp-Takers. Two Cheyenne warrior societies allowed women to participate in feasts and dances.

Among the Cheyenne, boys between the ages of thirteen and sixteen, with some exceptions, could choose which society they wished to join. Most chose to enter their father's warrior society. Candidates were rigorously trained for membership and then initiated in an elaborate celebration that often lasted several days. Feasts were given by the new warrior or his parents to celebrate. Warrior society members gathered prestige through courageous actions in raids and warfare. They were expected to be brave in battle and not allowed to leave the battlefield alone. Members of the Sioux Sacred Bow Society were expected to fight to the death.

Age sometimes placed conditions on the society a candidate could join or affected their rank within the society. Teen members might still be considered in training. Older warriors could retire from the society or become inactive members. Some societies were formed specifically for older members, like the Sioux Chief's Society or the Crow Muddy Hands. The Mandan Dog Society had three strata to accommodate different age groups—the Little Dogs, Dogs, and Old Dogs.

Some warrior and hunting societies were temporary, formed for a specific purpose. When the Pawnee decided to conduct a raid, a Wolf Society was formed. The wolf was the spiritual patron of warfare and members of the society modeled themselves after their spiritual guide by covering themselves in wolfskin when going into battle. A Wolf Society raid was led by any man who presented himself as leader, usually an outstanding warrior. The leader could call off the raid at any time and was expected to be bravest in battle. Anyone wishing to follow the party smoked from a sacred pipe. Priests blessed the group through special prayers and ceremonies. Sacred bundles and special foods were carried to secure their power. Successful or not, the society disbanded when the party returned.

Warrior societies also performed ceremonies that demonstrated their power and recounted stories of the warriors' successes and failures. The dances and rituals purified society members and renewed the power of warriors and their weaponry. Each society had its own songs, dances, body paint, and regalia. The Horse Dance of the Great Basin not only honored the society's guiding spirit, but rallied support and increased tribal unity.

Some warrior societies provided other services to the tribe. The Blackfoot Prairie Dogs acted as an internal camp police force. At times, the Cheyenne Dog Soldiers, which contained up to half of the Cheyenne warriors, controlled tribal politics. Older members of the Warrior or Scalp Society guarded Pueblo Indian medicine society meetings.

Ceremonial and Secret Societies. Ceremonial and secret societies were the keepers of tribal history, legend, and customs. The rites and celebrations performed by these societies entertained and renewed tribal identity, heritage, and pride. Some ceremonial societies developed into religious movements.

Many of the secret societies of the Northwest coastal culture region were formed as prestigious, ritual dance fraternities. Members performed an elaborate series of dances at feasts, potlatches, and ceremonies. These dances were inspired by powerful spiritual beings encountered by the society's ancestors. Dancers dramatized the spiritual encounter, its possession of and exorcism from the societal elder. Dancers of the Northwest coast utilized elaborate masks, rattles, costumes, and body paint and performed amazing physical feats during ceremonies. The Kwakiutl Cannibal Society appeared to eat human flesh. Members of the Fire-Throwing Society swallowed or walked on hot coals.

Northwestern secret societies usually had strict membership qualifications and were often stratified. Nobles were allowed to join higher grade societies. The Wakashan and Bella Coola secret societies required individuals to inherit or marry into the right to be initiated. The Bella Coola Sisaok Society was restricted to relatives of certain chiefs. Women were allowed to participate in the lower dances, but there were no secret societies exclusively for women. Tribesmen could join as many societies as desired and societal memberships were proudly displayed at feasts and public ceremonies.

Ceremonial presentations performed by the Bella Coola Kusiut included demonstrations of their supernatural powers. Young male candidates for the Kusiut, or Black Face, Society were forcibly recruited. Masked Society members grabbed potential candidates, painted their faces black and took them to a secret hut outside the village for instruction on the methods used to deceive audiences. Any nonmember who discovered the society's secrets was either initiated or killed. Any member who divulged society secrets was killed.

The Midewiwin, or Medicine Lodge, Society of the Northeast was one of the most influential in the region. The Midewiwin Society began as a nativistic medicine society and later controlled many aspects of tribal life. The Midewiwin Society officiated at many feasts and celebrations. Members of the Mide priesthood were the keepers of tribal traditions, history, mythology, and legends. They possessed knowledge of curative plants, medicine bundles, and other objects that hurt or healed.

Midewiwin Society practices varied among the different tribes. Among the Chippewa, Midewiwin membership began when a person became ill or dreamed he should join the society. The candidate then sought advice from a Midewiwin priest who agreed to instruct him. Substantial fees were required and were sometimes paid in the form of blankets and pails. Candidates were expected to host a number of feasts. During a period of training, candidates learned the society's curative secrets, stories, and songs. At initiation, new members received birchbark scrolls with pictographic representations of Mide songs and Mide bags containing healing herbs. The Ottawa and a few other tribes allowed women to join their Midewiwin Society.

Spiritual Societies. Spiritual societies protected their tribe from evil spirits and delivered the gifts of kind spirits. Dances and rituals performed by the society worshiped and glorified the spirit world and warded off wicked spells. Members were often considered shamans because they had the ability to keep evil spirits at bay.

The Plains Bundle Societies existed to honor sacred bundles that had been given to the tribe or society as ancient gifts from the stars. Members of the society were not only responsible for the physical sacred bundle but the legends and ceremonies surrounding it. Sacred bundles ensured successful raids, hunting, warfare, and the well-being of the tribe. Separate societies were formed around each bundle.

Candidates for membership in a Pawnee bundle society, such as the Horse, Brave Raven, or Those Coming Behind societies, had to undergo tests specific to the bundle society before initiation. If the candidate failed the test, he was forever barred from that bundle society, but he could apply to others. Those who could not pass any test might form their own society.

Some societies were formed by members who shared similar spiritual guides, such as the Iroquois Bear, Buffalo, and Otter societies. Society rituals glorified and gave thanks to the society's spiritual mentor, who provided food and materials for the tribe. Society members often took on characteristics of their spiritual animal and imitated its traits at ceremonial dances.

Male or female members of the California Kuksu secret societies were held in high regard by other members of the tribe. Kuksu ceremonies recreated gods, ghosts, spirits, and sacred times prior to the creation of man in order to renew the spirit of the tribe. Candidates were invited to join based on birthright or personal achievements. Candidates underwent strenuous rites of passage and instruction before initiation into the society.

The southwestern kachina societies honored the ancient spirits of the various kachinas believed to live in the mountains and lakes surrounding the tribes. Kachinas were kind, benevolent, fun-loving, and sometimes comical creatures who provided the tribe with many of their needs. Society members impersonated kachina characters in their dances and retold stories of their lives, adventures, and kindnesses in order to cure the ill and ensure a good harvest.

The Iroquois False Face Society, so named for their use of masks, existed to counteract witch societies believed to be in league with the Evil Spirit. Members were people who dreamed they should join and left when they dreamed they should. The society was proficient at curing nosebleeds, toothaches, swellings, and eye inflammations, as well as at protecting the tribe from evil spirits.

Miscellaneous Societies. Additional societies included the Contraries of the Plains, Great Basin, and Southwest tribes. If a Sioux Indian dreamed of clowns, it was a sign he should join the Heyoka or Thunder Dreamers Society. Members talked and walked backward. They ate scalding hot food and complained that it was too cold. The Crow Contraries, or Crazy Dogs Wishing to Die, was a more serious, and usually very temporary, society. Members were motivated to join by feelings of desperation resulting from the loss of a relative or personal embarrassment. Crazy Dogs also did ordinary things backward. Members painted themselves in black war paint during peacetime or ignored an enemy attack on their camp. Crazy Dogs also performed "courageous" deeds in battle, however, coming closest to the enemy and usually dying first.

A few tribes had Berdache societies. Society members were men who dreamed or decided they should take on the role of a woman. After a ceremony in which they were initiated by the other sex, they dressed and acted as women. Among some tribes, berdache were considered powerful shamans. Others took a berdache with them into battle because they were considered good luck.

Several tribes had women's societies or allowed women to

join men's societies. Female members usually did not acquire the same status or privileges as male members. Women were allowed to become active members of the Californian Kuksu secret societies. Plains Indians had Shield Bearer Societies for the mothers and wives of great warriors. Normally, women were not allowed to touch weaponry, but Shield Bearers were allowed to carry weapons during special ceremonies. Other women's societies acknowledged skill in artistry. The Plains Indian Quill Workers were women adept at weaving with porcupine quills.

Non-kin-based societies suffered as a result of population declines, acculturation, and dispersion of tribes. Memberships dwindled, and many societies dissolved. Other societies have witnessed a resurgence in popularity as a result of interest in renewing tribal heritage and tradition. Midewiwin ceremonies are still practiced in the Northeast when tribes gather. A number of Native Americans consult medicine society members to cure illnesses, and many of the kachina and warrior society dances are still performed.

Leslie Stricker

Sources for Further Study

Laubin, Reginald, and Gladys Laubin. *Indian Dances of North America: Their Importance to Indian Life*. Norman: University of Oklahoma Press, 1977. Describes ceremonial rituals performed by North American Indians. Details dances, costumes, and ceremonial objects used and the meanings behind their use.

Murie, James R. *Pawnee Indian Societies*. New York: The Trustees, 1914. Vol. 11, part 7, in the series Anthropological Papers of the American Museum of Natural History, published by the museum's trustees. This work details Pawnee societies as well as other aspects of Pawnee life.

Oswalt, Wendell H. *This Land Was Theirs: A Study of North American Indians*. 7th ed. Mountain View, Calif.: Mayfield, 2001. This work takes representative tribes from each culture area and describes their spiritual life, social relations, subsistence activities, technology, and history.

Sturtevant, William C., gen. ed. *Handbook of North American Indi-*

ans. Washington, D.C.: Smithsonian Institution Press, 1978-2001. This multivolume set is an excellent reference for every aspect of North American Indian tribal life. It also includes maps, charts, and photographs.

Underhill, Ruth M. *Red Man's Religion: Beliefs and Practices of the Indians North of Mexico.* Chicago: University of Chicago Press, 1965. Details the origins and beliefs of many North American tribes from each culture area. Describes songs, dances, prayers, and rituals practiced and the societies in which they were practiced.

Wissler, Clark. *Societies and Ceremonial Associations in the Oglala Division of the Teton-Dakota.* New York: The Trustees, 1912. Vol. 11, part 1, in the series Anthropological Papers of the American Museum of Natural History, published by the museum's trustees. Gives insight into Plains warrior societies by concentrating on the Oglala Sioux.

See also: Clans; Hamatsa; Husk Face Society; Kuksu Rituals and Society; Midewiwin; Military Societies; Secret Societies; Women's Societies.

Spirit Dancing

Tribe affected: Salish
Significance: *Male members of the Salish tribe danced the Spirit Dance to communicate with their personal spirits.*

Spirit dancing was practiced by male members of the Salish tribe, a group of Indians living along the Northwest Coast. The reason for this dancing was to welcome the visitation of a participant's spirit. Since the Salish people believed that the spirits were on the other side of the earth during the summer, the visitations were always in the winter, when the tribal members had more time for leisure.

Whenever a spirit paid a visit to a person, that person would begin to sing his spirit song, while others would join in as they learned his particular song. In addition to this singing, the person undergoing the visitation would have his face painted. He would then sing and dance wildly around a fire within the confines of his house. As he danced, he uttered low moans and glanced about as though he were in a trance. Spectators helped to ensure that the dancer, in his frenzy, did not hurt himself by running into the posts of the house or jumping into the fire.

Ruffin Stirling

See also: Dances and Dancing; Music and Song.

Sports Mascots

Tribes affected: Pantribal

Significance: *Indian mascots, logos, and names for athletic teams are widespread in the United States, and with the rise of Native American activism ignited controversy in the 1970's and again in the 1990's. Many saw such names and mascots as dehumanizing and proliferating misunderstandings about Indian peoples; others maintained that Indian mascots honor Indian people and the strength of their cultures.*

History. Professional and collegiate athletic teams began adopting Indian mascots and names toward the end of the nineteenth century and early in the twentieth century when football and baseball became important pastimes in the United States. In many instances, the team names were drawn from historic tribes who had lived in the geographic locale; other teams drew the names from romanticized ideas about Indians. During this period many well-respected historians and social scientists predicted that Indians would soon vanish as a race. Indian populations were dwindling due to poor health conditions and difficult economic conditions on reservations. On most reservations in the west and southwest deaths exceeded births, and it seemed that the predictions would soon be true—Indians as racial and cultural groups would soon cease to exist. This incited romanticism and nostalgia for the "noble red man" along with a interest in Indian lifeways, customs, dress, and histories. Such interest translated into team names intended to memorialize and honor Indian warriors and their fighting spirit. Many teams, professional, amateur, or collegiate, created highly romanticized and fictional stories of tribal customs and even tribal names. Over time many tribal cultural traditions and customs were highly embellished, and among other things, mascots began to beat drums, dance and leap around, mimic scalping, whoop and yell, and wear odd clothing.

Indians did not vanish, but the fascination with Indian mascots, nicknames, and logos continued to grow, particularly among institutions of higher education and professional or amateur teams. Cleveland's baseball team became the Indians in 1914. Previously they were known as the Naps after legendary second baseman Napoleon Lajoie. During the 1930's, as intercollegiate sports rivalries deepened, numerous colleges and universities renamed their teams and adopted Indian mascots. As examples, Arkansas State University dropped their nicknames Aggies or Farmers and officially became the Indians, and the University of North Dakota abandoned Flickertails, the name of the state bird, in favor of the Fighting Sioux. Most teams invented their Indian mascots, which had little or no connection to any tribal group.

Controversy. During the 1970's, the civil rights movement brought heightened awareness of racial and ethnic issues, and American Indian groups began to raise issues about the inappropriateness of the Indian mascots, their antics during games, and their mockery of Indian people and culture. In 1972 the American Indian Center of Cleveland, Ohio, launched a $9 million lawsuit against the Cleveland Indians for its insulting and stereotypical logo, Chief Wahoo. This prompted some college and university campuses to reevaluate their Indian mascots and halftime shows depicting Indian culture. Eventually, some schools changed their mascots in response to student and faculty protest. The Dartmouth Indians became the Big Green, the Stanford Indians became the Cardinals, and the Syracuse Indian mascot, the Saltine Warrior, became the fruit Otto Orange. Over the years many universities have retired their Indian mascots.

Professional sports teams have been the target of protests and lawsuits enjoining them to discontinue using a particular Indian mascot, logo, or nickname because it is derogatory and harmful. In 1992 seven prominent American Indians brought suit against the National Football League and petitioned the United States Patent Office to cancel federal trademark protections. The basis of the lawsuit was that the name Redskins is insulting to American Indians and causes them to be regarded with contempt. In 1999 a federal panel of judges ruled on the side of the Indian plaintiffs in this case, *Harjo et al v. Pro Football*, and found cause to cancel the federal trademarks. The case was appealed by team owners.

The Road to Reform. The protests over the Washington Redskins rekindled the issue of Indian mascots on college campuses, and there were calls to drop all such mascots. Typically, at universities pressure to change Indian mascots originated with student groups or faculty on the grounds that such mascots were perpetuating inappropriate, inaccurate, and harmful images of living people, their cultures, and their histories. Opposition to changing Indian mascots tended to come from the Greek societies, alumni groups, and school administrators and trustees, who appealed to the sense of tradition at the school and asserted that Indian mascots honor Indian people. In many instances, alumni groups pressured their alma maters, threatening to withdraw monetary support if school mascots were dropped.

In 2003, more than eighty institutions of higher education maintained Indian mascots, logos, or nicknames. The activism surrounding the mascots had led universities to tone down raucous halftime exhibitions, ensure that mascots were dressed in attire appropriate to the tribe represented by the mascot, and develop sensitivity courses for the athletes. Today a number of institutions of higher education offer scholarships to American Indian students. At most schools with an Indian mascot, there are unresolved controversies.

Innumerable elementary and high schools still have teams with names such as the Braves, Warriors, Indians, and so on, and these too have been challenged. The states of Michigan, Nebraska, Minnesota, and Wisconsin have asked all schools in their states to rename teams, retire their mascots, and redesign their logos. School districts have also mandated change in some areas. Schools in Los Angeles, Dallas, and other locales have replaced their Indian mascots.

Within American Indian communities the mascot issue is controversial. For many Indian people, economic development, tribal sovereignty, and education are more important issues, and this group tends to resist becoming embroiled in the mascot controversy. Other American Indian people believe that the controversies surrounding mascots speak to basic cultural and human dignity, and they are convinced that until all Indian mascots and nicknames are dropped, they will not be able to advance their rights in other areas of life.

Carole A. Barrett

Sources for Further Study

King, C. Richard, and Charles Frueling Springwood, eds. *Team Spirits: The Native American Mascots Controversy.* Lincoln: University of Nebraska, 2001.

Sigelman, Lee. "Hail to the Redskins? Public Reactions to a Racially Insensitive Team Name." *Sociology of Sport Journal* 15 (1998): 317-325.

Slowikowski, Synthia Sydnor. "Cultural Performances and Sports Mascots." *Journal of Sport and Social Issues* 17, no. 1 (1993): 23-33.

Spindel, Carol. *Dancing at Halftime: Sports and the Controversy over American Indian Mascots.* New York: New York University Press, 2002.

See also: Stereotypes.

Squash

Tribes affected: All agricultural tribes
Significance: *One of the earliest domesticated foods in North America, squash was widely eaten and used for implements.*

"Squash" covers a variety of related plants, divided into the hard squashes (including pumpkins and many gourds) and soft squashes (such as zucchini). Hard squashes can be stored for several months and have high sugar content; they were domesticated in Mesoamerica and diffused to North America at least by 4500 B.C.E. The soft squashes are bountiful but somewhat less nutritious and impossible to store simply. Recent research suggests that soft squashes were domesticated in Arkansas around 1000 C.E.

Hard squashes were eaten baked or boiled, and their seeds usually also were eaten, either raw as snacks or ground into flour. Soft squashes usually were eaten boiled, often as part of stews.

While squashes were used primarily for food, they also were important for the making of tools. Hard gourds provided ready-

Preserved squash seeds. *(Payson D. Sheets)*

made bottles; a hole was drilled, the seeds were removed, and a stopper was added. Slightly more ambitious cutting created spoons, ladles, cups, and other implements. Left completely intact, a gourd will dry, and its seeds will separate from the shell, creating a natural rattle. The early spread of squashes may have been hastened by the exchange of rattles, since the dried seeds remain viable for many years.

Russell J. Barber

See also: Agriculture; Beans; Corn; Food Preparation and Cooking; Subsistence.

Star Quilts

Tribes affected: Pantribal
Significance: *Star quilts, which feature elaborate and colorful eight-pointed designs, are a fixture of American Indian life in many culture areas of the United States and Canada, particularly among the Plains tribes.*

Star quilts play an important role in modern Native American life. These quilts are made to give away in traditional ceremonies to honor individuals such as high school graduates or veterans; babies are wrapped in star quilts made by grandmothers and aunts; those participating in rituals such as making-a-relative or vision quests wrap up in star quilts made specially for the occasion; and star quilts form a source of economic development for some women who make them to sell.

Traditionally, Plains tribes used buffalo robes as blankets, as robes for protection against the cold, and as tipi liners. The robes were elaborately decorated with intricate painting and quillwork. Customarily, men painted realistic scenes on their robes, often depictions of their exploits in battle, while women painted geometric designs. One of the most prized of the women's designs was the war bonnet motif, a series of diamonds arranged in concentric circles.

Native Plains women may have been introduced to quilting through mission schools and churches. As part of their missionizing effort, churchwomen taught Indian women how to sew and sponsored quilting bees. When Indian children were placed in boarding schools, Native American girls were taught quilting techniques. The star quilt designs are a series of diamonds arranged in a large and colorful eight-pointed pattern reminiscent of the war bonnet patterns on the robes. Plains Indian women therefore seem to have adapted their traditional designs for use in making the star quilts.

Traditionally, the most skilled women artisans among the Plains tribes were honored for their craftsmanship and were invited to become members of women's societies. During the large summer encampments, these women's societies sponsored feasts and put on displays of their work. The most gifted artisans were highly acclaimed by both male and female tribal members. About 1880, in the early days of the reservation period, Indian women also began to display their quilts at annual summer church gatherings, much as they had displayed their earlier quillwork and beadwork. The best quilters were admired for their sense of design and artistry. By this time, animal hides, especially buffalo hides, were scarce, so the Plains women's ability to incorporate their designs into quilts served to extend their cultural traditions. Star quilts replaced the hide blankets used to wrap babies; children now stood on star quilts rather than buffalo hides when they received their Indian name. The quilts were also given as gifts to honor individuals on special occasions or for notable accomplishments. Quilting became a significant part of early reservation life and facilitated extension of many of the old traditions into reservation life. Making quilts continues to be an important part of many contemporary native communities, and the women who make them are deeply respected and admired by their people.

Carole A. Barrett

See also: Blankets; Gifts and Gift Giving; Hides and Hidework; Missions and Missionaries; Weaving; Women; Women's Societies.

Stereotypes

Tribes affected: Pantribal
Significance: *Outmoded stereotypes of Native Americans have long dominated various media; these stereotypes may affect public policy as well as individual perceptions.*

Stereotypes are generalizations concerning groups of people. Because they are commonly based on false or incomplete information, they are frequently inaccurate. A central problem with stereotypes is that behavior toward individuals may be based on stereotypical assumptions concerning a group to which they belong, which means that people may be penalized (or occasionally rewarded) for traits which they as individuals may not in fact possess. Such behavior is manifestly unfair, and for this reason it is important to understand stereotypes concerning Native Americans and to correct these misconceptions.

Stereotyping of American Indian groups is not a recent phenomenon, and it is not confined to non-Indian stereotyping of Indians. Many Indian groups' names for themselves simply mean "the people" in their native tongues. Outsiders, however (including other Native Americans), often used names for them which were considered derogatory, such as Eskimo (said to mean "eaters of raw flesh") or Atakapa ("eaters of people"). Traditionally, many Indians considered those who did not speak their languages or share their cultural norms to be less than human. In anthropological terms, such behavior is called "ethnocentric," a reference to people's tendency to esteem their own culture and denigrate those of others, describing others' behavior as deviant or inappropriate.

Early European Stereotyping. With the arrival of Europeans in the Americas, additional stereotypes emerged and were soon recorded in various media. The first stereotypes appeared in the print media, such as literature, journalism, and government archives, and visual media, such as drawings, paintings, and photographs. Later came film and video images and aural recordings of music and spoken dialogue. Since the Europeans and their descendants in the Americas maintained extensive written and visual records, most studies concerning stereotyping of Native Americans concern the historic period.

The earliest historic descriptions of "New World" cultures were written by the Spanish about peoples of the Caribbean and Central and South America. They did not describe the Aztec and Maya as possessing different but worthwhile cultural traits; rather, Spanish narratives characterized them as lacking Christianity and "civilization." These distinctions allowed the Spanish to place native populations in a category apart from Europeans and to justify their own horrific treatment of aboriginal peoples.

The later colonization of North America by the English and French (among others) incorporated the assimilated Spanish preconceptions. The terms "Indian," "savage," "infidel," "barbarian,"

An engraving from a sixteenth century German history book that falsely depicts the character of Native Americans. *(Library of Congress)*

and "heathen" were widely used by the seventeenth century English to identify a large number of different Native American cultures and to treat them all as members of the same group. The French used the term *sauvage* for the same purpose. This collapsing of individual and cultural differences into broad generalizations was typical of the colonial period in North America. Such mental templates occasionally justified illogical policies, such as plans to relocate different cultural groups onto the same tract of land. The planners did not seem to recognize, or did not care, that such policies often resulted in severe cultural conflicts.

It was common (and, given the mindset of Europeans at the time, probably unavoidable) to describe Indians not simply as they were but in terms of their differences from Europeans; the differences were generally regarded as deficiencies. Europeans often evaluated Native Americans according to their own Christian moral code, dismissing as immoral behavior that which was perfectly appropriate and sensible within the distinctive cultures they were so judging.

"Good" and "Bad" Indians. Colonialism gave rise to two general categories of Native American stereotypes that, with variations and refinements, continued for centuries: the "good" Indian and the "bad" Indian. These categorizations had far more to do with intellectual currents among Europeans than with Indian cultures themselves. If Europeans wished to criticize their own society, they often turned to accounts of American Indians, supposedly unspoiled by the artificiality and constraints of civilization, to demonstrate the deplorable state of European culture. These conventions are most apparent in eighteenth century French literature and philosophy, as in the works of Jean-Jacques Rousseau and his notion of the "noble savage." Conversely, when Europeans wished to uphold the worth of their own social mores, they often called upon the stereotype of the Indian as dirty, wretched, and bloodthirsty to enhance, by comparison, the value of European society.

Among early English colonists, Puritan publications such as captivity narratives had didactic and social motives, namely to trumpet the virtues of Christianity, to support Christian conversion of Native Americans, and to justify colonial settlements on Indian lands. The "good" Indian motif was not prevalent in America until independence from England. At that time, American literature with indigenous themes came to seem patriotic. American literary nationalism discovered the "proud and noble" Indian, and this theme was later incorporated into the works of painters and photographers. By the mid-1880's, authors had turned their frontier obsession to cowboys. "Wild west" shows became a popular form of public entertainment, combining stereotypical images of cowboys, soldiers ("Indian fighters"), and Indians.

Modern Times. With the arrival of the twentieth century, radio, films, and television continued to popularize various outdated views of Native Americans. A general misconception, still prevalent, is that Indian culture was timeless and unchanging until contact with the Europeans, at which time it was destroyed. This denial of both Native American history and survival suggests that the only true Indians existed before European contact and that their descendants somehow do not exhibit real "Indian-ness." This type of misconception underlies accounts of North American history which describe white settlement as progress advancing across a huge expanse of seemingly unoccupied land and pushing the frontier west. Such accounts ignore native peoples as prime movers in their own right, and they deny the ethnicity and cultural diversity of a significant proportion of the North and Central American populations. Since the 1970's, American Indians themselves, in addition to non-Indian scholars, have confronted these and other stereotypes. Through publication and educational reform, they work to break the pattern of ongoing stereotyping.

Susan J. Wurtzburg

Sources for Further Study

Allen, Paula Gunn, ed. *Studies in American Indian Literature: Critical Essays and Course Designs*. New York: Modern Language Association of America, 1983.

Barnett, Louise K. *The Ignoble Savage: American Literary Racism, 1790-1890*. Westport, Conn.: Greenwood Press, 1975.

Bataille, Gretchen M., and Charles L. P. Silet, eds. *The Pretend Indians: Images of Native Americans in the Movies*. Ames: Iowa State University Press, 1980.

Berkhofer, Robert F., Jr. *The White Man's Indian: Images of the American Indian from Columbus to the Present*. New York: Vintage Books, 1979.

Hilger, Michael. *The American Indian in Film*. Metuchen, N.J.: Scarecrow Press, 1986.

Howard, Helen Addison. *American Indian Poetry*. Boston: Twayne, 1979.

Larson, Charles R. *American Indian Fiction*. Albuquerque: University of New Mexico Press, 1978.

Mihesuah, Devon A. *American Indians: Stereotypes and Realities*. Atlanta, Ga.: Clarity, 1996.

Muñoz, Braulio. *Sons of the Wind: The Search for Identity in Spanish American Indian Literature*. New Brunswick, N.J.: Rutgers University Press, 1982.

Nichols, Roger L., ed. *The American Indian: Past and Present*. 4th ed. New York: McGraw-Hill, 1992.

Rollins, Peter C., and John E. O'Connor, eds. *Hollywood's Indian: The Portrayal of the Native American in Film*. Lexington: University Press of Kentucky, 1998.

Washburn, Wilcomb, E., ed. *History of Indian-White Relations*. Vol. 4 in *Handbook of North American Indians*, edited by William C. Sturtevant. Washington, D.C.: Smithsonian Institution Press, 1988.

See also: Captivity and Captivity Narratives; Gender Relations and Roles; Sports Mascots; Women.

Stomp Dance

Tribes affected: Creek, Seminole

Significance: *Marking the beginning of the Creek and Seminole yearly ceremonial cycle, the Stomp Dance is an all-night dance first performed in the early spring, then repeated several times between spring and fall.*

Referring both to the nighttime dances held at the Square Ground (the physical center of religious and political life) and to a specific form, the Stomp Dance is a principal feature of Creek and Seminole ceremonial life.

After purifying themselves by washing and drinking *Hoyvniji*, an emetic, men begin the Stomp Dance at the Square Ground, where a sacred fire is burning. Like most Creek and all Seminole ceremonial dances, the fire is a focal point for the dancing ritual.

The Stomp Dance consists of a leader who begins dancing in a clockwise circle around the fire, inviting other experienced male dancers to join him. The dancers are accompanied by "shell-shaker girls" wearing leg rattles who provide the rhythmic background for the dance. After all the male dancers are participating, women are permitted to join them. A principal ceremonial feature of the dance is the sacrifice of meat, which is fed to the sacred fire.

Stomp dances are performed in early spring, in May and June as preliminaries to the Green Corn Ceremony (the major ceremonial observance of the year), and also in August and September.

Mary E. Virginia

See also: Dances and Dancing; Green Corn Dance.

Subsistence

Tribes affected: Pantribal
Significance: *In their thousands of years of residence in the Americas, Native Americans have obtained their food by various strategies.*

The Asians who crossed the Bering land bridge and became the first American Indians were hunter-gatherers, relying entirely on the plants and animals provided by nature for their food supplies. Over the millennia, their descendants developed a great variety of ways of gaining their livelihood, some continuing to exploit nature exclusively, some domesticating and cultivating crops, some herding domestic animals, and some combining these subsistence modes. Choices regarding what modes of subsistence to follow were neither capricious nor dictated by ignorance of other options: rather, they were rational decisions based on the advantages and disadvantages of each. The option that was chosen carried strong implications for the way of life, often leading a people down a path from which later departure was difficult.

Hunting-Gathering. The hunting-gathering way of life was based on utilizing food sources as they occurred naturally. Berries were picked from the berry patches, but no berry seeds were planted to create new berry patches; deer were stalked and killed, but they were neither herded nor bred to intensify characteristics preferred by the hunter. Fish were netted, but they were not impounded in ponds for breeding and harvest.

This simplified view of hunting-gathering overlooks some purposeful human modification of the environment. Indians in both the Northeast and California, for example, selectively burned areas, encouraging the growth of certain plants that colonize disturbed areas. Many of the weeds that first grow in burned areas were excellent eaten as greens and often bore starchy seeds that could be made into flour. Berry bushes also entered such areas soon after burning, and hunter-gatherers could take advantage of their fruits. Most important, deer (the most common meat source for North American hunter-gatherers) would find more browsing fodder in recently burned areas, and their numbers would increase. Burning, then, provided a measure of control over the foods that nature produced, encouraging the types desired by people; nevertheless, hunter-gatherers remained basically dependent on what nature offered.

Dependence on nature did not limit the ingenuity of American Indian hunter-gatherers in designing and using technology to aid hunting and fishing. Clever traps and weirs captured game and fish while the hunter or fisher was doing something else; spear-throwing aids effectively lengthened the hunter's arm in throwing a spear, increasing the power generated; plant poisons that stunned fish but did not render their flesh toxic to human beings were used widely in quiet stretches of rivers. In contrast, the gathering of plants remained labor-intensive, with few devices to improve its efficiency.

Hunting-gathering provided a generally good life. Except in marginal environments such as deserts, hunter-gatherers typically could obtain a day's food for their families with only a few hours' work, leaving much time for other activities. The wide variety of foods eaten by most hunter-gatherers provided sufficient nutritional diversity to maintain good health. Hunter-gatherers found it desirable to move with the seasons, taking advantage of the seasonal abundance of one or another food source and settling near it for the period it was available; this movement ensured hunter-gatherers of clean, new quarters on a regular basis, again helping preserve good health.

The requirements of hunting-gathering, however, placed some restrictions on American Indians following this mode of subsistence. Seasonal movements were necessary to take advantage of natural distributions of food sources over time and space; therefore, hunter-gatherers were limited in the amount of material items they could accumulate or transport. Duplicate tools could be made and stored at the different settlements in anticipation of next year's return, but it was difficult or impossible to stockpile large quantities of food. This was a limitation in seasonal environments, such as northern regions where several months of winter saw limited food supplies and sometimes starvation. The limitation of available food for the lean season meant that populations could attain only moderate densities in most environments. The same problem meant that the number of people in a settlement could not be too large, since the surrounding locale could provide only so much food.

Hunter-gatherers usually had relatively uncomplicated ways of governing themselves. Their leaders typically served at the pleasure of the community, and leaders rarely could do more than encourage people to follow the course of action they deemed appropriate. Hunter-gatherers usually had religions that stressed individual relations to spirits, and shamans often were the primary religious functionaries. Kinship relationships usually were patrilineal (traced through the male lines).

Transition to Agriculture. While hunting-gathering was a successful way of life, the limitation on the amount of food available during the lean season was a serious one. Hunter-gatherers searched for ways to increase the amount of food they provided their families, but the limitations remained. Food scarcity in the lean season resulted in higher child mortality. Rarely did children starve, and parents usually tried to protect them from the worst shortages, but undernourishment resulted in lowered resistance to disease, and children probably bore the brunt of lean-season deaths.

All peoples have realized the connection between seeds and plant growth. Hunter-gatherers doubtless turned to cultivating plants in an attempt to limit the problems of the lean season. Some of the earliest plant cultivation in the Americas is known from the Tehuacán Valley of central Mexico around 6000 B.C.E. Avocados and chili peppers were grown there by American Indians as an adjunct to hunting-gathering. These same Indians began growing corn by 5000 B.C.E. and beans and squash within the next few centuries. Not until 3500 B.C.E. or later, however, did these cultivators establish year-round settlements. Instead, they continued their

Primary Subsistence Types

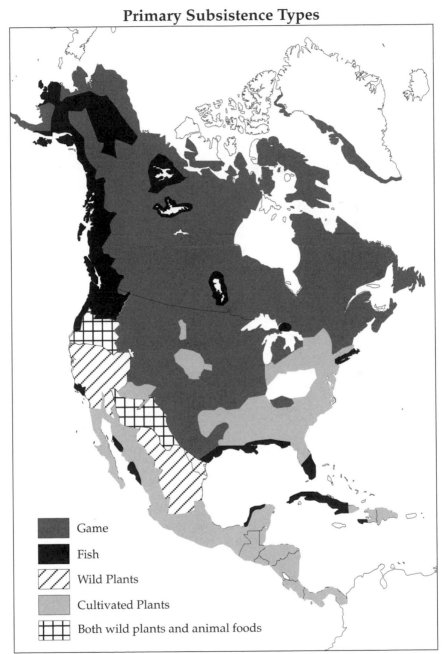

Game

Fish

Wild Plants

Cultivated Plants

Both wild plants and animal foods

Source: After Driver, Harold E., and William C. Massey, *Comparative Studies of North American Indians,* 1957.

seasonal movements and emphasis on hunting and gathering nature's bounty. Eventually, however, they became dependent on agriculture and placed their primary efforts in that field, utilizing wild plants and animals only as adjuncts to their agricultural produce. At this point, their ties to fields and storage facilities became greater than the benefits of seasonal movement, and they became sedentary.

The same process that took place in the Tehuacán Valley occurred in many other places in the Americas, though at different times. Between 3500 and 500 b.c.e. in the Southwest, the same process of using a few cultivated crops as an adjunct to hunting-gathering evolved into agricultural dependence; between perhaps 1200 b.c.e. and 800 c.e. in the Illinois Valley, a parallel process occurred.

As people became dependent on agricultural crops, they no longer were satisfied to continue growing wild plants. Instead, they modified them, choosing those with the fastest growing season, the largest fruits or seeds, or the greatest resistance to drought. By selecting the seeds or cuttings of these individual plants, the next generation would have a higher frequency of the desired trait, and gradually the plant was modified. This is the selective breeding process used in modern agronomy to establish new varieties of crops, and it achieved tremendous success in pre-Columbian America. Over thousands of years, tiny cobs of corn no larger than a little finger were converted to the sausage-sized cobs of historic times; beans became larger and more drought-resistant; squash became larger and sweeter. The process of domestication was so successful that some crops, corn included, lost their ability to reproduce themselves without human intervention.

Agriculturalists domesticated and cultivated a large inventory of crops in the Americas, including chili peppers, avocados, corn, squash, beans, sunflowers, tomatoes, potatoes, sweet potatoes, manioc, pineapples, and amaranth, a tiny seed crop eaten extensively in various places. The most important crops always were ones that could be stored effectively. In this way, agriculture helped reduce the problem of the lean season, and regional populations always grew at the onset of agricultural dependence. After a few generations, the ability to return to hunting-gathering probably was lost, since the higher population levels required the greater amounts of food that came with agriculture, especially during the lean season.

At some point as agriculture became more important, people had to settle down. Moving from one place to another with the seasons became impractical, since carrying their supply of stored foods would require unreasonable amounts of labor. With this sedentism, people could begin accumulating larger amounts of material goods, and they could live in larger communities. These communities often found it desirable to have a leader who had greater authority than any individual did under the hunter-gatherer system. In some places, populations were large enough that the people submitted to leaders who wielded coercive power, permitting these chiefs to enforce their decisions. The ultimate in this development was the Aztec Empire of Mexico, with its divine emperor who had life-and-death power over every member of the empire.

The relations between the sexes also changed under agriculture. Most hunter-gatherers assigned men the more dangerous task of hunting and women the more time-consuming chores of gathering plants, which typically formed the greatest part of the hunter-gatherer diet. Fishing might be assigned to either sex. As hunter-gatherers invested more in agriculture, women transferred their control of wild plants to domesticated crops. Fields often were controlled or even owned by women, who passed them on to their daughters. In this manner, the emphasis shifted in many cases to reckoning kinship primarily through women: matrilineality. A concern with the success of agriculture also began a greater focus on group-oriented religious ceremonies.

Pastoralism. For reasons that are unclear, American Indians never domesticated many animals. In South America, llamas and other camelids were domesticated for food and transportation, but in North America and Mexico, only turkeys and muscovy ducks were important domestications. (Dogs probably had been domesticated by the time they crossed over the Bering land bridge with the first American Indians.) When Europeans came into the Americas after 1492, they brought a variety of domesticated animals with them, especially horses, cattle, and sheep. These provided North American Indians with the first opportunity to begin pastoralism, the raising of domestic animals as a primary mode of subsistence.

The death and dislocations that accompanied the European conquest of the Americas kept most Indian groups from adopting pastoralism, but a few groups in the Southwest have done so successfully, notably the Navajo, some Apache groups, and the Tohono O'odham.

The Navajo serve as the prime example of pastoralists, since they typically move with their flocks. They focus on sheepherding, and most rural Navajo family groups have at least a few sheep. The demands of these livestock mean that the family must maintain considerable flexibility. If the grass runs out, the sheep have to be shifted to new pasturage, and bad years mean many shifts. If circumstances are particularly bad, relatives must be called upon for assistance, and flexibility in reckoning kinship ties is important. The size of the household must reflect the size and viability of the herd, and a bad year may mean that the family splits up for a time.

Pastoralists rarely can meet all their needs, and they usually have strong trading ties with settled agriculturalists. Because of this trade, some pastoralists may be able to accumulate a fair amount of wealth, at least enough to permit them to settle in a town and live off their profits. These individuals, called "ricos" among the Navajo, often abandon their former pastoralist ways.

Culture Areas and Subsistence. In traditional times, North American Indians in certain portions of the continent shared similar lifestyles and patterns of culture. In part, these similarities were engendered by living as neighbors, interacting and communicating with one another. Other similarities, however, probably were more the result of similar modes of subsistence.

In eastern North America, for example, Indian tribes shared considerable similarity. All tribes south of the latitude of central Maine were agriculturalists, relying heavily on corn, beans, and squash. All of these plants had been domesticated in tropical Mexico, and it had taken centuries for them to be transported this far and to be adapted to the rigors of the colder climate in eastern North America. These same plants had been adopted earlier in the Southeast, and population levels had risen, achieving higher levels there than in the Northeast. The largest towns in the Southeast before European contact were probably two or three times as large as their counterparts in the Northeast.

As a result, many of the Southeast tribes had developed the chiefdom form of government, with a coercive leader. The Natchez, for example, had a single ruler called "the Sun," who had total control over his subjects, though he could be removed from office for lack of bravery or other offenses. In the Northeast, government was less strong and intrusive, and leaders were more likely to lead by example than decree. The leadership of the Iroquois tribes, while more coercive than that of their Algonquian neighbors, was far less able to enforce an unpopular decree than were most leaders in the Southeast.

Before the advent of Europeans in North America, the Plains tribes were mostly similar to Eastern Woodlands tribes. They were agriculturalists, carving farms out of the tough sod of the prairies and living in villages of rarely more than a dozen families. Their leaders led by example, and religious ceremonies largely were conducted by kin groups and voluntary societies. Kinship was primarily matrilineal.

The coming of the Europeans, however, brought the horse, and it changed Plains life massively. Tribes formerly had hunted bison on foot seasonally, but the inefficiency of the process meant that this could not be relied upon as the primary means of subsistence. The horse, however, made bison hunting efficient, and most Plains tribes abandoned farming in favor of a new lifestyle based first on bison hunting and later augmented with raiding on neighbors and

Europeans. As the tribes converted from agriculturalists to hunter-gatherers, they returned to reckoning kinship through the male line, and many group-oriented ceremonies became less central to the community.

The Indian tribes of the Southwest before the coming of the Europeans fell into two groups: settled agriculturalists (the Pueblo peoples and the Pima and Tohono O'odham) and the mobile hunter-gatherers (the Apache, including those that later would become the Navajo) that lived in the areas between their settlements. The matrilineal agriculturalists lived in quite sizeable settlements, practicing group-oriented religious ceremonies and recognizing leaders who ruled by example. The hunter-gatherers exploited the foods of nature, traded with the settled peoples for corn and other goods, and occasionally took advantage of their mobility to raid the settled villages for goods.

The Northwest Coast of North America is a great exception to the generalizations presented about the relationship between subsistence and way of life. Tribes of this culture area never adopted agriculture, but the Northwest Coast possessed great natural bounty, especially in terms of salmon and other fish. As a result, dense populations developed and settled into sedentary villages along prime fishing rivers. The control of fishing areas was largely in the hands of the chiefs, and they often developed considerable power over others, in part through their personal wealth, in part through the coercive power given them by the people. This is one of the few cases known around the world where coercive leadership has developed among a hunting-gathering society.

In the far northern parts of North America, the growing season was too short to permit agriculture of any kind, and hunter-gatherers were the exclusive residents of these areas. The environment dictated small group sizes, great seasonal mobility, and the uncluttered government that is desirable under these characteristics. While hunter-gatherers typically gain most of their food from plants, far northern Indian tribes and the Inuit are exceptional. In this area, plants are few and the growing season is short, so people must resort to a diet dominated by animal flesh. Such a diet is likely to be short of vitamins, but the eating of internal organs, a major source of vitamins, helps offset that deficiency.

Russell J. Barber

Sources for Further Study

Brody, Hugh. *The Other Side of Eden: Hunters, Farmers, and the Shaping of the World*. New York: North Point Press, 2001. An analysis of the beliefs, thought processes, and practices that differentiate hunters and farmers.

Byers, Douglas S., ed. *Prehistory of the Tehuacán Valley*. Austin: University of Texas Press, 1967. This multivolume work provides great detail on all aspects of the archaeology of the Tehuacán Valley. Articles by Richard S. MacNeish summarize changes in subsistence, plant domestication, and associated adjustments in settlement size and seasonal movement.

Flannery, Kent V. "The Origins of Agriculture." In *Annual Reviews in Anthropology 2*. Palo Alto, Calif.: Annual Reviews, 1973. An excellent review of thinking on why agriculture developed and the adjustments it required from the hunting-gathering lifestyle. Emphasis is on agriculture in the Americas.

Kupferer, Harriet J. *Ancient Drums, Other Moccasins: Native American Cultural Adaptations*. Englewood Cliffs, N.J.: Prentice Hall, 1988. An overview of ten Indian tribes, approached from the viewpoint of the relationship between subsistence and culture. Accessible and nontechnical, but not very detailed.

Lee, Richard B., and Irven DeVore, eds. *Man, the Hunter*. Chicago: Aldine, 1968. A classic collection of essays on hunter-gatherers around the world. They explode many myths—that hunter-gatherers work long hours, that they do not understand seed growth, and so forth. The articles by Suttles and Sahlins on the Northwest Coast are particularly relevant.

Panter-Brick, Catherine, Robert H. Layton, and Peter Rowley-Conwy, eds. *Hunter-gatherers: An Interdisciplinary Perspective*. New York: Cambridge University Press, 2001. An examination of the demography, history, social organization, and technology of assorted hunter-gatherer societies.

Steward, Julian. *Basin-Plateau Aboriginal Sociopolitical Groups.* Bulletin 120. Washington, D.C.: Bureau of American Ethnology, 1938. A truly classic discussion of how ecological constraints and hunting-gathering shaped the social and political structures of tribes in western North America's desert.

See also: Agriculture; Buffalo; Fish and Fishing; Hunting and Gathering; Ranching; Weirs and Traps.

Suicide

Tribes affected: Pantribal
Significance: *The destruction of traditional culture and the corresponding economic deprivation of much reservation life has made suicide epidemic in the Indian population.*

Traditionally, Native Americans recognized the sanctity of life and stressed family and community responsibility. Suicide was thus uncommon, though it was permitted in some cultures under exceptional circumstances. Throughout North America, the aged and infirm often asked to be left to die rather than impose a burden. Among Plains Indians, suicide was sometimes regarded as preferable to social disgrace or severe physical deformity. Some saw suicide as permissible to avoid pain if all responsibilities had been fulfilled. Others, such as the Navajo, discouraged suicide, believing that it left behind a dangerous ghost.

Studies begun in the 1940's, however, uncovered a disturbing trend. With the breakdown of cultural traditions, family instability, poverty, and lack of opportunity, Indian suicide has become commonplace, especially among young males. The overall suicide rate for Indians is 30 percent higher than for the general population, and for young males (ages twelve to twenty-four), the rate is double. After age forty-five, the comparative rate begins to decline, and for the elderly it is significantly below the national average.

Charles Louis Kammer III

Sources for Further Study

Chandler, Michael J., et al. with commentary by James F
   Personal Persistence, Identity Development, and Suicide
   Native and Non-Native North American Adolescents. N
   well, 2003.
Lester, David. *Suicide in American Indians.* New
   ence, 1997.
Rhoades, Everett R., ed. *American Indian Health: In.*
   Health Care, Promotion, and Policy. Baltimore: Johns Hopkins
   University Press, 2000.
Trafzer, Clifford E., and Diane Weiner, eds. *Medicine Ways: Disease,*
   Health, and Survival Among Native Americans. Walnut Creek, Ca-
   lif.: AltaMira Press, 2001.

See also: Alcoholism; Disease and Intergroup Contact; Employment and Unemployment.

Sun Dance

Tribes affected: Arapaho, Arikara, Assiniboine, Blackfoot, Crow,
   Dakota, Gros Ventre, Hidatsa, Kiowa, Lakota, Ojibwa, Plains
   Cree, Sarsi, Shoshone, Siseton, Ute
Significance: *Conducted primarily to ask the Spirit to bring the tribe a*
   successful bison hunt, the Sun Dance also celebrates the creation of the
   world, re-creating the interaction of time, space, mass, and energy as
   mythologically perceived by various tribes, all of whom added their
   own sequences of steps to signal syncretic features unique to their own
   perceptions.

"Ceremony is a picture of one's relationship to that which is being
honored," said Nicholas Black Elk. Ritual is a ceremony repeated
at specific times for specific purposes. To gaze at the sun while
dancing and be gazed at by the sun while dancing was the only
calendrical ritual of the Plains tribes done by a group, band, or
tribe. It was (and is) held annually either during the full moon

when the berries ripen (June-July) or during the moon when the cherries blacken (July-August). Various bands gathered for the great "making of meat"—the hunting, cutting, spreading, drying, preserving, and storing of buffalo meat. The bison were central to the economy of the Plains tribes, and the bison is "of the earth." It occupied a central place in the mythology of many tribes.

History. The Sun Dance goes by different names—"dance without drinking" (Cree), "ceremony of the life renewal" (Cheyenne), "the sacred or mysterious dance" (Ponca), and "the sun gazes at the dance" (Dakota). Sun Dancing was most elaborate among the Arapaho, Cheyenne, Crow, and Sioux. The Pawnee, Comanche, Kiowa, and Ute copied it as late as 1890, the time when the wave of Ghost Dances was sweeping many Indian nations. When the horse was introduced to Indian cultures, it changed the syncretic sequences of various dances, and since that time immediate histories of various tribes have been inscribed onto the Sun Dance.

Following the years 1890-1891 and the massacre at Wounded Knee, and under reservation strictures, the pattern of the dance was curbed and changed drastically. From 1881 to 1920 the Sun Dance involving piercing of the flesh went underground. Semisecret Sun Dances without piercing were held in the 1920's. Following the Indian Reorganization Act of 1934, Sun Dances without piercing were held openly. In the late 1950's, enthusiasm revived, and Sun Dances including piercing became common on Plains reservations. The Pine Ridge Tribal Council even promoted them as a tourist attraction, "a re-enactment of the old ways," and presented a dance in conjunction with the Fourth of July Fair. A number of descriptions of Sun Dances have been published, dating from as early as 1882. No two Sun Dances even in the same tribe are conducted the same; perhaps they never were.

Honoring and Giving Back. The Sun Dance is a picture of the tribe's "relationship to that which is being honored," and that relationship changes with time and with the various Sun Dance intercessors' (holy men's) interpretations. In the old times, the "Tree

An artist's rendering of an early twentieth century Sioux sun dance. *(National Archives)*

of Life," the Sun, the Buffalo, the "Center of the Universe," and warrior societies were honored. These icons were honored with thanksgiving prayers for their very existence. In the long underground years from 1881 to 1934, many of the original instructions were reinterpreted. Much Christian, especially Catholic, influence came to bear. The Sun Dance, originally a thanksgiving rite, changed to a rite of repentance and self-mortification. In the old days there were flesh offerings, dragging of skulls, and suspension from skewers in the skin attached by rope to scaffolds or the center tree of life, but such acts were considered "giving back." In the beginning, according to Albert White Hat, Jr., a tribal archivist at Sinte Gleska College on the Rosebud Reservation, the very first power created all there is by "opening a vein" and letting energy flow. Thus, returning some of one's own flesh and blood to the Creator was considered a thanksgiving, a giving back; it was not considered immolation, mortification, or torture.

Originally those who vowed to dance for personal reasons usually did so because their life or a loved one's life had been spared or because a medicine was given and instruction for its use granted. Personal vows often took months, sometimes a year of preparation. Proper preparation for a Sun Dance requires months of constructing and readying the instruments used in the ceremony. Abstinence from sexual activity is recommended, varying with tribes from four days to four months before the ceremony.

Sun Dances were powerful and deeply emotional rituals lasting four days from opening to close and involving much personal sacrifice. Dancers abstained from food or water during the dance. They suffered from the heat and from hyperventilation caused by blowing continually on an eagle bone whistle. Some dancers also used the ritual to make giveaways of personal possessions. In giving thanks by making a blood sacrifice in one of several ways at this communal annual ritual, people prayed for the welfare of the entire tribe.

To paraphrase Frances Densmore's *Teton Sioux Music* (1918), a vow to dance was usually made at sunrise and was made to the daybreak star of understanding. A proper offering of bison fat was held in the left hand, and the right hand was raised as the vow was spoken. The spoken vow was only that the man would participate in a Sun Dance, but in his heart was the secret vow of the form of that participation. The man would vow either to dance, to be suspended from poles, or to drag buffalo skulls.

In mid-June of 1876, many bands gathered along Rosebud Creek in southeastern Montana. It was known that the U.S. Army was coming at them from three sides. Sioux, Cheyenne, and some Arapaho decided to hold the Sun Dance rather than run. Sitting Bull, among all the great men who were there, was chosen leader. Surrounded by the army, the Plains tribes held to their ancient beliefs and sought the power and a successful bison hunt. Sitting Bull knew that the army was close, but he also knew that the Indians would be safe during the Sun Dance. On June 17, two days after the dance, the bands were attacked by General Crook. One thousand Indian warriors forced seven hundred army troops into retreat. The Indians then moved to a river called the Little Bighorn, where they were attacked again by General George Custer. It was their last great victory.

The Sun Dance Today. Today the dance seems to be primarily a celebration of personal renewal. There is a special relationship between the dancer and the spiritual world, and the Sun Dance is an event of a highly religious nature. The revival of this ritual in our times is more than a visual representation. This ritual takes place on both mythological and real planes of existence and is the source of symbolic and expressionistic power. Because the mythological element is still so evident, many Indians do not understand why nontribal members would want to Sun Dance. They believe that non-Indians who dance without any clear understanding of the mythology being re-enacted are probably dancing for personal gratification or egotistical need. Purists also complain about the crass commercialism and religious degeneration of these dances.

The most visible Sun Dances held in the United States in modern times are on the Pine Ridge and Rosebud reservations in South Dakota and on the Crow Reservation in Montana. Many modern Sun Dances have become arenas where traditionalists and those who wish to capitalize on the ritual vent their anger toward one another. Yet modern Sun Dances satisfy the social needs of the tribes, whether members are traditionalists or modernists. Thousands of tribal people attend the Sun Dances, setting up old-style nomadic camps and catching up with friends and relatives from other reservations. Regardless of whether the contemporary Sun Dance is a syncretic version of old and new, it exists as a powerful mediating force between factions on reservations and allows all in attendance to assert their religious beliefs.

Among all tribes there are certain similarities and consistencies in the Sun Dances. There is always the establishment of a sacred center, symbolizing the center of the universe. This helps any of the various tribes experience their place of emergence, as nearly all American Indians have myth stories describing their "emergence" into this plane of existence. At the finding of the center, prayers, songs, drums, and rattles are used to drive away evil. Members of the scout society who conduct their lives in an exemplary way are sent to find the tree which will be placed in the center. Every action pertinent to the ritual is supported by prayers and songs. Sweatlodges and purification by smoke from sage, sweetgrass, and cedar are central to the ritual. Sacred icons or instruments such as pipes, arrows, or sacred bundles are also central to the rituals. There is always a recitation of the mythology of the people. There are often naming ceremonies for children. At Sun Dances each year, tribal identities are upheld and sustained. There is always a feast at the conclusion of the dance.

The Sun Dance is conducted by holy men (interpreters), who talk with spirit forces. If the camp circle is very large and several holy men are present, they will decide among themselves who will conduct the dance. It is generally known who will be the intercessor, and often the same man will serve in this capacity for a number of years. Bearing this responsibility requires long and special preparation. The duties traditionally included offering prayers for all the people, singing certain ancient songs at exactly the right time, painting sacred objects, handling the most sacred instruments of the nation, and preparing the sacred place. A Teton Sioux man named Red Bird once told Frances Densmore that "the tribe would never appoint an unworthy man to the office of intercessor. In his prayers and offerings he represented the people, and if he were not a good man he might even send disaster upon the tribe."

There is much confusion surrounding Sun Dances today. Traditionalists say that one should dance to see and that there are too many now who are dancing to be seen. Many dance unprepared; others dance with little or no knowledge of the mythology of the people whose ceremony they are enacting. A proper Sun Dance may be likened to a carefully orchestrated symphony of the entire religion of the people. Power is called and set in motion for another year, "that the people may live."

Glenn J. Schiffman

Sources for Further Study

Bonnefoy, Yves. *Mythologies*. Translated by Wendy Donniger. Vol. 2. Chicago: University of Chicago Press, 1991.

Brown, Joseph Epes, ed. *The Sacred Pipe: Black Elk's Account of the Seven Rites of the Oglala Sioux*. Norman: University of Oklahoma Press, 1989.

Dorsey, George A. *The Cheyenne Indians: The Sun Dance*. Glorietta, N.Mex.: Rio Grande Press, 1971.

Hull, Michael. *Sun Dancing: A Spiritual Journey on the Red Road*. Rochester, Vt.: Inner Traditions International, 2000.

Mails, Thomas E. *Sundancing at Rosebud and Pine Ridge*. Sioux Falls, S.Dak.: Center for Western Studies, Augustana College, 1978.

_____. *Sundancing: The Great Sioux Piercing Ritual*. 2d ed. Tulsa, Okla.: Council Oak Books, 1998.

Neihardt, John. *Black Elk Speaks*. Lincoln: University of Nebraska Press, 1979.

Schiffman, Glenn, ed. *Black Elk Speaks*. Illuminated Books and Manuscripts: An Interactive Program. Los Angeles: IBM, 1990.

_____. *Relationship with Fire*. Los Angeles: Word of Mouth Press, 1988.

See also: Dances and Dancing; Ghost Dance; Okeepa; Religion.

Sweatlodges and Sweatbaths

Tribes affected: Pantribal
Significance: *Sweatlodges and sweatbaths are widely used for ceremonial, social, and medicinal purposes.*

The sweatlodge is a traditional ceremonial enclosure, usually circular in design. It is generally framed with saplings, wooden poles in a conical arrangement, or cedar planks. The enclosure can be from 4 to 8 feet across and 4 to 6 feet in height. It was traditionally covered with animal skins, bark, or earth. Today blankets or other coverings are often used. Lodge design is varied according to tribe and available building materials.

A shallow pit, approximately a foot across, is dug in the center of the sweatlodge floor. This pit is the receptacle for the seven to twenty-eight stones used to heat the enclosure. They are brought in, in one to four rounds of approximately fifteen to twenty minutes duration. Volcanic stones hold heat the best. Temperatures in the sweatlodge can exceed 200 degrees Fahrenheit.

Participants disrobe, either completely or partially, and walk clockwise around the lodge. They enter the lodge from the east side and sit on the earthen floor. It is covered with cedar or other evergreen boughs. The entry is closed, and the interior is dark except for the glowing stones.

Water is scooped from a gourd or other container and poured on the stones to make steam. A sacred pipe is sometimes passed. It is filled with tobacco, sage, and other medicinal plants which can

The entrance to a Yurok sweatlodge. *(Library of Congress)*

also be sprinkled on the stones, making the steam fragrant and healing. Prayers are made and songs are sung. This continues until the stones cool. The specifics of the structure of the sweatlodge and ceremony used vary from one community to another.

Michael W. Simpson

Source for Further Study

Bucko, Raymond A. *The Lakota Ritual of the Sweat Lodge: History and Contemporary Practice*. Lincoln: University of Nebraska Press in cooperation with the American Indian Studies Research Institute, 1998.

See also: Ethnophilosophy and Worldview; Medicine and Modes of Curing: Pre-contact; Religion.

Syllabaries

Tribes affected: Pantribal
Significance: *Syllabic writing systems first made it possible to record American Indian languages; Sequoyah, a Cherokee, produced the first syllabary for an Indian language.*

A syllabary is a phonetic transcription of a spoken language. It is distinct from pictographs, which are symbols of objects and actions. Technically, it may also be distinguished from an alphabet; in a syllabary, symbols represent syllables, whereas in an alphabet, they represent shorter units of sound (consonants and vowels).

It is generally accepted that the first knowledge the Indians had of alphabets was when they were contacted by European explorers starting in the late fifteenth century. Among the explorers were Christian missionaries, who were very much interested in converting the natives and therefore tried both to teach them European languages and to transliterate native languages into European alphabets. Considerable difficulties were involved, however, and early attempts were unsuccessful.

In 1821 a Cherokee leader named Sequoyah created the first syllabic writing system for an American Indian language. Sequoyah had been a volunteer under General Andrew Jackson, and he had been impressed with the white people's method of writing that enabled them to communicate over great distances. Sequoyah's syllabary had eighty-six characters for syllables in the Cherokee language. Although he used some English characters, the sounds they represented were distinct from those they represented in English. The Cherokee tribal council, impressed at its effectiveness, sanctioned its use.

The *Cherokee Phoenix*, begun in 1828 and called the first American Indian newspaper, printed articles in both English and the Cherokee syllabary. As use of the syllabary spread, books were translated into the Cherokee language; soon books were being written using the syllabary. The Bible was translated into the Cherokee syllabary by missionary Samuel Worcester. Soon other missionaries and tribal leaders alike began to use the syllabic approach. Missionary John Fleming developed a syllabary for the Creek language; Cyrus Bovington created one for the Choctaw language that could also be used by the Chickasaws. Farther north, a syllabary came into use among the Cree people of Canada and was adapted by some Inuit groups.

Eventually the alphabet used by the European settlers and their descendants won out over syllabic systems in most areas. One reason is simply that most books were available in European languages and were not available in the syllabaries. There has always been difficulty in translating native languages into the Roman alphabet because the phonetic systems are extremely different; scholars and linguists have grappled with these problems for many years with varying degrees of success.

Marc Goldstein

See also: Language Families; Pictographs.